BECOMING FAULKNER

BECOMING FAULKNER

The Art and Life of William Faulkner

PHILIP WEINSTEIN

OXFORD
UNIVERSITY PRESS

OXFORD
UNIVERSITY PRESS

Oxford University Press, Inc., publishes works that further
Oxford University's objective of excellence
in research, scholarship, and education.

OXFORD NEW YORK
Auckland Cape Town Dar es Salaam Hong Kong Karachi
Kuala Lumpur Madrid Melbourne Mexico City Nairobi
New Delhi Shanghai Taipei Toronto

WITH OFFICES IN
Argentina Austria Brazil Chile Czech Republic France Greece
Guatemala Hungary Italy Japan Poland Portugal Singapore
South Korea Switzerland Thailand Turkey Ukraine Vietnam

Copyright © 2010 by Philip Weinstein

Published by Oxford University Press, Inc.
198 Madison Avenue, New York, New York 10016
www.oup.com

First issued as an Oxford University Press paperback, 2012.

Oxford is a registered trademark of Oxford University Press

Library of Congress Cataloging-in-Publication Data
Weinstein, Philip M.
   Becoming Faulkner : the art and life of William Faulkner / Philip Weinstein.
      p. cm
ISBN 978-0-19-534153-9 (hardcover); 978-0-19-989835-0 (paperback)
  1. Faulkner, William, 1897–1962. 2. Novelists, American—20th
century—Biography. 1. Title.
   PS3511.A86Z98548 2009
   813'.52—dc22   2009013181
   [B]

9 8 7 6 5 4 3 2 1

ACKNOWLEDGMENTS

All of one's book are indebted to others beyond the power to acknowledge, but this one benefits from an indebtedness both more obvious and more profound.

Some seven years ago I received a telephone call from Alice Tasman, of the Jean V. Naggar Literary Agency in New York. As an undergraduate (years earlier), she had studied Faulkner with my brother Arnold, at Brown University. An agent now, she wanted to coax into being a biographical study of Faulkner that would do justice to the impact his work had had on her. I responded that I was at that time immersed in writing a larger study of modernism (*Unknowing: The Work of Modernist Fiction*), and that I was—however invested professionally in Faulkner's work—no biographer. During the next four years, three events occurred that changed my mind. I finished writing *Unknowing*, and I read in draft form Jay Parini's *One Matchless Time: A Life of William Faulkner* (2004) and André Bleikasten's *William Faulkner: Une vie en romans* (2007). The more I reflected on these formidable biographies, the more I warmed to the idea of connecting otherwise the life and the work, the work and the life. I called Alice, and she responded enthusiastically: the project was underway. I expanded the argument, Alice took it to a range of presses, and Oxford signed on. Suddenly, all I had to do was find the time—and figure out how—to bring to birth an idea that had begun as a gleam in the eye, but whose becoming was now a promised and contracted reality.

As often in my academic career, my home institution, Swarthmore College, provided me with the time: a full-year sabbatical leave (thanks to a Lang Fellowship) in 2007–2008. The wind in my sails, I began to conceptualize the book in a more sustained fashion. That is when—intent on (re)establishing for myself the story of Faulkner's life—I began to incur indebtedness on a broader scale. I reread Joseph Blotner's authorized biography, and I marveled (as I had not before) at the scope and scrupulousness of his work: the countless interviews conducted, the thousands of pages of unpublished and published work scrutinized, the contextual frames considered, in order to put Faulkner's life into perspective. In his wake, a host of critical biographers—David Minter, Judith Wittenberg, Judith Sensibar, Frederic Karl, Richard Gray, Joel Williamson, and James Watson, among others—produced (prior to Parini and Bleikasten) compelling work seeking to interrelate Faulkner's life and his creative output. Although I was undertaking a different kind of book, I benefited massively from their biographical labors. (My debt to Blotner is beyond accounting: he looms behind a third of my pages.) Finally, having come to grips as I could with previous biographies, I encountered (a few weeks before turning in my final manuscript) Sensibar's just-published *Faulkner and Love: The Women Who Shaped His Art* (2009). Since she reads his life in terms that differ from my own, I have sought, in half a dozen notes, to engage her argument.

In between taking Alice Tasman's phone call in 2002 and pondering Judith Sensibar's argument in 2009, I have incurred a host of other debts. David Riggs (himself a biographer) generously read the biographical précis. Academic friends and colleagues—Robert Bell and Robert Roza—read each chapter, critically and sympathetically. John Matthews engaged the argument—as he has engaged all my work on Faulkner for the past twenty-five years—with an eye at once demanding and supportive. Jay Parini—familiar with both the territory I was pursuing and the challenges I would encounter—graciously perused the entire manuscript, and André Bleikasten attended to its argument as he could, while struggling with health issues. My twin brother Arnold gave me his unstinting attention, as he considered my take on materials he and I have been discussing together—and writing on—for decades.

Oxford University Press has supported this book in a number of ways. Shannon McLachlan who first saw and said yes to the project, Brendan O'Neill who labored to help me secure the photos in the book, Martha Ramsay who kept me on the right side of gender usage and even enjoined—at full page length!—several of my claims, Jessica Ryan who has given me the good of her response to my revisions: these Oxford professionals have made this a better book. Locating and getting permission to use the photos I wanted turned out to be a task of greater magnitude than anticipated. Fellow Faulknerian Robert Hamblin (head of the Center for Faulkner Studies at Southeast Missouri State University) both bailed me out and helped—along with Donald Kartiganer—to keep up my morale. Thanks also to Pamela Williamson, Curator of the Department of Archives and Special Collections of the University of Mississippi Libraries—home of the Coldfield Collection of Faulkner photos. Thanks finally to Marcus Gray, whose unerring eye has greatly facilitated my task of correcting errors as *Becoming Faulkner* goes into paperback.

I close by dedicating this book to three people: Alice Tasman, whose belief in it galvanized me; my wife Penny, whose belief in me underwrites everything I have written; and André Bleikasten, peerless Faulknerian, *in memoriam.*

CONTENTS

ABBREVIATIONS

FAULKNER EDITIONS CITED

AA   *Absalom, Absalom!* (1936), in *Faulkner: Novels 1936–1940* (New York: Library of America, 1990).

AILD   *As I Lay Dying* (1930), in *Faulkner: Novels 1930–1935* (New York: Library of America, 1985).

ELM   *Elmer* (1925), in *William Faulkner Manuscripts 1: Elmer and "A Portrait of Elmer,"* with an introduction by Thomas L. McHaney (New York: Garland, 1987).

EPP   *Early Prose and Poetry,* ed. Carvel Collins (Boston: Little Brown, 1962).

ESPL   *Essays, Speeches & Public Letters,* ed. James B. Meriwether (New York: Random House, 1966).

FAB   *A Fable* (1954), in *Faulkner: Novels 1942–1954* (New York: Library of America, 1994).

FD   *Flags in the Dust,* in *Faulkner: Novels 1926–1929* (New York: Library of America, 2006).

FIU   *Faulkner in the University,* ed. Frederick L. Gwynn and Joseph Blotner (Charlottesville: University of Virginia Press, 1959).

GDM   *Go Down, Moses* (1942), in *Faulkner: Novels 1942–1954* (New York: Library of America, 1994).

HAM   *The Hamlet* (1940), in *Faulkner: Novels 1936–1940* (New York: Library of America, 1990).

HEL   *Helen: A Courtship and Mississippi Poems,* ed. Carvel Collins and Joseph Blotner (New Orleans: Tulane University Press, 1981).

ID   *Intruder in the Dust* (1948), in *Faulkner: Novels 1942–1954* (New York: Library of America, 1994).

IIF   *If I Forget Thee, Jerusalem* (1939) (originally published as *The Wild Palms*), in *Faulkner: Novels 1936–1940* (New York: Library of America, 1990).

LA   *Light in August* (1932), in *Faulkner: Novels 1930–1935* (New York: Library of America, 1985).

LG   *Lion in the Garden: Interviews with William Faulkner, 1926–1962,* ed. James B. Meriwether and Michael Millgate (New York: Random House, 1968).

MAN   *The Mansion* (1959), in *Faulkner: Novels 1957–1962* (New York: Library of America, 1999).

MF   *The Marble Faun* (1924), in *The Marble Faun and A Green Bough* (New York: Random House, 1965).

MOS   *Mosquitoes* (1927), in *Faulkner: Novels 1926–1929* (New York: Library of America, 2006).

PYL   *Pylon* (1935), in *Faulkner: Novels 1930-1935* (New York: Library of America, 1985).

RN   *Requiem for a Nun* (1951), in *Faulkner: Novels 1942–1954* (New York: Library of America, 1994).

SAN   *Sanctuary* (1931), in *Faulkner: Novels 1930–1935* (New York: Library of America, 1985).

SF   *The Sound and the Fury* (1929), in *Novels 1926–1929* (New York: Library of America, 2006).

SL   *Selected Letters of William Faulkner,* ed. Joseph Blotner (New York: Random House, 1977).

SP   *Soldiers' Pay* (1926), in *Faulkner: Novels 1926–1929* (New York: Library of Amerca, 2006).

TN   *The Town* (1957), in *Faulkner: Novels 1957–1962* (New York: Library of America, 1999).

OTHER FREQUENTLY CITED SOURCES

ALG   Meta Carpenter Wilde and Orin Borsten, *A Loving Gentleman: The Love Story of William Faulkner and Meta Carpenter* (New York: Simon and Schuster, 1976).

CH   John Bassett, *William Faulkner: The Critical Heritage* (London: Routledge & Kegan Paul, 1975).

CNC   Ben Wasson, *Count No 'Count: Flashbacks to Faulkner* (Jackson: University Press of Mississippi, 1983).

F   Joseph Blotner, *Faulkner: A Biography: One-volume Edition* (New York: Random House, 1984).

F2   Joseph Blotner, *Faulkner: A Biography,* 2 vols. (New York: Random House, 1974).

FCF   Malcolm Cowley, *The Faulkner-Cowley File: Letters and Memories, 1944–1962* (New York: Viking Press, 1966).

FOM   Murry C. Falkner, *The Falkners of Mississippi: A Memoir* (Baton Rouge: Louisiana State University Press, 1967).

MBB   John Faulkner, *My Brother Bill: An Affectionate Reminiscence* (New York: Trident Press, 1963).

NOR   David Minter, ed. *The Sound and the Fury* (New York: Norton Critical Edition, 2nd ed., 1993).

OFA   Judith Sensibar, *The Origins of Faulkner's Art* (Austin: University of Texas Press, 1984).

OMT   Jay Parini, *One Matchless Time: A Life of William Faulkner* (New York: Harper Collins, 2004).

TH   James G. Watson, *Thinking of Home: William Faulkner's Letters to His Mother and Father, 1918–1925* (New York: Norton, 1992).

WFSH   Joel Williamson, *William Faulkner and Southern History* (New York: Oxford University Press, 1993).

BECOMING FAULKNER

"CANT MATTER"

Because you make so little impression, you see. You get born and you try this and you dont know why only you keep on trying it and you are born at the same time with a lot of other people, all mixed up with them, like trying to, having to, move your arms and legs with strings only the same strings are hitched to all the other arms and legs...like five or six people all trying to make a rug on the same loom only each one wants to weave his own pattern into the rug; and it cant matter, you know that, or the Ones that set up the loom would have arranged things a little better.

—*Absalom, Absalom!*

What would a life look like if its inner sense conformed to this passage? How might someone else try to tell such a life? We assume that a life worth the telling involves a shaping force and weight, eventually cohering into something more than "so little impression." But this passage insists on messiness and waste, on fruitless labor. It focuses on the failure of personal coherence to emerge in time. Others are there, alongside you from the beginning, and they get in your way. They desire as urgently as you do; their desire interferes with yours. The scene is mystifying. Each individual struggles to make something, but the larger cultural loom on which the individual "patterns" are plotted and pursued is defective, in ways that those striving below might guess at but cannot alter.[1] All the actors become entangled like stringed puppets helplessly careening into each other's space. The more they strive, the more inextricable the entanglement.

Becoming Faulkner: my title seems to invite us to consider the notion of "becoming"—of making something out of a life—in a more positive light. It promises the story of Faulkner's becoming a writer and eventually a world-renowned artist. One anticipates a narrative of obstacles encountered and eventually dealt with. One expects Faulkner to achieve his becoming—to get his arms and legs (and mind and feelings and imagination and typewriter) into the clear. "Becoming" implies a gathered coherence, an achieved project not unlike Judith's sought-after weaving, something gaining in sense and wholeness as it progresses. William Faulkner did become a great novelist (who would deny it?), I have become a writer about his achievement (my book is in your hands), and you may become a reader of my book. *May*—there's the rub. Inasmuch as you are now where he and I once were—in the uncertainty of the present moment—you are in a position to recognize the concealed time-trick on which all claims of *becoming* are premised. You might *not* become my reader. In the present moment, this is something that has started but not yet concluded. You could put the book down. Move back a bit further in time, when this book was still to be written, and I might not have become its author. Move back further yet, to the present time of Faulkner, and Faulkner might not have become Faulkner. We know what any becoming looks like only because, *after* it has taken place, its force and weight are recognizable. Retrospection magically transforms the messy scene of ongoing present time into the congealed order it (later) appears always to have been headed for. But in the turbulent present moment—prior to an achieved becoming—there is…what?

In the vortex of the present moment there is frustration and confusion. Confined to that moment (which is where all human beings are confined, the time frame in which life itself is lived), one experiences—whenever the unanticipated arrives—bafflement rather than recognition. And one's ability to cope with the unexpected is inseparable from the resources culturally bequeathed for coping. In Faulkner's desiccated early-twentieth-century South—a place stubbornly facing backward—these resources were especially tenuous. Buffeted by events, one's strenuous moves entangled with the countermoves of others, the Faulkner protagonist—like Judith Sutpen in that passage from *Absalom*—feels certain of one thing: *I cant matter.* Judith experiences her life not as a project in the process of becoming but as an inexplicable derailment. Whatever undivulged purpose "the Ones that set up the loom" had in mind, it was hardly her own prospering. Judith goes to her grave not enlightened by the calm that follows a storm but marked by the storm that precedes any calm. Likewise, the trajectory of Faulkner "becoming Faulkner" took shape as a risk-filled project in ongoing time. Indeed, once his incapacity for progress ceased to torment him, his work began to lose its capacity to startle, awaken, disturb. The outrage of unpreparedness is the traumatic experience he learned to

narrate—an outrage that, could he have avoided it in his own life, he might
well have done so. And been freed perhaps from writing masterpieces.

Faulkner's life registered—and his art explored—the priority of storm
over calm, priority in both senses: before, and more (mis)shaping. Calm is
a function of retrospective clarification—a seductive ordering after the fact.
On completing *Requiem for a Nun* (a novel of failed recognitions), Faulkner
wrote his friend Else Jonsson: "I am really tired of writing, the agony and
sweat of it...I feel like nothing would be as peaceful as to break the pencil,
throw it away, admit I dont know why, the answers either" (SL 315). We
expect lives to make sense over time (we certainly want our own to do so),
and we insist that narratives show us such becoming. Perhaps our deepest
anticipation when reading fiction is to experience, once again, that precious
sense of complex lives coming into focus and revealing their depth over
time. By contrast, Faulkner's great work all but heroically refuses the premise—hardwired into narrative itself—that time brings illumination. Time
hardly did so for him. If that is true, then—to return to the question raised
above—how should one narrate a life whose underlying sense of itself was
"I dont know why": it *cant matter?*

Biographers typically refuse this question. And no wonder. We go to
biography in order to see a human life composed from the later vantage
point of the biographer—the life made sense of as a completed passage
through time, even if (for the subject of the biography) it didn't make much
sense while it was happening. Faulkner's authorized biographer, Joseph
Blotner, labored for some twelve years following Faulkner's death in 1962
(and many years prior to it) to complete his massive eighteen-hundred-
page biography. Blotner drew on the passage of time for all his chapter
titles: periods as long as "Summer, 1897—September, 1902" (chapter 9,
the first on Faulkner's own life) and as short as "Autumn 1921" (chapter
20, a tumultuous few months). More openly than in most biographies,
Blotner's chapter titles signal his employment of linear time as a structural principle for plotting his subject's life. Between the opening time-
title and the closing one ("May–July 1962"), Blotner was able to order a
life span of sixty-five years, to shape its becoming. Looking back at the
celebrated achievements of the men and women who are their subjects,
what can biographers do but narrate their subjects' lives coming into focus
over time? Biographies go from birth and insignificance to death and the
loss of someone who, finally, mattered so much. But what if, to himself, the
subject of the biography remained persuaded that life did not add up, that
life was "the same frantic steeplechase toward nothing everywhere and

man stinks the same stink"—himself included—and that his own experience *cant matter* (FCF 15)?

Faulkner was convinced that his own life was not worth the telling. The more Malcolm Cowley attempted (in 1946) to wrest from him a biographical narrative (as part of Cowley's introduction to *The Portable Faulkner*), the more Faulkner resisted. A few years later, when Cowley sought approval for a larger biographical essay, Faulkner eloquently rebuked the entire enterprise: "this [the biographical essay] is not for me. I will protest to the last: no photographs, no recorded documents. It is my ambition to be, as a private individual, abolished and voided from history, leaving it markless, no refuse save the printed books....It is my aim, and every effort bent, that the sum and history of my life, which in the same sentence is my obit and epitaph too, shall be them both: He made the books and he died" (FCF 126). This memorable statement (one finds variations of it throughout Faulkner's pronouncements) deserves consideration. And not just because Faulkner's insistence is motivated in part by his determination to stop lying about his role in World War I. More deeply, the rebuke intimates an insight into the pitfall of biography itself. It is as though Faulkner glimpsed that biography is incapable of doing justice to the inconsistency and waywardness of its subject's actual life in time. The life itself loses its messy authenticity when it enters the monumentalizing mangle of biography: it emerges straightened out, time-ordered, false.

From Blotner in 1974 through Jay Parini (2004) and André Bleikasten (2007), Faulkner's biographers rehearse not *cant matter* but their various constructions of why the life of Faulkner does matter. This is what biographers do. And yet they all run into trouble. Grateful as one is for their detailed account of the events that make up Faulkner's life—and my debt to the authorized biographer, Joseph Blotner, is enormous—one comes away with the sense of something crucial missing: something that might compellingly connect the disturbed life with the disturbing work that arose from it. Too often the two are treated as parallel tracks that do not meet. We get Faulkner's story but not, as Henry James would put it, the story of that story, the yeasty possibilities of its troubled inner structure. Or, to use Faulkner's own metaphor in *Absalom*, the biographers scrupulously provide a multitude of sticks—the innumerable twigs and branches of the life and the work—but not their incandescence when brought together, not the bonfire. We do not get the composite *gesture* that an imaginative placing of the life against the work—the work against the life—might let us glimpse.

The biographers' admiration for the work—which certainly *does matter*—motivates their desire to find in Faulkner's life a kindred story of achieved becoming. But one ends up discovering, as Jonathan Yardley put it in his review of Parini's *One Matchless Time*, "there isn't all that much of a story to tell. Apart from his writing—which in Faulkner's mind seems to have taken place in its own separate universe...he really didn't do much." Faced with this imbalance between the unforgettable events in the fiction and the forgettable ones (often sodden as well) in his life, biographers have employed a number of strategies. Blotner (who knew Faulkner and admired him greatly) tends to whitewash the life, making it more unblemished than it was. Frederic Karl tends to estrange the life into oppositions, juxtaposing it against the Southern frame in which it had its tangled roots. Parini, for his part, tends to reveal that Faulkner's life was...just a life. Nothing "matchless" about it. In each of these biographies, we encounter grandeur in the art contrasted with messiness in the life, but a reader seeking to understand how this particular man was able to write this particular body of work keeps wanting more.

How might we reconceive the two realms so that parallel lines begin to meet? The answer to this question requires treating what is failed in the life not as the opposite of what is achieved in the work—and therefore in need of whitewash or massaging—but rather as the work's secret sharer, its painfully enabling ground. What tends to be missing from the biographies is a dialectical sense for how the life and the art come together as—so Faulkner put it in *Absalom*—"strophe and antistrophe." On this model, the life is the negative of the work, the earthbound quarry for its splendid flights. Dialectical: the life's relation to the work does not involve a recycling of personal experiences. Rather, Faulkner's fiction revisits the dark, arresting stresses of his life, illuminating and transforming them unpredictably, diagnostically. The life and the work share a kindred turbulence. This is the turbulence of experience in ongoing time, suffered at first by the human being, then retrospectively grappled into verbal form by the writer. Grappled, not tamed. As Sam Fathers says of the wild dog Lion in Faulkner's great story "The Bear," "we don't want him tame." The work to be done requires wildness under harness—the wildness under harness that readers recognize as Faulkner's signature.

I do not delude myself that Faulkner would have welcomed this book. But his reasons might have differed from his repugnance toward biographical investigations that began with Cowley in the 1940s and continued unabated. The biographical portrait proposed here has no interest in straightening his life out by way of retrospective fiction-making. It tries not to offer—he might have recognized—a monumentalizing of a life often gone badly wrong during its actual unfolding. More, this portrait attaches no blame to its subject's missteps. My attempt is guided by one of the stunning dimensions of Faulkner's great work: its refusal to judge, even as it does not sentimentally excuse. The causes for stumbling, his work lets us extensively see, are too inextricable and incorrigible to warrant the fatuousness of judgment. Finally, I see the messiness of Faulkner's life as the fertilizing loam for his novelistic soaring. Although he would have resisted this intrusion into his privacy, I fondly hope he might nevertheless have recognized himself in the mirror of my pages. And, more fondly yet, that he might have conceded my premise: that his extraordinarily troubling work was rooted—where else?—in his ordinarily troubled life.

Faulkner's life revealed micro and macro causes for experiencing time as unmanageable turbulence. At the micro level, he suffered a number of traumatic events. A primary one involved his ill-timed and mismanaged erotic life, launched by his early failure (1918) to marry Estelle Oldham, his childhood sweetheart. Instead of eloping with him, she married Cornell Franklin and departed from Oxford, Mississippi, to live in Hawaii and, later, the Far East. During the next decade she returned often to Oxford, bringing with her not only the burden of a failed marriage but the two children who embodied the change it had wrought. Seemingly against his own better judgment, as well as against his underlying sense of this returned Estelle as "damaged goods"—no longer his "still unravished" Keatsean bride—Faulkner could not resist renewing relations with her. She finalized her divorce from Cornell Franklin in 1927, and they married in 1929, sealing a (re)union as foredoomed as it would prove to be inextricable. Theirs was a marriage Faulkner would spend the rest of his life committed to, suffering from, betraying, but never severing.

Inseparable from Faulkner's mismanaged, ill-timed love life was his mismanaged, ill-timed war experience. Wounded by Estelle's marriage to another man, he was determined to enter the Great War. This was easier said than done, since Faulkner—mindful of his ancestor, Colonel William C. Falkner of Civil War fame—was not eager to enter *his* war as a foot soldier. But he was too short, by half an inch—too light as well—to be accepted into the aviation section of the U.S. army. Undaunted, he made his way to Toronto, and—masquerading as the scion of an aristocratic British family—joined a flight training program with the Canadian air force. Although he did not earn his wings until late December 1918 (over a month after Armistice), Faulkner returned to Oxford in the role and uniform of a war veteran, full of stories of European flights—with self-declared wounds in his head and his knee to bear out his claims. Parading through Oxford's streets, he came to be referred to as "Count No 'Count."

Later, there was his brother Dean's fatal crash (in 1935) in a plane that Faulkner (who had taken up flying for real after years of pretended wartime flight) had sold to him at a much-reduced price. Amateur aviation was all the rage in the early 1930s, and Dean's disastrous love affair with the plane might have occurred without input from his older brother. Yet there is no way Faulkner could have viewed it with detachment, free of blame. In these instances, we can see how Faulkner mismanaged the event and came to be haunted by possibilities passed rather than seized, menaces signed on to before they later blew up in his face. His moves in time seemed out of joint, careening at a pace he did not master. Belated, untimely, he emerged more as the shaped creature in his own life drama than (as he would be) its lordly, shaping creator.

Macro time for Faulkner was no less disorienting. Born in 1897 into a once illustrious Mississippi family now down on its luck, Faulkner grew up as a son of the New South ambivalently enthralled to an Old South, impotent since 1865. His mind was stocked with the manners, extravagances, and racial norms of an earlier time. Faulkner thus experienced repercussions set loose by ancestors long dead, troubles more broadly regional, if not national, yet for all that troubles he could not disown. He was war-wounded not just by the Great War he tried to participate in, but by the Civil War of his great-grandfather's romantic exploits—the defining war of Southern manhood, that other war he missed. So micro time exploded upon him—as sudden assault, a moment's invasion—before he could get his bearings and read its promise/menace, while macro time affected him no less damagingly, because of its long-accumulated burden of implication. Inasmuch as nothing passed (once and for all) in Faulkner's time-arrested South, the dead of 1865 lost none of their deforming power. Under the impress of the old ways of doing things, he bought (in 1930) his own "big house," Rowan Oak. There his traditional model of largess and noblesse oblige prompted him to support a retinue of black servants. He took financial responsibility for parents and siblings and their orphaned offspring as well. Finally, imbued with a residual sense of the charm of older ways, Faulkner remained throughout his life a hunter and a horseman. Such behavior led to his getting thrown repeatedly and further damaging an already badly damaged back. Much of this lifestyle was belated—consisting of insistent (and, often, once-aristocratic) roles summoned into play by the call of a past that refused to pass.

What was missing in Faulknerian time was manageability: time as neither micro (shard-like, invasive) nor macro (accumulated over decades, overwhelming), but in-between and negotiable. Manageable time fuels the Western liberal narrative of progress—the story of individual struggle and resolution. But neither Faulkner's life nor his art featured progress. In his life he experienced, and in his art he explored, the unwanted "other" of progress. Both the life and the work reveal an individual incoherently aggregated in time. Social space in Faulkner's life and work appears, likewise, as aggregated rather than ordered. Ostensibly segregated spaces fail to quarantine difference; leakage occurs everywhere. Genealogies of scandalously mixed blood haunt his novels, perhaps his life as well. In so doing, they complicate the tidier narrative of American exceptionalism, revealing the underweave of the American success story.

Such, in outline, is the gesture of unpreparedness—of belatedness in time and inefficacy of role—constituted by Faulkner's life. In the pages that follow I amplify, enrich, and supply nuance to this gesture. But I have no interest in laying out, extensively, the multitude of known facts about Faulkner's ancestry, his family, his acquaintances, his part-time jobs, his escapades in New Orleans, his interludes in Hollywood, his travels for the State Department (in the 1950s, after he had been awarded the Nobel Prize and become famous), his teaching stints at Princeton and the University of Virginia. I attend to these, but I want to center on the bonfire, not get enmeshed in the innumerable sticks and branches of data that may, at best, have contributed indirectly. Biographies regularly seek to provide an exhaustive anatomy of a life's sticks and logs: too rarely do they reveal the conflagration these made possible.

Like all writers concerned with Faulkner's life, I am embarked on a narrative of why he matters. But in order to keep the priority of *cant matter* in mind, I have sought to minimize the traps of linear time, retrospective clarity, achieved becoming. I pursue his career in time in ways that make room for the role of stumbling—of being in the dark, under assault rather than gaining control—in both the life and the work. Life as a forward-moving and unrehearsable lurching, art as a retrospective and precious ordering: can this opposition—once it is transposed to the scene of writing—even be contested? Can *cant matter* be *put into words* at all? When Faulkner insisted (repeatedly) that his work never escaped failure, however grand or even magnificent, he was being neither coy nor falsely modest. Writing—because it operates otherwise than life—is condemned to failure. It is not the experience of stumbling through time, it can never substitute for that experience. Faulkner became a great writer when he first realized (or wrote as though he realized) that there is something intrinsically mendacious about narrative's treatment of time. Narrative seizes life trajectories condemned to stumbling and—by the act of *telling* them—binds those trajectories into retrospective order. Dedicated to the fiction of becoming—the calm finally attained, after the storm—rather than attempting (impossibly) to say the real in its present incoherence, narrative seems shaped so as to console. Or at least to domesticate, render tame. Its normal mission is to supply what we surely have too little of in our moment-by-moment lives: grace, cogency, purpose.

How can I bring to life a condition that biography as a genre is designed to transcend? How convey—in what is after all a narrative—the reality of Faulkner's stumbling in time, and of his learning how to write that stumbling? I attempt to do this in several ways, with certain attendant costs and consequences.

I have chosen to thematize Faulkner's life and art as a narrative—in five different keys—of trouble encountered but not overcome. Devoting an extensive chapter to each of these keys, I begin chapter 1 with an exploration of Faulkner's tormented life between November 1927 (when his publisher rejected *Flags in the Dust*) and June 1929 (the month of his marriage, sought yet dreaded, to now-divorced Estelle). That chapter then turns a doubt-darkened eye on Faulkner's earlier writings. It homes in retrospectively, as he might have done, on their greatest weakness: their playing it safe, their refusal to expose and tap their author's vulnerability. Such self-risking would emerge full-blown in the masterpieces soon to appear, *The Sound and the Fury* and *As I Lay Dying*.

Chapter 2 opens with an earlier crisis—perhaps the most anguishing experience in Faulkner's life—his failed elopement. That chapter traces his careening life for the next dozen years, ending with a consideration of the masterpieces that emerged between 1929 and 1932: *The Sound and the Fury, As I Lay Dying, Sanctuary,* and *Light in August*. In chapter 3, the biographical and the cultural lenses widen as I probe Faulkner's ways of living and writing his region's racial confusion. I seek to lay out arguably his greatest claim on us—his extraordinary entry into the nightmare of Southern race relations, in *Light in August, Absalom, Absalom!* and *Go Down, Moses*.

Chapter 4 illuminates the countermoves—drunken binges and love affairs—Faulkner pursued as bids for peace (or failing that, at least as temporary escape from the insoluble predicaments of his life). This chapter ends by probing the novels of erotic passion—*If I Forget Thee, Jerusalem* and *The Hamlet*—that he wrote while enthralled with Meta Carpenter. Finally, chapter 5 ("Tomorrow and Tomorrow and Tomorrow") attends to the replays and repetitions—as well as the frustrations and the fame—that filled Faulkner's later years. At the same time it proposes, in summary fashion, a brief account of the later work from *Intruder in the Dust* through *The Reivers*.

None of these chapters scrupulously respects chronological order (although my narrative does advance—erratically—in time). Instead each chapter, entering the life at a moment of sudden or cumulative stress, stays with the dynamics and fallout of that stress in ways that no biography committed to progressing responsibly from 1897 to 1962 can afford to do. In this sense, I seek to "compose Faulkner," rearranging the materials of his life and art so as to seize on latent patterns within a larger troubled weave.

I "compose" him in another sense as well. I pretend now and then to "become Faulkner," to narrate—as subjective experience not seen past or later diagnosed—some of his moment-by-moment dilemmas. In these vignettes I seek less to recuperate the life into meaning than to articulate it as process, to fashion—and pass on to my reader—something resembling its turbulent texture. Although the biographical data buttressing these simulations are well established, such sequences involve—of course—invention on my part. I am not so naïve as to believe that I could actually "become Faulkner"! My aim is heuristic: to simulate (at crucial instances) the precious life-reality that escapes all biographies—what it might have felt like *to be Faulkner,* in present time and cascading trouble. Invention, then, not for its own sake, but to put flesh on the primary bones of my argument: that unmanageable trouble in time emerges as the fault line joining Faulkner's discretely disturbed life with his inexhaustibly disturbing novels.

I approach the great novels as the bonfire that it took his stumbling and off-balance life to make possible. After all, the fundamental reason we write (and read) biography is that its subject produced work of great magnitude. We want to know in what generative soil that work was rooted. We want to know about the man's life—the sticks and branches that make it up—but mainly in the service of a larger desire: how does such magnificent work come out of this particular life?

That question guides my book. Nothing guarantees that I will succeed, but—as Faulkner might have said—this is at least the right way to fail. Exploring the turbulence that marked his life, I seek to do justice to the ways in which the feel and texture of his great novels—their enabling assumptions and tortuous procedures—reprise and unforgettably transform such turbulence.[2] The measure of my success can only be the extent to which my work inspires you to go to the novels themselves. There, in the temple of his prose, the identity of Faulkner that matters most resides.[3]

CHAPTER I

CRISIS AND CHILDHOOD

I'm inclined to think that…maybe peace is only a condition in retrospect, when the subconscious has got rid of the gnats and the tacks and
the broken glass in experience and has left only the peaceful pleasant
things—that was peace. Maybe peace is not is, but was.

—*Faulkner in the University*

CHALLENGE

Faulkner had probably just returned from the annual deer hunt at General
Stone's lodge, thirty miles west of Oxford, Mississippi, on the edge of the
Delta. He was two months past his thirtieth birthday and had reason to
be feeling good. Thanks to Phil Stone's friendship over the years, he had
grown accustomed to spending time with the larger Stone family—wealthy,
privileged, and planterly, as Faulkner's family was not. One of the pleasures of this connection was the renewed hunting it afforded. He may even
have remembered Phil's telling of his first bear—a vignette so vivid that
it was as though it had happened to Faulkner too. Just fifteen years old,
Phil had seen the bear, stood his ground, fired, and closed his eyes. When
he opened them, the bear was sprawled out before him, dead. The other
hunters put Phil through the ritual "blooding" that attends a boy's first
kill. They smeared his face with the bear's blood, initiating him into the
yearly hunting of wild creatures, in the company of men. Throughout his
life, Faulkner would find ways to reenact the ceremony of hunting in the
big woods, in the company of men. It confirmed—graciously, wordlessly—
his sense of himself. So as he was returning home that last day of November
1927, he was no doubt in an expansive mood. When he came upon the
unopened letter from Horace Liveright—of Boni & Liveright Press, the
man who had published him twice in the past two years—his mood might
have brightened further. He knew that this latest novel, *Flags in the Dust*,
was far and away his best. As he had written Liveright six weeks earlier,

when mailing in the typescript, "At last and certainly, I have written THE book, of which those other things were but foals. I believe it is the damdest best book you'll look at this year, and any other publisher" (F 204).

Opening Liveright's letter, he read:

> It is with sorrow in my heart that I write to tell you that three of us have read *Flags in the Dust* and don't believe that Boni & Liveright should publish it. Furthermore, as a firm deeply interested in your work, we don't believe that you should offer it for publication.... *Soldiers' Pay* was a very fine book and should have done better. Then *Mosquitoes* wasn't quite as good, showed little development in your spiritual growth and I think none in your art of writing. Now comes *Flags in the Dust* and we're frankly very much disappointed by it.... The story really doesn't get anywhere and has a thousand loose ends. If the book had plot and structure, we might suggest shortening and revisions but it is so diffuse that I don't think this would be any use. My chief objection is that you don't seem to have any story to tell and I contend that a novel should tell a story. (F 560)

He was stunned. The new book had broached for the first time the teeming materials of family and region—of the South as he had unthinkingly absorbed it, never knowing he could write it too. Yet Liveright saw *Flags* as a dead end, so dead that showing it to other publishers could damage his career before it had really begun. Faulkner responded jauntily—"It's too bad you don't like *Flags in the Dust*," and later: "I think now that I'll sell my typewriter and go to work—though God knows, it's sacrilege to waste that talent for idleness which I possess." Beneath the insouciant pose he was disoriented, stopped in his tracks. During the months that followed, he sought to revise *Flags* on his own, getting nowhere. To his great-aunt Alabama he wrote, "Every day or so I burn some of it up and rewrite it, and at present it is almost incoherent." Two years later, he still remembered the wound vividly:

> I was shocked: my first emotion was blind protest, then I became objective for an instant, like a parent who is told that its child is a thief or an idiot or a leper; for a dreadful moment I contemplated it with consternation and despair, then like the parent I hid my own eyes in the fury of denial." (all quotes in F 206)

"Child," "parent," "idiot," "fury": these terms suggestively bring to mind the breakthrough novel—*The Sound and the Fury*—that he would write in the months following Liveright's assault on *Flags*. But in November 1927, he had nothing new to show as counter-evidence. Worse, the big things published up to then—the volume of poetry, the two apprentice novels—were beginning to appear in an unsettling light.

That trio of successes, looked back on, revealed liabilities he may have suspected, but which had appeared minor so long as the acceptances kept coming in. (As he was to write years later, in *Absalom, Absalom!* "He seemed to kind of dissolve and a part of him turn and rush back through the two years... like when you pass through a room fast and look at all the objects in it and you turn and go back through the room again and look at all the objects from the other side and you find out you had never seen them before, rushing back through those two years and seeing a dozen things that had happened and he hadn't even seen them before.") He had been writing poetry ever since he could remember, but the poems had attracted little attention—published (apart from *The Marble Faun* [1924]) maybe in the University of Mississippi's literary journal, or hand-bound and offered to a friend or sweetheart. If he looked at it squarely, even *The Marble Faun* seemed to lose its status as counter-evidence. Had Phil Stone not generously supplied $400 to meet production costs, the Four Seasons Press of Boston would not have published it, knowing—as Faulkner may also have known in the back of his mind—that sales would never match their outlay.

If Phil Stone made that first publication possible, it didn't take a lot of guesswork to identify who made the next two possible. The connection with Sherwood Anderson—meeting him in New Orleans in late 1924 after having become friends with his wife-to-be three years earlier in New York—had been a rare stroke of luck. Faulkner would later take sardonic pleasure in repeating Mrs. Anderson's remark "that... if he [Anderson] don't have to read it [*Soldiers' Pay*], he will tell his publisher to take it" (F 146). Amusing to remember later, but less so if recalled in November 1927. The terms of the deal—Anderson's telling the publisher to sign the book—might now have suggested a different portent. Sherwood Anderson was a celebrated writer who could, and did, dictate terms to Liveright. Thanks to the best-seller success of *Winesburg, Ohio,* Anderson was currently enjoying a huge advance from Liveright on his next novel (which became *Dark Laughter*). In his contract, Liveright had urged Anderson to be on the lookout for new talent. What Anderson wanted, Anderson was likely to get. Was *Soldiers' Pay* in print mainly because the great man, who hadn't even read it, had given his imprimatur? Take away Phil Stone and Sherwood Anderson, and where was William Faulkner?

The fragility of his position increased the more he probed it. When Liveright gave *Soldiers' Pay* (1926) the green light, what was he actually endorsing? Did he glimpse its awkward lyricism? Or did he envisage, more pragmatically, a salable variation on "the war story," such as what Dos Passos (*Three Soldiers*) and cummings (*The Enormous Room*) had already cashed in on a few years earlier? More, did he now view it, in late 1927, as an apprentice piece of work still in search of itself, if silhouetted against Hemingway's masterly *The Sun Also Rises* (also 1926)? Yet another nihilistic report from a casualty of World War I, another testimonial from the Lost Generation? ("A fitting complement and wind-up to the literature of the War," Richard Hughes would write of it in 1930—*Soldiers' Pay* as a novel nicely finding its niche within a familiar genre of 1920s fiction [CH 60].) If this were so, Faulkner's unease might have deepened because he knew—as neither Liveright nor anyone else knew—that he was a specious reporter of that war, a self-proclaimed veteran who had actually never seen military action. If Faulkner explored his discomfort further, the thoughts became darker. What about *Mosquitoes?* Did Liveright give it a green light mainly because it was fashionably alienated, disaffected, superior to the New Orleans antics it acidly narrated? A publisher like Liveright, committed to shocking bourgeois complacency and to supporting the most abrasive modernist texts, might have seen in the freewheeling corrosiveness of *Mosquitoes* plenty to applaud, even though he had his reservations. Finally, what did it mean that the novel in which Faulkner had most revealed his talent—*Flags in the Dust*—struck Liveright as a mirror in which nothing of interest could be seen? Did Faulkner himself intimate such a disparaging assessment of his first two novels when he proposed to Liveright to "bang... out a book to suit you—though it'll never be one as youngly glamorous as 'Soldiers' Pay' nor as trashily smart as 'Mosquitoes'" (F 206)?

Worse, he owed Liveright money, the $200 advance on *Flags*—a lot of money in 1927. How could he pay that off? Would Liveright bind him further by refusing to return the typescript of *Flags* until he had replaced it with something else—something that Liveright might not care for either? Not for the first time, Faulkner sought to erase debt by placing his short stories in one of the popular national magazines, and not for the first time, struck out. None was accepted in 1928. Thirty years old, he had been writing poetry, and then fiction, for over half his life, yet his professional identity was suddenly more in question than it had ever been. Just hitting his artistic stride, he had been grounded at the very moment his wings were unfolding. And that was only to speak professionally. Emotionally, he had—without planning it, yet without avoiding it either—entered an area of even greater turmoil.

Not that he was in the habit of explaining things, but even if he were, he could not explain this. Not to himself, much less to others. Estelle Oldham was poised to become his again. She had been his childhood playmate and then his sweetheart for over a decade. She had wanted to elope with him, they had failed to bring it off, and she had gone on to marry another man. Now, all but extricated from that marriage, she would soon be free to become his wife. This approaching event looked like a dream about to come true. Was that the problem—that dreams don't come true, shouldn't come true? On perhaps the worst day of his life—April 18, 1918—she had disappeared from him, a Eurydice descending into darkness, marrying Cornell Franklin and heading for an exotic world in which he had no part. As that fateful day in April had approached, his distress had mounted unbearably, and he had fled. He put over a thousand miles between them, visiting Phil Stone at Yale and working at a munitions factory in New Haven. He was plotting to enter the Great War before it ended. Even so, the distance had failed to calm his heart. It had not kept him from seeing the wedding service inexorably taking place, from hearing the church bells confirming it. None of this could be undone. Yet it was being undone even as he pondered it. Her marriage had failed, and she was going to be his again, soon, sooner than he wanted.

Estelle had returned to Oxford shortly after her wedding and recurrently thereafter, bearing incontrovertible evidence of its reality—first her daughter, Victoria, born in 1919, and four years later her son, Malcolm. Faulkner had continued to write poetry for her, visiting with her often at her parents' home, incoherently straddling the gap between an intimacy unbroken and an intimacy ruptured. Her married life in Honolulu was exotic—a world of wealth and elegant clothes, of dances and garden parties, like nothing he knew or desired. Still, her unpossessed image continued to stir him into poetry, spurring an outburst of poems during her 1919 visit, then even more at the time of her 1921 visit. In a volume of Swinburne he gave her, she found an inscription so passionate that she had to tear it out of the book before returning to her husband in Honolulu. He could not extricate himself from her spell.

Change or die, he often told himself. Though still in love with Estelle, he had survived her abandoning him by changing. By 1927, he had become a published poet and novelist, a denizen of the New Orleans literary world, a traveler to Europe. He had also taken up more dubious roles: local dandy, barefoot and shaggy vagabond, criminal bootlegger, bohemian extraordinaire. None of these roles accommodated a spouse. None involved income producing, home owning, tax paying, child raising, wife sustaining. How could he help but recognize that he had become, during her decade of marriage, a bachelor again, on the voyage out, his horizons expanding? Half a dozen future novels clamored inside him, their opening premises already sketched on paper or circulating in his head. Estelle had inflicted on him his most grievous wound, but she belonged more to a past he had somehow survived and left behind than to a future in which he could see himself flourishing.

Yet she seemed inextricably part of his present those last days in November 1927. Almost three years earlier, her marriage with Cornell Franklin had apparently reached a state of crisis. She and her husband both spoke of wanting out. Since divorce could be granted in Mississippi only on grounds of adultery, they agreed that—if it came to that—they would seek divorce in Shanghai (where they had been living since 1923). They had consented to a sort of probationary separation for six months—he in Shanghai, she in Honolulu—to see if the bond could be salvaged. As that period came to an end, they both knew that the marriage was beyond saving. It seems that Franklin, rather than Estelle, actually initiated the divorce proceedings in Shanghai, in the U.S. Court for China, on November 13, 1928. He was eager to remarry, and if Estelle had done the filing, she would have had to prove two years of prior residence in Shanghai—a requirement that her extensive returns to Oxford during that time made it impossible to fulfill. (Indeed, Franklin's official motive for divorce was his wife's "desertion.") By February 15, 1929, the divorce was finalized, although the divorce decree reached the Oxford courthouse only on June 6, 1929. The conditions Franklin imposed were severe: he would provide $300/month for the support of his two children, but no alimony for her. By then Estelle wanted out so badly that she did not contest these conditions.[1]

She had thus become a thirty-one-year-old divorcee without income and with two young offspring to think about. Her life was now all but unmanageably messy, and Faulkner could not help but realize that in her eyes, the right man for straightening out this mess was available, apparently had been waiting all along. During the last few years, as her marriage turned increasingly unworkable, her horizons had shrunk and her nerves had become alarmingly frayed. He was the gateway toward a larger life they could create together. He would ground her and make her right again.

From his perspective, too much had changed. He had abandoned their past; he could not sign on to their future. In between, unbearably, was the present moment: *is*. How could the scenarios of *was* differ so utterly from his predicament of *is*? Much later—well into his middle years—he would say to a class of students at the University of Virginia, "maybe peace is only a condition in retrospect, when the subconscious has got rid of the gnats and the tacks and the broken glass in experience and has left only the peaceful pleasant things—that was peace. Maybe peace is not is, but was" (FIU 67). They probably didn't understand what he was talking about; at their age he hadn't either. But what he now knew in his bones, and what he sensed overwhelmingly in November 1927, was the unbridgeable gap between the peace of *was*—once the dust had settled—and the turmoil of *is*. He glimpsed even then that such peace owed everything to the currying retrospective mind—to that interior broom that rids experience of the gnats and tacks and broken glass that give it its bitter reality. And more: that the ideal is never anything but the not-here, not-now, not-experienced. The ideal cannot take on those gnats and tacks and broken glass and remain ideal. Was this true for his beloved Estelle? Was she a woman whose image compelled him only so long as it remained unpossessed? Would she remain Estelle once he married her? Perhaps he remembered the moment when—thanks to Phil Stone's tutelage—he had discovered in Keats's "Ode on a Grecian Urn" the paradox that was already engraved in his heart: "She cannot fade, though thou hast not thy bliss / Forever wilt thou love and she be fair."

The peace of *was*, the turmoil of *is*. Are the crucial moments of experience—those that Faulkner's art would later find a way to grasp and explore—instants in which *is* explodes in the face of *was*, shatters all "the devious intricate channels of decorous ordering" (as he would put it in *Absalom*)? Does one's life come to life only when the patterning that made it recognizable as one's life ceases to function? Is personal outrage, intolerable affront, a condition of being itself? Much later, in a 1955 interview, he would claim that "There's always a moment in experience...that's there. There all I do is work up to that moment. I figure what must have happened before to lead to that particular moment, and I work away from it, finding out how people act after that moment" (LG 220). A core moment, an all-disturbing perception or outrage: the turmoil of *is*. His life was now in that turmoil. He could not marry her, he had to marry her; he knew he would. This tension was incandescent. Obscurely he realized that for all the poems he had written and novels he had published—including the latest that Liveright had turned down and that was, he knew, his best—he had never written such an unbearable moment. Never centered a novel on an image of the real as sheer exploding presence—an image radiant and inexhaustible in its trouble-making implications. Maybe only now did he glimpse that words *exist* to ward off such moments, to keep the unbearable at bay. That the real in its disturbing presence is wordless, that trying to write it is both doomed to failure and the only justification for writing. Perhaps Liveright had unknowingly set him free. Perhaps, in a novel that no one would read because no press would publish it, he could actually begin "with the picture of a little girl's muddy drawers in a pear tree," a girl who had climbed high enough to see through a window where her grandmother's funeral was taking place, while her brothers—who lacked her courage—were waiting below, unaware of the death she was seeing as they focused on her muddy drawers.

Whatever the particulars of his thought process, the period spanning Liveright's rejection of *Flags* in late 1927 and his marriage to Estelle in June 1929 surged with conflict and anxiety. His life was out of control, challenging him as it had not since 1918. His career ground to a halt. Then, suddenly—rather than continue trying to figure out what they did want, since they didn't want *Flags*—he took the leap. He would go the other way, where no publishers were waiting. "One day I seemed to shut a door between me and all publishers' addresses and book lists," he would write in 1933. "I said to myself, Now I can write" (NOR 227). Thus he plunged, in the early spring of 1928, into his most lyrical novel, *The Sound and the Fury*. This creative work—the happiest he was ever to engage in—occupied him well into the fall of that year. At the same time, *Flags* was morphing (under his friend Ben Wasson's editorial labor) into a shorter, publishable version entitled *Sartoris*. All the while, Faulkner was drifting toward the desired and dreaded marriage. It can hardly be accidental that during the wedding-shadowed five months of 1929 leading up to their June marriage, he conceived and drafted his darkest novel, *Sanctuary*. I shall attend later to *Sanctuary*, but the following passage may suggest its relation to his marital crisis: "When you marry your own wife, you start from scratch...scratching. When you marry somebody else's wife, you start off maybe ten years behind, from somebody else's scratch and scratching" (SAN 190).

Scratch and scratching: marital intercourse figured as sordid bodily moves—like the irritable response to mosquito bites—that a man and a woman inflict on each other, and that a second husband experiences as a form of cuckolding. No Keatsean "still unravished bride" here. Once married, he and Estelle seem to have experienced a honeymoon that was hardly honeyed. Neighbors near the Gulf Coast cottage where they stayed heard them often quarreling. Late one night—they had both been drinking heavily—a startled neighbor was urged by the frantic Faulkner to rescue Estelle from drowning. Ophelia-like, she had walked into the Gulf in one of her elegantly brocaded Shanghai gowns, heading for deeper waters. The neighbor rushed after her, reaching her just before she slipped away. As Faulkner would write later of Ellen's doomed union with Sutpen in *Absalom, Absalom!*, "Yes, she was weeping again now; it did, indeed, rain on that marriage" (AA 47).

What had gone wrong between the two of them? Dream-lovers for so many years, they seemed to be in actuality almost strangers. The ten years apart had marked each of them indelibly, their differences strengthening and becoming impassable barriers. Always a social butterfly, she delighted in the give and take of passing flirtations. The male/female "ballet" was a dance she both delighted in and performed flawlessly. As Faulkner's friend Ben Wasson later put it, "one would have thought, watching her as she listened to a man, that he was the most fascinating and brilliant creature in the world" (CNC 77). Playful conversation often laced with erotic innuendo sustained her equilibrium. It was true that as her first marriage had begun to come apart, she found herself increasingly dependent on alcohol to maintain that equilibrium. Even so, despite the emotional barrenness of her union with Cornell, there had been compensations. Her life with him was replete with money, maids, social encounters, and cultural activities. It had furnished a splendid setting for the public performance of her identity. Married life with Faulkner, she couldn't help but realize, would provide none of these backdrops. For his part, the brooding misfit of twenty had become a determined loner by the age of thirty. He neither danced nor made small talk. Capable of long silences ever since childhood, he had alarmingly extended the range of occasions in which he found it appropriate to say nothing. (He would probably never realize how hard on her was the mere fact of his prolonged, unpredictable silences.) For the past decade, he had protected and nurtured his unconventional traits, turning them into facets of a stubbornly maintained maverick identity. They were, by this point, virtually destined to get on each other's nerves.

Moreover, he had not sought out this wedding. It took an urgent phone call from Estelle's sister, Dot, to make him concede the depth of Estelle's plight and the necessity of their marriage. Even so, he recoiled, desperately writing to his new publisher, Hal Smith, a few days before the wedding:

> I am going to be married. Both want to and have to. THIS PART IS CONFIDENTIAL, UTTERLY. For my honour and the sanity—I believe life—of

a woman. This is not bunk; nor am I being sucked in. We grew up together and I don't think she could fool me in this way; that is, make me believe that her mental condition, her nerves are this far gone....It's a situation which I engendered and permitted to ripen which has become unbearable, and I am tired of running from the devilment I bring about. (OMT 138)

Their commencement of life together appears as an ending neither can avoid. Weddings often darkly punctuate his fiction—as funerals not yet understood as such. As he finished drafting *Sanctuary* in May 1929, he contemplated his heroine Temple Drake entering the courthouse and about to commit perjury. Since he had her do so on the same date (June 20) on which he would publicly utter his marriage vows, he might have been pondering his own approaching perjury, envisaging with dread the portal he was about to pass through.[2]

At any rate, Faulkner's concession to marriage may have been more apparent than real. Physically present at the church ceremony and the Pascagoula honeymoon, he was spiritually absent, inextricably involved in the page proofs for *The Sound and the Fury*. These had just arrived, and the contrast between the beauty of his book and the mess of his life was not lost on him. Ignoring for hours on end the bodily bride who shared his actual space in those late June days in Pascagoula, he worked his way more deeply into the fabric of his novel, focusing on its central figure, Caddy Compson, whom he thought of as his "heart's darling." Of his entire gallery of created characters, she was the one he would cherish most throughout his lifetime. Whatever tarnish she sustained in the harrowing course of the novel she inhabited, she would remain for him a still unravished Keatsean bride, protected in the sanctuary of his art.

What extraordinary light might the conceiving and writing of this new novel have shed, what disturbing view might it have provoked, on his entire earlier output? What is at stake in claiming that *The Sound and the Fury* thrust him upon a world stage? That Faulkner before it is not yet Faulkner? That Faulkner without it would not have become Faulkner?

RETROSPECT

"A Sort of Cocktail of Words": Faulkner's Poetry

In *The Sound and the Fury* (as I will go on to explore) words themselves were the enemy Faulkner learned to recognize as such, then struggled to outwit. Their conventional ordering loomed as cottony insulation softening the ferocity of *is* into the tameness of *was*. In the light of that recognition, his long-sustained output of poetry might have suddenly appeared problematic, even defective. He had been ardently writing poems since his midteens—so ardently that his guide and would-be mentor, Phil Stone, would often proclaim that his destined form was poetry, not fiction. By the late 1920s Faulkner himself was less sanguine. In *Mosquitoes* (1927) he had Dalton Fairchild read aloud a modern poem and then ask another character, "What do you make of it?" The latter responds, "Mostly words, a sort of cocktail of words"—an assessment probably not far from Faulkner's own, since the unidentified poem is one Faulkner had written. Was the rest of his poetry also just a heady brew of words?

It had hardly seemed so at the time. But he could not deny that his withdrawal from the routines of school and work occurred simultaneously with a turn inward toward the construction of a substitute universe—a private and poetic word-world. The making of poems served as both anesthesia and a strange blend of discipline and release. It supplied a lifeline for performing his otherwise inarticulable specialness, the "youthful gesture" (as he later put it) "of being 'different' in a small town" (HEL 163). Not just any poems, moreover, but aggressively rhyming, rhythmic ones—full of fauns and nymphs, pastoral woods and streams, erotic quests and histrionic collapses—poems that articulated his alienation from the mundane pieties of Oxford, Mississippi. Among the late nineteenth-century poets whose practice threw him this lifeline, the one who mattered most was Algernon Charles Swinburne. "At the age of sixteen, I discovered Swinburne," he wrote in 1924. "Or rather Swinburne discovered me, springing from some tortured undergrowth of my adolescence, like a highwayman, making me his slave" (163). (Such attachment never entirely disappeared. His daughter Jill would remember his teaching her Swinburne in the 1940s. Of the two hundred of his books in Jill's library, the Swinburne volume is the most worn [OFA 78].)

Swinburne appealed as an intoxicating word-man. Faulkner's modeling his verse on the earlier poet's also permitted him—as he wryly put it in 1924—to further "various philanderings in which I was then engaged" (HEL 163). The point seems trivial but is not. The young Faulkner's versifying recurrently joins hands with the aim of impressing or seducing its intended female reader—usually Estelle (mostly absent between 1918 and the late 1920s) but also, at least twice, Helen Baird (the young woman to whom he proposed in the mid-1920s and who turned him down flat). If the release embodied in *The Sound of the Fury* is inseparable from his believing no one else would care for it, the abortiveness of the poems owes something to their never-forgotten bid for impressiveness. This, too, he was to recognize in *Mosquitoes,* where Fairchild says to his audience, "I believe that every word a writing man writes is put down with the ultimate intention of impressing some woman that probably dont care anything at all for literature" (MOS 460).

One eye on the page, another on the woman it is to impress: the poems are written in the mirror of other poets' already distinctive styles. T. S. Eliot's "Prufrock" reappears throughout the 1921 *Vision in Spring* ("Let us go then; you and I, while evening grows / And a delicate violet thins the rose"). Although critics have argued that Faulkner strategically rewrites his sources, there is no denying their priority. In addition to Swinburne and Eliot (each serving different moods), A. E. Housman's *Shropshire Lad* marks his verse recurrently: "Once he was quick and golden, / Once he was clean and brave. / Earth, you dreamed and shaped him: / Will you deny him grave?" (MF 35). In these lyrics (published later in *A Green Bough*) one hears Housman's elegantly shortened lines, his pastoral ambiance and world-weary melancholy. Finally, the poetry of Conrad Aiken both aroused Faulkner's generosity (rarely proffered to other living writers) and inspired his imitations. Ben Wasson recounts showing Faulkner some Aiken lines suspiciously similar to Faulkner's own. Glancing at them, Faulkner wryly responded: "Anyhow, you'll have to admit I showed good taste in selecting such a good man to imitate" (CNC 41).

The Marble Faun (1924) reveals most clearly the failure of Faulkner's poetic vocation. Failure means different things in Faulkner's lexicon. At the high end, there is the failure that attaches to language's intrinsic incapacity to say the real, as in "the splendid magnificent bust that [Thomas] Wolfe made in trying to put the whole history of the human heart on the head of the pin" (FIU 144). Failure at this level of aspiration was unavoidable—it involves language's attempt to transcend its own condition as language— and Faulkner regularly assessed his own great work accordingly. I shall argue later that despite his own negative judgment (which was sincere, not posture), such work was uniquely successful. By contrast, the poems fail at the low end. Rather than seek to escape the limit imposed by words, they indulge in words, swoon over them, aspire toward a word-world elsewhere. Though *The Marble Faun* ostensibly recounts a specific time (April through June) and place, the cycle of poems establishes no location:

With half closed eyes I see
Peace and quiet liquidly

Steeping the walls and cloaking them
With warmth and silence soaking them;
They do not know, nor care to know,
Why evening waters sigh in flow;
Why about the pole star turn
Stars that flare and freeze and burn;
Nor why the seasons, springward wheeling
Set the bells of living pealing.
They sorrow not that they are dumb:
For they would not a god become. (MF 48)

"Half closed eyes": the entire cycle circulates around landscapes "liquidly" glimpsed in the mind's eye, not vividly delineated for the reader. The insistent end-rhymed lines, the vaguely allegorical "peace and quiet," the generic stars and seasons and bells: there are no specifying hooks in this language, no detail that pins the words down and lets them deliver a nonverbal experience. Its aim is to anesthetize—a "cocktail of words" that functions all too often (as in Gail Hightower's reverie in *Light in August*) as "fine galloping language, the gutless swooning full of sapless trees...like listening in a cathedral to a eunuch chanting in a language which he does not even need to not understand" (LA 634).

True for everything but that closing couplet, its last line the most provocative in the entire poem cycle. What ordeal do we alone undergo in the scene of natural space and time—undergo because only we seek, but cannot attain, god-status? How do space and time themselves shape the prison that we inhabit from birth to death? What limiting conditions do they impose on our desire for completeness, conditions that only a god could transcend? Faulkner hardly knew in the early 1920s how to answer these questions. The melancholy of the immovable faun testifies to the failure of a "word-world" to supply completeness to the human creature painfully caught up in real space and time. The experience of loss is the scandalous human lot, Faulkner would come to realize. The cheat of words—including those that make up most of his poetry—involved pretending to repair or transcend this loss. He would later develop a comprehensive term for all attempts to evade the loss of being that comes with life in ongoing time: *sanctuary*. To Jean Stein he said in 1955, "There is no such thing as *was*—only *is*. If *was* existed there would be no grief or sorrow" (LG 255). Long before 1955—in *The Sound and the Fury* (1929)—he was to articulate the explosion of life in moment-by-moment time. There would be no more "fine galloping" words that served as a fantasy word-world of escape from the unpreparedness and fleetingness of here and now. Rather, he would bend language downward, toward the earth, until it shed all pretence of plot, teetered on incoherence. He would strip language of its illusory orderliness, twisting it until it conveyed the grief and sorrow of *is*—the specific moment exploding in its defenseless exposure, flaring incandescently before disappearing into the nothingness of *was*.

Faulkner's Early Prose

Such, in 1929—after the breakthrough of *The Sound and the Fury*—might have appeared the poetry he had been writing for the past two decades. What about the prose? Had Sherwood Anderson's endorsement persuaded Liveright to publish work not otherwise compelling? He remembered Anderson's warning: "You've got too much talent. You can do it too easy, in too many different ways. If you're not careful, you'll never write anything" (ESPL 7). Too much talent might do him in: what did that mean? He had written a lot of fiction since Anderson said those words. Did it all fall under the rubric of "never write anything"? Had his linguistic facility itself—the ease with which he generated plot and character and setting and mood—allowed him to remain on the surface, doing it "too easy, in too many different ways"? Without Anderson and the bohemian ambience of New Orleans, he might never have turned seriously to prose at all. Before Anderson, there were a few unpublished stories. But after Anderson— thanks to that fabulous New Orleans spring of 1925, drinking and talking and carousing and writing—he had become a writer of fiction. It began as sketches published in the *New Orleans Times-Picayune,* and continued as the drafting of *Soldiers' Pay.* By the time he left the city for Europe, six months after his arrival, his writerly identity had begun to crystallize. A first novel with Anderson's imprimatur was awaiting Liveright's approval, and the elements of a second novel were coiling inside his mind—one that would do mocking justice to the pretensions of New Orleans bohemian life.

The New Orleans sketches had launched him, and looking back on them, he could still savor their feisty energy. Week after week he would turn out portraits of the underworld he had begun to frequent—gamblers, beggars, immigrants, bootleggers, criminals, backwoodsmen, and perhaps most memorably, an idiot with "eyes clear and blue as cornflowers" and a disoriented black man who crazily sought to make his way back to Africa. Violence abounded in these sketches. What plot he used was neat and clear, slipping into knot-like focus by the end of the sketch. Further, he was beginning to access characters whose interest exceeded his current uses, who had more to give—at some future time. All his life, moreover, he had been absorbing the vernacular expressiveness of blacks and poor whites. His remarkable capacity for silence nourished a no less remarkable capacity for listening to and remembering spoken rhythms. Finally, the "failed poet" had not so much disappeared as changed genres. The "poetry" now appeared in descriptions of brooding landscape, moments of reverie and anguish, phrases of haunting or longing. The sketches tapped and expanded his resources. They were good in themselves and even better in what they promised. They were also unfailingly picturesque. Not a one of them escaped the limitations of "Can you beat this?" Hard-boiled, droll, poetic, alienated, the voice of these sketches risked little. Did that uncommitted voice signal the trap of having "too much talent"?

He continued to write sketches and reviews for the *Times-Picayune* as he headed to Europe, and he began to think of more ambitious formats. Apart from diligent sightseeing, he was trying—off and on for several months, mainly in Paris—to write a different kind of fiction, one in which he risked more of his own interiority. The manuscript entitled *Elmer* is as strangely static, arrested, as *The Marble Faun* was—"Who marble-bound must ever be." But Elmer lacked the costumed distance supplied by pastoral landscape. He moved in slow motion, tentatively, almost viscously. He was immured not in a scene of woods and seasons, but rather in a remembered setting of his desired mother's body and his adored sister's tenderness and anger, as well as his current lover's soul-less seductiveness. A remarkable eight-page sequence involving the child Elmer's entry (almost second by second) into a bed shared with his sister Jo-Addie concludes as follows:

> His hand went out with quiet joy touching his sister's side where it curved briefly and sharply into the mattress. It was like touching a dog, a bird dog eager to be off. . . . Jo neither accepted nor rejected his touch: it was as though she were somewhere else. Without moving or speaking she said That's enough and Elmer withdrew his hand and lay relaxed and happy for sleep. Suddenly Jo moved: a breath of cold air about his shoulders told him that she had risen to her elbow.
>
> "Ellie," she said suddenly, putting her hand on his head, grasping a handful of his hair and shaking his head roughly, "when you want to do anything, you do it. Hear?"
>
> "Yes, Jo. I will," he promised without question.
>
> She released his hair and warmth settled again about his shoulders. "Don't you let nobody stop you," she added.

"Yes," repeated Elmer happily burrowing his round yellow head into the thin pillow, sleeping. (ELM 15–6)

The uncanny moment narrated here is modest, moving, and specific. It resonates with the vulnerability that would later mark the tormented brother-sister relationships of *The Sound and the Fury*. The vignette is at once inside and outside—a precisely rendered set of bodily moves in a believable bedroom, but also a hushed articulation of a child's longing and neediness, and of his sister's silent recognition of his plight. If, in *Elmer*, Faulkner began to explore his own pathos—no longer decked out as troubled faun or impotent Prufrock—he seems to have come to a pathway too emotionally demanding to continue. The most revealing dimension of *Elmer* may be Faulkner's refusal—or incapacity—to complete his narration. At any rate, he abandoned *Elmer* on his return stateside in December 1925. Instead, he turned toward the swirling New Orleans materials that would culminate, several months later, as the completed typescript of *Mosquitoes*. There, as in *Soldiers' Pay*, he could "do the hard-boiled" with the best of them. There was no need to reenter the charged emotional territory of a sensitive boy obsessed by his older sister.

"When Am I Going to Get Out?": Soldiers' Pay

Soldiers' Pay opens on cadet Julian Lowe, a would-be soldier whose tragedy, like Faulkner's, is swiftly stated: "they had stopped the war on him" (SP 3). Hurtling homeward on a fast-moving train, post-Armistice, Lowe is nicely positioned for Faulkner to explore what it felt like *not* to make it to the war. Faulkner knew this feeling only too well, but could never divulge it to others and was unwilling to explore it here. Instead, Lowe's silence gives way to the aggressive voice of Joe Gilligan, a veteran whose abusive witticisms and alcoholic consumption set the stage for the novel. The gap between combat and noncombat emerges as absolute. Gilligan has been there but will not describe it; Lowe has not been there and can never make up the deficit. Faulkner soon looks beyond Lowe, but not before having him and Gilligan usher in Margaret Powers and Donald Mahon. These two death-shadowed figures—she war-widowed and tersely wise, he war-wounded and scarred beyond recognition—carry the emotional freight of *Soldiers' Pay*. "When am I going to get out?" (136) Mahon asks Gilligan—when will I be able to die? The unspoken answer is: not until all the betrayals that circulate around your dying have taken place, and there is nothing more for you to lose.

Soldiers' Pay returns obsessively to two concerns: frustrated desire, and loyalty silhouetted against betrayal. Powers and Mahon embody the book's gesture toward a death-suffused loyalty, as though all forms of postwar life were variations on infidelity. Both characters are permanently marked by war violence; neither has, nor wants, a future. Faulkner makes their weirdly destined marriage at the end of the novel appear as simultaneously a funeral—as though, in a world of illusory colors, they share the single authentic hue: black. Powers is awkwardly imported into this plot. Placed by the writer onto that fast-moving train without prior appropriateness, she exists only to be drawn to the dying Mahon. The logic of the novel demands this pairing as a fitting sequel to her having survived her husband. As she attends to Mahon, Lowe and Gilligan paw at her, trying unsuccessfully to reach her feelings. When, at the end of the book, Gilligan presses her one last time, she responds, "Bless your heart, darling. If I married you you'd be dead in a year, Joe. All the men that marry me die, you know" (SP 245). Her utterances are oracular and absolute. A sexually alluring woman yet a deadly mate, she is also the missing mother for these war-orphaned young men. A mother, however—like Faulkner's own?—whose impress is sinister, if not fatal. Each of the young men seeks out her embrace, yet to enter it erotically is to die. Unshakably wise, she calls the shots in this book. Or we could say that she shares that role with Donald Mahon.

Mahon seems mutely to harbor Faulkner's own longings. His wound anneals him from all possibility of intimacy, both orphaning him and con-stituting an impenetrable sanctuary sorely unavailable to his creator. "The man that was wounded is dead," Powers says, "and this is another one: a grown child. It's his apathy, his detachment from everything that's so terrible" (SP 92). Though his former fiancée, Cecily, continues to betray him, Mahon has reached a position of final indifference. It is as though Faulkner bestowed on him both the war wound he never received and the love wound he would never recover from. Mahon is at ease with both these wounds, finally safe behind his scar. He appears as a figure through whom the writer fantasized the immunity that death brings to the dying. Perhaps this is why *Soldiers' Pay* reads like a burial ceremony—a roundabout means of getting the damaged Mahon properly dead and into the earth.

Surrounding Mahon's ceremonial descent into death are a choir-like set of antic figures—inconstant Cecily Saunders and her stop-and-start flir-tations, drunken George Farr and his frustrated lust for Cecily, goat-like Januarius Jones and his freewheeling predations on whatever female will submit to them. Faulkner makes none of these minor figures interesting.

They seem to inhabit a different universe from that of Powers and Mahon. *Soldiers' Pay* fails to interrelate its cast of characters persuasively, as though there remain ghostly unwritten materials behind the palpably written ones. The writer's energy—balked from release in either plot or character (Mahon is an unplumbable center, and Powers does not develop)—finds its outlet in gorgeous, overwritten settings: "Beyond the oaks against a wall poplars in restless formal row were columns of a Greek temple, yet the poplars them-selves in slim vague green were poised and vain as girls in a frieze. Against a privet hedge would be lilies soon like nuns in a cloister and blue hyacinths swung soundless bells, dreaming of Lesbos" (SP 46). Yet another cocktail of words, poetic phrases doing duty for an ordeal of the spirit that Faulkner does not know how to narrate. No one in or outside the novel cares about the poplars or the privet hedge, the lilies or the blue hyacinths. "When am I going to get out?" the dying Donald Mahon murmured. Behind that question lies another this novel does not pose: when are we going to get in? When will we be enabled, by the writer's experimental language, to encounter not Mahon's deathly immunity but the living anguish inside his wounded mind and body? *Soldiers' Pay* dances around the surface of this question. *Mosquitoes*, stuffed to the gills with its own artistic and erotic questions, never even takes it up.

"It's Like Morphine, Language Is": Mosquitoes

Mosquitoes moves with a narrative assurance lacking in *Soldiers' Pay*, and Faulkner must have known at least one of the reasons why. He had actually experienced its main events. If the war in *Soldiers' Pay* imposed a wound-ing he elaborately faked, the mosquitoes in *Mosquitoes* inflicted a kind of sting—bodily, but also verbal, sexual, artistic—he knew only too well. In 1925 he had been aboard an abortive cruise on New Orleans's Lake Pontchartrain. Rain assailed the party, the yacht's motor gave out, and they were unable to move. Hordes of mosquitoes descended on them. The same event, reconfigured, gives *Mosquitoes* its plot. More broadly, Faulkner was sorting out his New Orleans experience—what he had come to know of its artistic and intellectual pretensions—into a ship of fools. Each character is reduced to essential traits—the loquacious writer Fairchild, the idealistic sculptor Gordon, the sexually engorged Jenny, the lean and epicene Patricia, the gnomic semitic man, and so on. Like epithets in eighteenth-century poetry, their leading traits serve as straitjackets. No one can change in this novel (the phrase "the semitic man" accompanies Julius Wiseman like a mantra, endlessly repeated, never varied). The central figure in this cast of characters is the hapless Mr. Talliaferro, who "often mused with regret on the degree of intimacy he might have established with his artistic acquaintances had he but acquired the habit of masturbation in his youth" (MOS 161). This piece of "information" is provided on the novel's opening page. It refers to a sexual activity never elsewhere named in Faulkner's novels, never elsewhere pertinent to their concerns. It is as though the writer were saying, abandon spiritual striving, all you who enter here!

Although Faulkner insinuates his name once into this novel—as "a little kind of black man" (MOS 371) whom Jenny met once and considered crazy—he stays out of *Mosquitoes*. The consequences are considerable, for his willingness to pass judgment correlates with his distance from his materials. Faulkner would never again be so imaginatively indifferent, so insistently mocking. The shameless self-display of artistic convictions, the nonstop aesthetic and cultural manifestoes that he encountered among Anderson's New Orleans coterie: for a man who treasured silence, these were not only sterile but offensive. "Talk, talk, talk: the utter and heartbreaking stupidity of words. It seemed endless" (408). Faulkner's later often-stated conviction—those who can, do, while those who can't, write—might have dated from the heady logorrhea of New Orleans literary life.

On the boat, an endless stream of pontification, punctuated for the males by steady drinking (heading toward stupor), and for the females by aimless chatter and flirtation. Off the boat, no better. When Pat and David romantically jump ship in order to elope, Faulkner subjects them to a fate crueler than on-board boredom. Bombarded by mosquitoes, lost in a swamp, brutalized by the penetrating summer sun, their romance fizzles. They almost die of exposure. Their rescue is as unchivalric as that Temple Drake receives two years later in *Sanctuary*. A sweat-stained local appears, glares at them, spits near their feet: "You folks been wandering around in the swamp all day? What you want to go back fer, now? Feller got enough, huh?" He spits again, "Aint no such thing as enough. Git a real man next time" (MOS 431). If Faulkner was thinking of his own failed elopement with Estelle, he granted no reprieve in this sordid replay. The novel reads more broadly as a refusal of all reprieve. There is no escaping the itch and scratch of desire stimulated and frustrated, of art contemplated but not created, of ceaseless talk that goes nowhere. "It's like morphine, language is" (516).

Only the aloof and silent sculptor, Gordon, operates above this infecting realm of talk and tease. Faulkner opens the book inside Gordon's studio, letting us see the real thing that the others' verbal antics merely play at: "it was marble . . . motionless and passionately eternal—the virginal breastless torso of a girl, headless armless legless, in marble temporarily caught and hushed yet passionate still for escape" (MOS 263). Such lyrical language appears in *Mosquitoes* only one other time. Seeing in Pat an intolerable embodiment of the wrought torso that obsesses him, Gordon suddenly swings her into the air: "and for an instant she stopped in mid-flight . . . Sunset was in his eyes: a glory, he could not see; and her taut simple body, almost breastless . . . was an ecstasy in golden marble, and in her face the passionate ecstasy of a child" (320–1). Flight, marble, ecstasy: these signal an exercise of spirit that nothing said or done on the novel's yacht can match. Flight will always enkindle Faulkner's imagination, and it will usually involve—what is absent here—the mortal danger that attaches to transcendence.

On the ground, as on the water, *Mosquitoes* rehearses its suffocating rituals. "They rolled smoothly, passing beneath spaced lights and around narrow corners, while Mrs Maurier talked steadily of her and Mr Talliaferro's and Gordon's souls" (MOS 270). To talk of one's soul is, for Faulkner, to have no soul. Apart from the two moments identified earlier, *Mosquitoes* has no genuine interest in the soul. Nothing is more than skin deep here. The "profound" talk, saturated in self-consciousness, is especially skin deep. "You become conscious of thinking, and then you start right off to think in words. And first thing you know, you don't have thoughts in your mind at all: you just have words for it" (445). Words appear as the ceaseless outpouring of open-mouthed beings, as the tiresome gesture—arousing and irritating—with which portentousness would pass itself off as spirit.

Before taking on this book, Faulkner had been hesitant—he wasn't sure he knew enough yet to manage its materials—but the problem was deeper than lack of knowledge. He loved New Orleans for its encouraging a free-living, free-drinking release of the spirit and the body. But New Orleans as a scene where pontificating artists and philosophers endlessly talked of work they never created: toward that city he felt contempt. Some writers—like Aldous Huxley, whose example served him here—make good use of contempt, creatively deliver a scene saturated in corrosive ironies. Not Faulkner. His great work to come would involve unthinking projection into the materials, would center on the ordeal of outraged spirit. The talkiness of words, their cheap exchangeability and the social/cultural jockeying that accompanied them, was outside the fictional territory he could imaginatively bring to life.

Dorothy Parker once confided to Ben Wasson that Faulkner's attempts at social repartee were awkward and embarrassing: "He should leave it to the likes of us to see how feather-brained we can be. My God, his wit is execrable. He's too great a man for our kind of foolishness" (CNC 109). Did Faulkner glimpse that foolishness—not folly but foolishness—was outside his fictional range, when he characterized *Mosquitoes* to Liveright as "trashily smart"? If so, it would have been an unwelcome recognition, since the man whose *Flags in the Dust* had just been turned down was hardly regarded as a "great" man. Parker was speaking of the Faulkner she met in the early 1930s; in November 1927 he was not yet that man. Three masterpieces—*The Sound and the Fury, As I Lay Dying, Sanctuary*—would appear in the next three years. Seen in the light of their brilliance, as well as the attention they had garnered, he might well have struck her as "great." But that aura was beyond his wildest fantasies in late 1927. All he wanted to do was to get *Flags* published, to stay on his feet. The future could wait; his insurmountable trouble was the present.

"The Company of Him Who Had Passed beyond Death
and Returned": Flags in the Dust

Despite Liveright's rejection, Faulkner knew that *Flags* was the best novel he had yet written. A glance at its opening paragraph intimates why:

> As usual old man Falls had brought John Sartoris into the room with him,
> had walked the three miles in from the county Poor Farm, fetching, like an
> odor, like the clean dusty smell of his faded overalls, the spirit of the dead
> man into that room where the dead man's son sat and where the two of them,
> pauper and banker, would sit for a half an hour in the company of him who
> had passed beyond death and returned. (FD 543)

"As usual": none of Faulkner's earlier fiction had risked—or reaped the rewards of—the "usual." From *New Orleans Sketches* through *Mosquitoes,* he had sought the unusual, the extraordinary. A certain desire to grandstand— "Pay attention to me!"—insinuates itself throughout that earlier work. It may not be too much to say that such work (poetry as well as prose) was damagingly invested in his need to demonstrate his difference. *Flags* opens instead on a familiar Southern town engaged in one of its identity-confirming rituals: rehearsing how the South lost the Civil War sixty years ago.

New, as well, is Faulkner's willingness to begin with old folks. *Soldiers' Pay* and *Mosquitoes* deal mainly with ardent and aggressive people younger than either of these old men, unspeakably wounded soldiers and the women they court, self-important artists and the theories they sport. Old man Falls carries into that room neither wound nor theory; he brings with him a past—and a ghost. Within a paragraph, Faulkner has found his way into his region's abiding neurosis. Its present is overshadowed, quietly suffocating under a past that has not passed. The South that is incidental to *Soldiers' Pay* and marginal to *Mosquitoes* is now center stage. Although Liveright seems not to have noticed it (he could find no unity in *Flags*), every vignette in the novel contributes to a diagnostic rendering of Faulkner's South. Diagnostic, not adversarial: could Liveright have missed *Flags*'s unemphatic but sustained critique because he found nothing Mencken-like in it, nothing contemptuously dismissive?

Just a page further, old man Falls brings something else to this book: white Southern vernacular. Faulkner had used black vernacular (often heavily stylized) in both the New Orleans sketches and *Soldiers' Pay*, and *Flags* goes on to delight more amply in black speech. "Delight" is the right verb, though a troublesome one. Delight in black vernacular fuels innumerable passages of white-authored Southern literature, testifying to racial affection cushioned on an unthinking conviction of white superiority. Little Southern white vernacular, however, had appeared in Faulkner's earlier work (urban gangster and underclass idioms are a different matter). In making old man Falls speak, Faulkner began to tap what would become one of his greatest novelistic resources:

> "They was times back in sixty three and fo' when a feller could a bought a section of land and a couple of niggers with this yere bag of candy. Lots of times I mind, with ever'thing goin' agin us like, and sugar and cawfee gone and food scace, eatin' stole cawn when they was any to steal and ditch weeds ef they wa'nt; bivouackin' at night in the rain, more' n like." (FD 730)

Did Faulkner recognize that Falls's voice was worth a dozen Swinburnes? That the poetry he had been recycling from other sources was all around him—in a different form—in the spoken vernacular of his region? There are many keys that help explain the master that Faulkner was to become, but one is that—in the figure of Falls, and later of Suratt and the MacCallums in *Flags*—he irresistibly sounds the vernacular rhythms of his place. No need to borrow from Housman or Eliot or Aiken; no need to tend an unspeakable wound; no need to sound "trashily smart" or to mock others for doing so.

The ritual of remembering the Lost Cause entails further rituals. Falls has come to Old Bayard's office to give him the pipe that belonged to Bayard's larger-than-life father, Colonel Sartoris, the Civil War hero. It is utterly pertinent (my next chapter will expand on the pertinence) that Faulkner—who smoked a pipe most of his life—was here recycling a ritual of his own great-grandfather, Colonel W. C. Falkner, also a Civil War hero. In *Flags*, the bond across time stretches across class as well; "pauper and banker" come together in the piety of shared memories. Bayard makes other gifts to the older man, supplying him annually with chewing tobacco. *Flags* registers this ceremony in common with a further one—this time bonding not classes but races—as it rehearses the "Christmas gift" ritual that moneyed whites enact with impoverished black servants and workers. Such rituals are far from innocent, and Faulkner does not justify them. The point is that he now *sees* them, puts them into narrative. The South in *Flags* may be moribund, but its author supplies it with tempo, texture, credible social norms.

Such Civil War–descended norms are useless for the young men returning from the Great War. Falls and Old Bayard have nothing helpful to say to the young—they can barely even hear each other since both are nearly deaf. Both are turned involuntarily toward the greater dead one, Colonel John Sartoris, who entered with them in that opening paragraph and broods on them. This dead Sartoris—more potent than when alive—dominates *Flags*. The book opens under his aegis and closes there as well: "He stood on a stone pedestal... one leg slightly advanced and one hand resting lightly on the stone pylon beside him... his back to the world and his carven eyes gazing out across the valley where his railroad ran and the blue changeless hills beyond, and beyond that, the ramparts of infinity itself" (FD 870). The ramparts of infinity: there is no space in *Flags* his marble statue does not oversee. To repudiate what he stands for is to have no standing at all. Young Bayard must enter *Flags* clandestinely, "like a hobo... [without] sojer-clothes... lak a drummer er somethin'" (546).

The implicit drama that Liveright missed in *Flags* involves the perverse and futile motions of the young who cannot follow the ancestral standard. Faulkner orchestrates this drama by way of a pair of twinned characters: young Bayard and young Horace, both orphaned, returning from the Great War. Critics have claimed that Phil Stone sat for the portrait of Horace (Stone often said so himself), but Faulkner amply endows Horace with elements of his own malaise, including his noncombat status. Horace suffers from bookishness, idealism, loneliness, love-misery. He is a figure of innocence catapulted into a world of unwanted experience: "It's having been younger once. Being dragged by time out of a certain day like a kitten from a tow sack, being thrust into another sack with shreds of the first one sticking to our claws" (FD 801). Although *Flags* cannot narrate that younger day—a failure *The Sound and the Fury* will powerfully redeem—the novel grants Horace a measure of the childhood-fueled amazement Faulkner never shed.

Sliding helplessly into the repellent sexual orbit of Belle Mitchell, Horace muses on the divorce she will engineer in order to marry him. He sees himself being set up to scratch a first husband's scratchings. More, he recognizes with disgust why he is unable to flee:

> a sort of gadfly urge after the petty, ignoble impulses which man has tried so vainly to conjure with words out of himself. Nature, perhaps, watching him as he tries to wean himself away from the rank and richly foul old mire that spawned him, biding her time and flouting that illusion of purifaction which he has foisted upon himself and calls his soul. (FD 800)

Impulse, words, nature, soul: this vocabulary appears in *Mosquitoes*, to be sure, but only in the argumentative voice of Fairchild or "the semitic man," never with the brooding openness of Horace Benbow. He sees humans as made up of chemicals "clotting for no reason, breaking apart again for no reason still" (799), their being violently removed from an earlier and happier realm and hurtled into this savagely new one for which they are unprepared, the "shreds of the first one" still sticking to them. These motifs of amazement would flower unforgettably in *The Sound and the Fury, As I Lay Dying,* and *Absalom, Absalom!*

Young Bayard Sartoris, the careening force at the center of *Flags,* is the most compelling character Faulkner had so far invented. (Ben Wasson was quick to identify him as the fulcrum for the shortened version that would become *Sartoris.*) He brings with him a war trauma Faulkner somehow suffered without experiencing. Bayard has survived his twin brother's being shot down by German fighter pilots. He is obsessed by the image of his brother John insouciantly mocking the death hurtling toward him in the air, even as the first Bayard Sartoris had gaily mocked his oncoming death fifty years earlier, shot down in the Civil War by a cook while raiding a Yankee commissary for anchovies. Young Bayard can neither match nor forget the glamour of his brother's exit. Every act of postwar violence that he compulsively launches—on a horse, in a car, in a plane—reenacts the death-drive of his twin. A figure of unspeakable trauma, young Bayard cannot get free of that earlier death. Readers cannot take their eyes off him, nor can Horace's sister, the serene Narcissa Benbow. She is drawn against her will into the orbit of his anguish. She "could see his bleak eyes and the fixed derision of his teeth, and suddenly she swayed forward in her chair and her head dropped between her prisoned arms and she wept with hopeless and dreadful hysteria" (FD 755).

What turmoil does his distress release in her—as though by contagion? Unable to narrate Bayard's war experience coherently, Faulkner sidesteps it with hifalutin rhetoric: "a meteoric violence like that of fallen angels, beyond heaven or hell and partaking of both: doomed immortality and immortal doom" (FD 643). We are back to "a cocktail of words," words thrown up as a screen against the real. The origin of Bayard's war-oriented misery may remain beyond articulation, but its damaging effects are vivid. The drinking scenes that awkwardly launch *Soldiers' Pay* and ritualistically punctuate *Mosquitoes* take on focus and power in *Flags*. Bayard's binges with young men in town and with the MacCallums in the backcountry eloquently convey his futile search for sanctuary: "It's my damned head. I keep thinking another drink will ease it off some" (658).

"It's my damned head": did Faulkner glimpse in this terse phrase the core of his dilemma as a writer? Did he recognize that *Flags*, for all its richness of regional description and analysis, did not find its way into the head—which is to say, into the heart? Faulkner himself had already learned to use alcohol to evade both head and heart. His heavy drinking would increase over time, becoming binge drinking. Usually, as he emerged from the booze, he would find that the drink had temporarily "ease[d] it off some." Temporarily. I examine Faulkner's alcoholism in some detail later, but for now the writerly problem of how to get into that "damned head" was before him. Despite the warmth with which *Flags* dilates on the routines and ritual of the South, it unmistakably emits an SOS of distress. Bayard and Horace—its orphaned young men in crisis—were suffering outside the reach of archaic cultural norms. Both were drowning in the *now*; neither could say why.

As Faulkner sought to revise *Flags* in late 1927, his mind turned repeatedly to Liveright's reasons for turning it down. "If the book had plot and structure, we might suggest shortening and revisions ... my chief objection is that you don't seem to have any story to tell and I contend that a novel should tell a story." Liveright had seen that *Flags* did not tell a story, but— Faulkner might now have pondered—had Liveright seen why it did not? Had Faulkner himself really seen why? In truth, if he looked at it hard, he had no story to tell. Perhaps what he had to tell, but had not yet learned how to tell it, was the breakdown of story. "It's my damned head," he had written in *Flags*. The unarticulated drama he had been unable to tell through

Donald Mahon or Horace Benbow or Bayard Sartoris was locked unspeakably inside their heads. All three men were wounded, arrested, incapable of
explaining themselves. None of them was a candidate for "story." Mahon
or Horace or Bayard eventually getting through their distress? Impossible.
But what might be possible was to give voice and heft to the distress itself.
Did he see that what had all along spurred his writing, but never gotten *into*
the writing, was distress? To say the gap between *was* and *is,* the collapse of
sanctioned expectations, to show how these roiled and derailed the "damned
head": he had not known this *could* be written. The outrage of being alive in
the present moment and unprepared for what is coming at you—an explosion of moments beyond story altogether. *The Sound and the Fury* would not
respond to Liveright's warning, and it would probably never get published.
But it would say distress as distress had not been said before.

The Sound and the Fury would locate distress where it originated—in
childhood. Of his earlier work, only *Elmer* risked the pathos lodging there.
The awkwardness of that unfinished text suggests Faulkner's discomfort,
his inability to go further in. *Soldiers' Pay* and *Mosquitoes* both achieved
fluency not least because, avoiding childhood, they protected his writerly
immunity. Even *Flags* could access childhood only in the form of young
Virgil Beard, an inexpressive child fixed somewhere between silent obsession and psychopathic rage. Young Virgil tortures insects and kills mock-
ingbirds; he would soon flower into *Sanctuary*'s Popeye. He does not prepare
us for a cluster of innocent children playing by a stream. Those children's
threatful future remains pastorally at bay, though continuously implicit in
their words and gestures—intimated to us, unknown to them. Their fate
lies compressed within a single radiant image—that of a little girl's muddy
drawers, seen from below by her hushed and hesitant brothers, while she
remains high up in a pear tree, looking on death. Childhood as a drama of
unpreparedness and exposure, of multiple times (the shaping past, the all-
consuming present, the approaching future): as he had unknowingly lived
it, as he luminously reconfigured it, later. His own childhood: that had been
missing from the work all along.

CHILDHOOD

He was his parents' first-born child, and—so he had always heard—his
entry onto the scene was not easy. He was colicky for much of his first year
(he would suffer from sleeping disorders off and on throughout his life),
obscurely unhappy at being there at all. His mother would rock him for

hours, the chair she sat in striking the floor and making their neighbors think the Falkners were chopping kindling all night long. He had come into the world on September 25, 1897, in the village of New Albany, Mississippi. His parents were almost as new to that setting as he was (they had moved in only a year earlier), and over the next five years the family would undergo two more displacements: to Ripley in 1898, and to Oxford in 1902. He didn't know why these moves occurred; no one consulted him about them. He would later remember how, during those four years at Ripley, some people would pass to the other side of the street to avoid speaking to his family (F 24). He didn't understand their motives then. Already, perhaps, he was registering what all infants experience, few later remember, and fewer yet go on to explore: that the past operates massively in the present, even if (especially if) you don't yet know what that past contained.

He suffered from other displacements more wounding than changes of residence. Each of his brothers' arrivals was hard on him. Murry Jr. (Jack) was born when he was less than two. Though free of colic, Jack was finicky about food and required incessant maternal care. The birth of John (Johncy), three years later, was even more difficult for him. Johncy was graceless enough to emerge on the scene only one day before his own fifth birthday, suddenly ousting him from attention. As though in revenge, he promptly contracted scarlet fever, and nearly died of it. To round it off, Dean's birth five years later—probably the only sibling birth he consciously remembered—was the most trying of all. Born in August 1907, after a harrowing eight months during which both of the children's grandmothers had sickened and died, Dean suffered from a severe case of cradle cap (an eczema on the crown of the infant's head). His mother, still anguished over the recent loss of her own mother, frantically attended to her newborn's needs. She had named him after her own mother (Lelia Dean Swift Butler) and could not bear to see him suffer.

Faulkner knew early on, without knowing why, that his parents were badly married. They were physically mismatched, but the troubling misfit was mental and emotional. Like other intractable troubles he would come to know, this one had a concealed prehistory. Maud Butler Falkner was petite, with a sharply focused face and an even more focused mind. "Don't Complain—Don't Explain," she had written in bright red letters above her kitchen stove. As Faulkner's brother Jack said later, this was "her philosophy of life, and she passed it on in full measure to her children" (FOM 15–6). Such a message signaled to them the cardinal need for backbone, staying power. What it signaled about the giving and withholding of love was something else. Her mark on all her sons was deep and permanent. They were each to write her regularly when traveling, throughout their lives. If in Oxford, Faulkner would rarely miss a day of sharing coffee and conversation with her, up to the time of her death in 1960. The brothers all married, but the first woman in their lives seems to have remained their mother. She safeguarded this position of dominance by keeping at bay the wives her sons had taken—a distancing the sons apparently accepted without much question. That Faulkner was to compose his fiction on a frail spindle-legged writing desk she had given him—while sitting on a tall-backed chair she had likewise given him—is enormously telling. His mother was inseparable from the exercise of his imaginative life, which is not to say that he regarded her with anything but ambivalence. Mothers were to fare badly in his fiction, perhaps worse than fathers; his sympathies would always lie with their damaged offspring. It was she who first encouraged him to read widely in canonical Western literature—the Bible, the Greeks, Shakespeare, Cervantes, Balzac, Dickens, Conrad. More, she steadfastly defended the novels he would produce over the years—including the notorious *Sanctuary*—whether or not she comprehended their purposes. ("Let him alone, Buddy," she reprimanded her angered husband during Oxford's outraged reception of *Sanctuary*, "he writes what he has to" [F2 1:687].)

Maud's childhood had not been easy, and she didn't make that of her children easy either. Her father, Charles Butler, had shocked everyone by abandoning his family in the late 1880s, taking with him money not his own. From that point forward, the fates of Charles's abandoned wife and daughter were entwined. Maud's dreams of higher education gave way to the need to support her suddenly vulnerable mother. The young woman Murry Falkner married in 1896 grimly knew what she knew about the world—and about men. As her mother's health began to fail later, Maud insisted that Lelia ("Damuddy") move into their new Oxford home, where she lived until her death in 1907. These were the years of Faulkner's early childhood. They cannot have been easy for anyone involved, though his parents at least knew why. Leila Butler had not concealed her disapproval of her daughter's choice. For years after the marriage, her letters continued to address her daughter as Miss Maud Butler, in care of Mr. Murry Falkner. Both mother and daughter possessed artistic talent and an appreciation for higher culture lacking in the Falkner family, conspicuously so in Murry. Murry might have struck Maud as a dubious bet as well.

Murry Falkner was a big strapping man, like his father before him and most of his sons. Only William was small, never to exceed five feet five and a half inches in height. As I mentioned, in 1918 he was judged too short and too light to qualify for the aviation division of the U.S. army. His small size was to affect him immeasurably, throughout his childhood, adolescence, and manhood. Perhaps the first thing all infants note about their parents is how big they are—how powerful and difficult to contest—and in Faulkner's case the question of size was exponentially laden. The boy had inherited Butler features, not Falkner ones—his mother's small compact body, her hooded almond eyes, thin lips, sharp nose. He knew his father found him different, inward, alien. When Murry would sometimes sneeringly refer to him as "Snake-lips," could Faulkner have recognized that the pain inflicted by this insult was intended for his mother as well—perhaps for her most of all? That the only target Murry could reach was that son who so obviously favored Maud?

Murry had attended the University of Mississippi, like his father before him, but would never be a scholar. He loved the outdoors, passing his time in the woods or in the stables, with men (black and white) and animals. Not a man of words, he preferred to be in bodily motion rather than exploring ideas or feelings. At first his luck held good. His father had granted Murry's supreme wish by allowing him to work for the father's railroad company. Murry loved this work and rose steadily up the ranks. By 1900 he was essentially running the Ripley railroad office. In 1902, however—when Faulkner was five—the railroad was suddenly sold out from under Murry. As a little boy in the years following this disastrous event, Faulkner could hardly help knowing that his father was often morose and embittered. But it would take time for Murry's sons to realize fully what wound it was he had never recovered from. When would they have grasped how much it meant when, as one of them later remembered, their father, at the sound of an approaching train's whistle, would stop in his tracks and stare?

Though he was punctual and could usually be counted on to fulfill his commitments, Murry was inarticulate, lacking the flexibility that comes with inner resources. The only reading he cared for—apart from the funny papers—was westerns. (He seems never to have read any of his son's novels.) After he lost his beloved railroad, he became irreparably aimless. His vision of the future, vaguely enough, involved leaving Mississippi altogether—getting clear of his domineering, job-removing, and job-imposing father—and becoming a rancher somewhere out west. Murry's tough-minded and practical wife was not about to indulge such a proposed change in residence. So—unindulged, hemmed in, caught in domestic and business arrangements he found suffocating—Murry took his revenge. As his own father and grandfather had, he periodically exploded in outbursts of anger and bouts of drinking.

Faulkner grew up in the presence of such explosions. When the drinking reached the state of uncontrollable binge, Maud would take over. She would cart Murry off to the same Keeley sanatorium (near Memphis) his father had used when he, too, had needed to be "dried out" professionally. More, Maud would take her sons along, ensuring that they absorbed the lesson of their father's irresponsible behavior and the humiliating treatment it required. Throughout his life, Faulkner would remember his father as awkward, incommunicative, not on his side. A vignette he later liked to tell involved one of his father's rare bids for sympathy. Murry approached his silent oldest son, at some point well into his teens, and said he had heard that the boy had taken up smoking. He took out one of his cigars and offered his son a "good smoke." William accepted the cigar, said "Thank you, sir," then reached into his pocket for his pipe. He tore the cigar in half, stuffed half of it into the pipe, and lit it. Murry watched in silence, then walked away. "He never gave me another cigar," Faulkner fondly remembered. What is most resonant about this story is less the meanness it brims over with than the son's delight in telling it later. Whatever the father-inflicted wound might have been, his eldest son did not tire of rehearsing his moment of revenge.

His parents' marital misery was amply before him, but not the details of its prehistory. Later he might have begun to piece it together, perhaps recognizing that his father's unhappiness participated in a pattern at least three generations old. It went all the way back to William's great-grandfather, mythologized (by all subsequent Falkners) as Colonel William C. Falkner of Civil War grandeur. This W. C. Falkner entered family lore as a fourteen-year-old boy arriving in Pontotoc, Mississippi, in 1839, a runaway from home thanks to a severe beating by his own father. Self-orphaned, he begged to be taken in by his maternal aunt and her husband, John Wesley Thompson. The Thompsons took him in, but some six years later Thompson refused to accept his nephew into his law practice. A few years after that, the nephew—a veteran of the Mexican war, now married and a father—lost his wife to illness. He decided to give the baby up to his uncle. They apparently agreed that the uncle would take care of the baby on condition that the nephew never ask to have him back. It seems that W. C. Falkner never did ask to have him back. Rather, he remarried and began a second family, in effect abandoning his first-born son. A few years later, in 1855, he challenged his uncle for a seat in the Mississippi legislature, and lost. Once the

Civil War broke out, W. C. Falkner went on to lead a memorably violent and achievement-studded life, to which I shall return later, since he was the ancestor who meant most to his great-grandson.

Meanwhile, that abandoned boy, J. W. T. Falkner, named for his great-uncle J. W. Thompson, who brought him up, was eventually invited to join his great-uncle's law firm (as his own father had not been permitted to do). In time, J. W. T. Falkner became a successful politician, banker, real estate owner, and railway tycoon. Called in his youth the "Young Colonel" and in later times "the Colonel," this colorful and imposing man—Murry's father—was fondly remembered by his grandson William. He dressed in courtly white linen suits and an elegant panama hat, both of which were complemented by his ever-present cigar. He delighted in a highly visible lifestyle while residing in the Oxford mansion he had built, The Big Place. His grandsons remembered his buying one of the first cars in town and—chauffeur-driven—touring around the countryside in it. They also remembered the story of how, fairly deep into the booze, he directed his black driver to circle around the bank he presided over. He then ordered his driver to stop the car. He carefully got out, picked up a good-sized brick, and hurled it through the bank's plate-glass window. When asked later about his reasons, J. W. T. Falkner responded: "It was my Buick, my brick, and my bank" (F 34).

J. W. T. Falkner may well have had his own filial/paternal issue to resolve—by recycling it, this time with himself in the position of power. After installing his oldest son, Murry, in his railroad business and shepherding his success there, J.W.T. abruptly—in 1902—sold the railroad out from under his son. He did this, moreover, when railroads were one of America's boom industries. The railroad that he sold for $75,000 had made a profit that year of nearly $35,000. A smart businessman who sells an enterprise earning an annual 45 percent of its sale price: that is an enigma begging to be explained. Perhaps J.W.T.'s banking and real estate commitments in Oxford really did require the supportive presence of Murry. Maybe they really did mandate the sale of the railroad and the uprooting of Murry's family from Ripley to Oxford. Perhaps not.[3] In any case, the Murry Falkners were soon installed in a house conspicuously smaller than J.W.T.'s Big Place, and Murry was now permanently at loose ends. Reflecting on a family pattern of paternal abuse and abandonment repeating itself over generations, it would hardly have been lost on Faulkner how strident present troubles have voiceless histories. He might even have generalized this insight and seen that fathers often find ways direct and indirect to destroy their sons. Only in the mid-1930s would he write *Absalom, Absalom!*—one of his greatest novels—but the paternal/filial concerns of that book were all around him thirty years earlier, alive in the dinner-table quarrels between his mother and his father. Alive there, but significant only if his mind moved from the immediate piece at hand to the far-reaching pattern in family history. Significant only if he could see that the abuse he himself suffered at his father's hands had a prehistory of abuse imposed and received, dating back to before the Civil War.[4]

How much damage did these mismatched parents do to their first-born son? The question cannot be answered, though there is good reason to think that in each of his supreme novels he was rehearsing and exploring it. The father's incapacity to enter his son's subjectivity cannot but have hardened the son's emotional defenses—Faulkner's default sense of being misunderstood. Ben Wasson once reported that Faulkner flared out at him, "Godamighty, fellow, if there's anything that upsets the world, it's people who do things because they consider it's 'well-meaning'" (CNC 74). This outburst was in immediate response to his mother having decided on her own to write a letter to Liveright, asking him to reconsider his dismissal of *Flags*. The outburst has a broader resonance. It conveys Faulkner's belief that others could not possibly put themselves in his shoes—even those who believed, because they loved him, that they shared his hopes and fears. Murry was unable to offer this needy child an open paternal heart, to see in William a version of himself. This closure worked to seal off Faulkner's own heart, persuading him that even the most intimate relationships were founded on distortion, guesswork, misunderstanding.

This wound is likely to have become compounded inasmuch as, despite Maud's many virtues and lifelong loyalty, she, too, seems to have suffered from a hardened heart. Perhaps she had been through too much before he was born. She powerfully modeled character and loyalty for him, but not empathic generosity of feeling. Self-discipline in the face of obstacles was her watchword. When she determined that, as a young teenager, he was falling into incorrect posture, she did not hesitate to make him wear a back brace for two years. What he thought of the discipline mandating this brace—which in addition to its discomfort embarrassingly resembled a woman's corset—he never said, but we do know that the odious Mrs. Compson in *The Sound and the Fury* forced her daughter Caddy to wear something similar. Maud's inability to confirm him in a bodily fashion—her need to improve rather than endorse his bodily being—seems to emerge in a 1925 letter he wrote to his great-aunt Alabama. Faulkner is referring here to her niece, Vannye:

> I will be awfully glad to see Vannye again. The last time I remember seeing her was when I was 3, I suppose. I had gone to spend the night with Aunt Willie [in Ripley] and I was suddenly taken with one of those spells of lone-liness and nameless sorrow that children suffer, for what or because of what they do not know. And Vannye and Natalie [her sister] brought me home, with a kerosene lamp. I remember how Vannye's hair looked in the light—like honey. Vannye was impersonal; quite aloof: she was holding the lamp. Natalie was quick and dark. She was touching me. She must have carried me. (SL 20)

To find anything like this bodily sensibility in his work before *The Sound and the Fury*, one would have to return to *Elmer*. The unpreparedness and vulnerability of infancy and early childhood resonate here, as they will so powerfully in the narratives of Benjy Compson, Vardaman Bundren, and the young Joe Christmas. Judith Sensibar has suggestively read this passage as a screen memory. Vannye and Natalie, she argues, are stand-ins for his mother Maud and his black nurse, Mammy Callie. Maud the impersonal and aloof caregiver, the figure of light; Callie the dark one who touches him, who must have carried him. I shall return to Callie later, when I explore the issue of Faulkner and race. Her importance to him is inestimable. His daughter once claimed that of the women in his life, "Mammy Callie meant the most to him" (OFA 237n34).

The deficiencies of his childhood do not enforce limitations in his art. Rather, such emotional withholding spurred him to his greatest work, strengthened his need to understand the failure of the heart in all its dimensions and fallout. Perhaps no other novelist has explored more pow-erfully the consequences upon the child of parents who—for the most intractable reasons—cannot love that child as it needs to be loved. That this emotional dilemma launches the fiction into greatness does not mean, however, that the author did not suffer from it his entire life. Self-yielding, self-opening: these are nearly absent in his life, and their near absence is inseparable from the notorious silences he would maintain, as well as his passionate defense of privacy.

There remains one further insight he might have garnered from his father's postrailroad sequence of failures: a sense for untimeliness, for the difficulty of being ready to take on what the present moment carries for good or ill. Murry chose to own a livery stable in the first decade of the twentieth century—just as cars were beginning to become the vehicle of choice. When that business failed, he turned to the coal oil (for lamplight-ing) business—just as electricity was beginning to replace gas light. It would be easy to mock Murry for these unpropitious choices. His oldest son might have reflected further and arrived at a rarer insight. He might have glimpsed that humans are typically not wise in present time—that wisdom is a ret-rospective angle of vision (and often useless because too late) whereby men and women see beyond the error of their earlier stumbling. Did Faulkner grasp that erasing the present moment's blindness was a way of denying experience itself? He would recurrently stumble throughout present-tense crises in his own life, and he would learn to respect his mistakes (which did not mean justifying them). In time, his art became supremely invested in the unavoidability of stumbling. And he discovered that the tradition of the novel—as he had inherited it from earlier practitioners in the West—was hostile to that insight, shaped so as to minimize it. Which meant—though he would never have put it to himself in this way—that he would have to reinvent the form of the novel.

His childhood was hardly limited to an engagement with the dilem-mas I have just explored. In fact, biographers have mainly portrayed it as a scene of idyllic, rough-and-tumble play, at least until his early teens. If his father's limitations damaged his emotional growth, his father's consolations for a failed career expanded his range of activities. It was Murry who intro-duced him to the delights of male camaraderie—who let him pass hours silently taking in the all-male activities and conversations that occurred in the livery stable. (To Malcolm Cowley he would say in 1945, "I more or less grew up in my father's livery stable" [FCF 67].) A hunter and a lover of animals, Murry introduced all his sons to the pleasures of life in the big woods. Mammy Callie enriched these pleasures by teaching the boys the names of the birds, the virtues of the plants that flourished in nature. All the boys became scouts, and Faulkner—whose tenderness toward children was notable his entire life—later served as scoutmaster.

The three older boys grew up as inseparable playmates, joined soon by their tomboy cousin Sally Murry. (The four Compson children of *The Sound and the Fury*—three boys and one radiant girl—owe much to his own childhood experiences.) Thanks to books written (after his death in 1962) by his brothers Jack and Johncy, we have a vivid picture of the Falkner boys' early adventures and shenanigans. As the oldest brother, William played the role of the boss who gives the orders. He participated equally in their escapades but did not need—or care—to explain his commands. Flying kites, rolling in mud, building a "steam engine," accidentally setting fire to the house, joining together to fight gangs of other kids (often using corncobs to do so): such scapegrace activities seem to have punctuated their childhood. Perhaps the most suggestive of them involved a (homemade) airplane. Under Faulkner's supervision, the brothers labored for weeks to jerrybuild a plane from designs taken from an *American Boy* journal—using rotten wood, rusty nails, grocery bags, and wrapping paper. The day arrived finally when their improvised craft was to take off. Boss Faulkner insisted that luckless Jack would serve as pilot. At the last moment, though, they couldn't make their plane slide down a bluff in order to begin its flight. Jack was given a reprieve, joining the others, who were to push as hard as possible. Faulkner honorably replaced his brother at the controls. Heaving together, the others finally launched the vehicle. The collapse that followed was the first, but not the last, air disaster in which he would participate.

The Falkner boys' childhood narratives evoke Mark Twain; a series of Tom Sawyerish pranks and experiments are pursued with innocent fanaticism, while the horrified parents arrive on the scene always just too late. For Jack and Johncy, their shared childhood may well have appeared thus in memory. Shared is the key word: such shenanigans give their childhood many of its sharable dimensions. We need to remind ourselves that both brothers wrote about a childhood that had taken place a half century earlier—childhood gathered retrospectively into a Twain-like story. Faulkner himself never wrote of his childhood at all, and, more curious, none of his fiction prior to *The Sound and the Fury* even broaches childhood. Childhood as a scene of play and pranks is something he is able to write only in his sixties, at the end of his career, in *The Reivers*. (Is it accidental that both brothers' narratives of their famous sibling resemble that last novel more than anything else he wrote?) What actually emerges in each of his brothers' memoirs is less the childhood life of William than his unapproachability, his self-protecting armor, which neither of them can penetrate. His inviolate separateness stamps their family stories with unintended pathos. He grew up in their midst, made indelible impressions on them, remained a loyal and responsible sibling, and won the Nobel Prize—but they did not know him.

Jack comes closest to understanding such guarded privacy when he writes of Faulkner's delight in horses and mules: "I think his feeling toward them was a sort of compassion born of reflecting that a mule is actually nothing more than a freak of nature.... He regarded animals in the same light as he did human beings: neither asked to be here, both were, and both had t exist the best way they could" (FOM 198). Jack goes on to say that Faulkner admired mules for "always standing on their own four feet and ... eternally daring anyone to try to push them off" (198). Don't complain, don't explain: hold your ground, maintain integrity, stay who you are.

When does the young Faulkner start to demonstrate his "mulish-ness"? Entering first grade at the age of eight, he adored his teacher, Miss Annie Chandler. He performed admirably for her, even giving her three of his watercolor paintings. As a token of her gratitude, she offered him a copy of *The Clansman: An Historical Romance of the Ku Klux Klan,* by Thomas Dixon—a racist novel that served a decade later as the basis of D. W. Griffith's (in)famous film *The Birth of a Nation*. A beloved teacher choosing to offer this book—as pedagogical encouragement—to one of her most promising students speaks volumes about racial norms in the early twentieth-century South. I shall revisit those norms when I later consider Faulkner's insertion in his region's drama of race. For the next three years, he continued to make the honor roll; he was even allowed to skip second grade. Such model behavior ceased after the fifth grade. By then he had turned to playing hooky, was regularly skipping school, and was refusing to do the chores his parents assigned. He had lost interest, giving no reasons for it. School no longer mattered, and it would never play more than a neg-ligible role in his fiction. Labove, one of the very few teachers in Faulkner's novelistic world, appears in *The Hamlet* as a young man starved for higher culture, one who has sacrificed much to obtain it. His misfortune is not long in coming. Irresistible Eula Varner ambles into Labove's classroom—a teenager exuding a deadly sexual attraction and not only indifferent to him but unaware of his uncontrollable lust. Smitten, he is helpless to repress the most humiliating attempts to embrace her, or failing that, to put his face into her just-vacated classroom seat, besotted by its still-present imprint. Labove's education project has vanished: his real education—degrading, involuntary, disastrous—has taken over.

"To me, all human behavior is unpredictable, and, considering man's frailty ... irrational" (FIU 267), Faulkner would later propose to the Univer-sity of   inia's Department of Psychiatry in the late 1950s. The enabling
                  ducation struck him as in large part self-doomed, inasmuch as
                  ofessors attempting to prepare students to deal with realities
                  et arrived. He knew they weren't real until they arrived. No
                  ich you how to manage them in advance. As he wryly put
                  students that year at the University of Virginia, "Actually,
                  e for you, you know. You've got to do that yourself" (133).
                  —what he would call in *Absalom* the "*citadel of the central*

I-Am's private own" (AA115, emphasis in the original)—marked his child-hood. The key things in your life: you've got to do them yourself. Fiercely protected privacy, on the one hand, menaced by unpredictable assaults, on the other. Such assaults were both dreaded and desired. In breaking into his "citadel," might they also spring him free from its confines? To quote his earlier poem, "marble-bound must he ever be?"

Perhaps his dearest hope for breakthrough rested on a girl who lived nearby. He had known her family since they were children together; his attraction to her had deepened over time. A half-year older, Estelle Old-ham was voluble and charming as he could never be. Carefully trained by her socially established and ambitious parents, she was well on her way to becoming a southern belle. Not a tomboy like her sister Victoria or his cousin Sally Murry, Estelle flourished on a feminine stage—she played the piano, danced the old and the new dances, engaged effortlessly in the art of conversation. Boys adored her. Yet she sought out the reclusive young Faulkner, sharing his private aspirations, his love of poetry and the arts. As they spent more and more time in each other's company, they forged a bond whose hold on them both exceeded their capacity to give it focus and direc-tion. They somehow knew they would remain part of each other's lives. Was he beginning to believe—without thinking it out in so many words—that a future life with her might, miraculously, both unlock him and render him intact as never before?

Childhood as he had actually experienced it had little of the playfulness that his brothers later remembered. It was not a sequence of boyish she-nanigans. "She must have carried me," he had written his great aunt about her niece, the "quick and dark" Natalie who "was touching me" during "one of those spells of loneliness and nameless sorrow that children suffer." Like Elmer, he was sensitized to touch as only a child who has not received enough of it can be. His own mother, so obviously there for him throughout his life—a model of loyalty and rectitude he never ceased to honor—was also, perhaps, at a deeper bodily level, not there at all. Not there because of earlier dilemmas she had suffered from, been scarred by; not there for her husband either. They all lived in the same household, but each inhabited the shared domestic space in his or her incommunicable way. Murry and Maud were his authoritative parents, yes. But he had seen enough of their parents—of Colonel J. W. T. Falkner and of Leila Dean Swift Butler—to grasp that though his own mother and father were no longer children, yet they were children still. Perhaps life, alongside its undeniable ongoing movement, did not move at all? Perhaps everything changed, but nothing changed, those earlier wounds both inflicted long ago yet still damaging, indeed immortal?

Childhood wrought upon him the experience of incapacity, of being little among others who were big. It gave him no less the experience of not-knowing, of coming on the scene not at the beginning but in the middle. Others acted out of motives he couldn't yet know—motives formed before he was born, but whose impact on him was unavoidable. Childhood was about unavoidability, about being in a body not yet able to avoid what it had not chosen to encounter. And if some of its sorrows would always remain "nameless," others would open up to understanding—later. That was when, he would discover, things did open up—usually too late to be of use. His own childhood had led him unswervingly, though without his planning it, toward silence and an inwardness he could not shed. Strangest of all, this had all occurred in the presence of others continuously sharing his space and attentive to his being there.

To narrate this experience of childhood would require an unconventional sense of how things occurred—a sense outside Mark Twain's narrative range. He would have to show that what is shared with others in common space is doubled by what is unsharable. He would also have to show that what namelessly assaults the child, in the moment of now, has its namable roots in what occurred earlier, before the child was born. Childhood was about double exposure: the nameless violence of *is*, juxtaposed against the name-filled mapping of *was*. He had never told this earlier because its strangeness had seemed untellable, hostile to narrative itself. Donald Mahon at least had an explanatory war behind his all-damaging wound. But Mahon's war, like the range of neurotic behavior represented in *Mosquitoes*, had not been unspeakably Faulkner's own. Childhood was unspeakably his own, and he had had to lose it before he could begin to see it. Lose it in the sense of getting past it, but lose it also in the sense of turning it into coherence. Could he tell it in such a way that his words would supply the coherence that words do supply, yet preserve the violence that was there before the saying? Could he make the clash of *is* and *was* penetrate, as heartbreak, yet also intimate, as beauty?

BREAKTHROUGH

"The Only Thing in Literature That Would Ever Move Me":
The Sound and the Fury

Perhaps the best brief summary of what happens in *The Sound and the Fury* is provided by Faulkner himself, in a letter to his friend and editor Ben Wasson. Editing the first chapter of the novel, Wasson was confused by Faulkner's use of italics to indicate sudden shifts of time. As a trusted friend, Wasson decided to improve matters. He took the liberty of substituting a spatial device (skipping a line of type whenever there was a time shift) for Faulkner's typographical one (italics that replaced roman script). He then sent the revised proofs to Faulkner at Pascagoula, where the newlyweds were honeymooning. Soon after came this response from Faulkner:

> I received the proof. It seemed pretty tough to me, so I corrected it as written, adding a few more italics where the original seemed obscure on second reading. Your reason for the change, i.e., that with italics only 2 different dates were indicated I do not think sound for 2 reasons. First, I do not see that the use of breaks clarifies it any more; second, there are more than 4 dates involved. The ones I recall off-hand are: Damuddy dies. Benjy is 3. (2) His name is changed. He is 5. (3) Caddy's wedding. He is 14. (4) He tries to rape a young girl and is castrated. 15. (5) Quentin's death. (6) His father's death. (7) A visit to the cemetery at 18. (8) The day of the anecdote, he is 33. (NOR, 227)

The time line described thus in sequential fashion—moving from an earlier death when Benjy is three to the present time when he is thirty-three— seems familiar enough. It includes a name change, a sister's wedding, a misdirected attempt to embrace young girls and its dire consequence, the death of an older brother, the death of a father, a cemetery visit, and the events occurring on his thirty-third birthday. This thirty-year span suggests a familiar plot of maturation, and not a few readers of *The Sound and the Fury* might wish that the book proceeded accordingly. But Benjy is an idiot, and he has not matured between the ages of three and thirty-three. (As his caretaker Luster's friend remarks, "he been three years old thirty years" [SF 889].) He experiences time otherwise. Rather than narrating events sequentially and coherently—as Faulkner's letter to Wasson does— the novel opens in Benjy's mind as follows:

> Through the fence, between the curling flower spaces, I could see them hitting. They were coming toward where the flag was and I went along the fence. Luster was hunting in the grass by the flower tree. They took the flag out, and they were hitting. Then they put the flag back and they went to the table, and he hit and the other hit. Then they went on, and I went along the fence. Luster came away from the flower tree and we went along the fence and they stopped and we stopped and I looked through the fence while Luster was hunting in the grass.

"Here, caddie." He hit. They went away across the pasture. I held to the fence and watched them going away.

"Listen at you, now." Luster said. "Aint you something, thirty three years old, going on that way. After I done went all the way to town to buy you that cake. Hush up that moaning. Aint you going to help me find that quarter so I can go to the show tonight."...

We went along the fence and came to the garden fence, where our shadows were. My shadow was higher than Luster's on the fence. We came to the broken place and went through it.

"Wait a minute. Luster said. "You snagged on that nail again. Cant you never crawl through here without snagging on that nail."

Caddy uncaught me and we crawled through. Uncle Maury said to not let anybody see us, so we better stoop over, Caddy said. Stoop over, Benjy. Like this, see. We stooped over and crossed the garden, where the flowers rasped and rattled against us. (SF 879–80)

This passage is quietly unnerving. Placed in Benjy's mind, we see only what he sees. His caretaker Luster is "hunting" for something, and a group of people are "hitting." Since there is a flag connected with their hitting, an adroit reader might pick up the next cue—"here, caddie"—and realize that these other people are golfers. They are putting on a green and then teeing off for the next hole, their caddies going with them. One might pick this up, but one might not. No green is identified, no fairway or tees. Benjy identifies the people as moving "across the pasture." Here we encounter the (il)logic of an idiot's insertion in space and time. Benjy's sense of space is untutored (the men's movement across it has for him no recognizable purpose), and he is unaware that he exists in time. He identifies the golf course as the pasture because when he was a child, it was the family's pasture. That earlier identification has remained unchanged; it is still the pasture. He does not know that his family sold it later to the town, to become a golf course, so that they could pay for their eldest son, Quentin, to attend Harvard. That sale occurred some twenty years earlier, and Quentin has been dead nearly that long himself. Benjy is incapable of knowing any of this.

His ignorance (as narrator) ensures ours as readers, and there are those who—irritated by such disorientation—refuse to read beyond this opening page. Only when a writer removes us from our anticipated moorings—the capacity, shared by reader and protagonist, to read location in space and time orientationally—do we realize how much we depend on such moorings. It is as though Faulkner were placing us in front of a television screen and showing images made strange because the sound had been turned off. Like that missing sound, the glue that organizes the flow of images is missing. Benjy sees phenomena in space and time (people hitting), not the conventional arrangement that makes these phenomena cohere (golfers playing). Benjy's perspective registers only brute sequence—a cascade of "then" and "and" rather than "thus" or "therefore." Yet this unmoored scene has its own beauty. He notices the unequal shadows, he hears the rasping flowers. His sensory notations are fresh and keen. More, Faulkner insinuates an undeclared emotional causality into this passage, as its moving from "here, caddie" to "listen at you, now" suggests. Since no first-time reader yet knows, however, that the dearest person in his life—his long-departed sister—is named Caddy, that reader cannot yet know why he bursts into tears when a golfer asks his caddie for a club. Cannot *yet* know. On rereading this passage, as Faulkner's procedure all but demands, we start to supply the overarching spatial and temporal logic that is missing—the golf game, caddie and Caddy, his tears. We begin to recognize the double exposure that marks Faulkner's narration of childhood. It is for Benjy all unenlightened present experience, punctuated by inexplicable repetitions, even as Faulkner writes it so as to reveal—to us, *later*—the cumulative coherence that retrospection provides. Pasture and golf course, hitting and playing, caddie and Caddy. In reading this opening page, we are pressed by Faulkner's experimental procedure to both not know and know what Benjy cannot know. The gap between the two stances—the disorientation of his moment and the ordering later supplied (yet latently there)—is unsettling.

Finally, there is that passage in italics. The sequence moves from Luster's unsnagging Benjy from a nail in the fence to "*Caddy uncaught me and we crawled through.*" A moment in 1928—Benjy's thirty-third birthday, in the care of his black attendant Luster—releases a similar moment occurring more than twenty-five years earlier. His being unsnagged again springs the earlier unsnagging back to life. (Faulkner allows Benjy to access all that he has experienced before.) So he remains for the next two pages immersed in a December 1900 event, before being summoned by the narrative back into the 1928 scene: "*What are you moaning about, Luster said*" (SF 881). Such a transition is impossible in nineteenth-century realist fiction. The narrative sequencing of those earlier novels—Austen's, Dickens's, the Brontës,' Hardy's—did not fail to imitate time's orderly, clock-measured movement forward. Such novels could not permit a moment in 1928 to release a similar one that occurred in 1900, both of them *in the present*. Faulkner dares to do this, and we see now why he needs italics to signal to his reader what is happening. The temporal logic of Benjy's narrative is subjective, not clock-determined. His narrative goes where his mind goes. It may engage all the events indicated in Faulkner's clarifying letter to Wasson, but no reader of this novel is granted the familiar sequence of eight events occurring in chronological order.

Of all of Faulkner's unprepared protagonists, Benjy is the most time-challenged. Off-balance whenever his moment escapes his idiot-insistent grooves and becomes chaotic, Benjy is doomed to remain behind the fence and watch people hitting on a golf course that he still sees as his family's pasture. He is the purest victim of ongoing time, hopelessly incapable of adapting to the changes that it brings.

No less, however, we can begin to recognize Faulkner's narrative countermove. Though Benjy is time's victim, *The Sound and the Fury* is *structured* as a challenge to time's relentless forward movement. Burrowing into the mind's rehearsal of what has passed yet not passed, Faulkner opens up an immense mental territory that oscillates between the extremes of trauma on the one hand and revisionary reseeing on the other. Ultimately, Faulkner seems to be staging a sort of revenge against ongoing time's theft of being itself. "There is no such thing as *was*—only *is*," he would later say to Jean Stein. "If *was* existed there would be no grief or sorrow" (LG 255). Objectively departed, *was* is an illusory phantom, yet it remains lodged in the remembering subject—sometimes evoking later "*a might-have-been*," as he was to call it in *Absalom*, "*that is more true than truth.*" Without such organizing retrospection and anticipation, who could bear the aggression of *is*, of life as a pell-mell assault of not-yet-domesticated moments? What does Benjy's ceaseless moaning say, if not his incapacity to bear it?

In a wide range of ways Faulkner's fiction will go on to explore this tension. To Loïc Bouvard he would say in 1952, "man is never time's slave" (LG 70). Four years later he would say to Jean Stein—this is perhaps his most cited claim—"so I created a cosmos of my own. I can move these people around like God, not only in space but in time too" (255). This is a claim for the artist that Balzac might have made—except for that last part. Moving his people around "in time too" signals a uniquely Faulknerian resistance to time's annihilating power. Unlike Balzac, Faulkner as creator seeks to convey—in the same text, often in the same sentence—both the blindness of present seeing and the oppressive immanence of what is latently at play, but not (yet) seen. The moment itself—radiant, violent, unmanageable—and the intricate patterning it already carries, unseen, and that it will later reveal.

This claim takes on specificity if we revisit the luminous image that inspired the novel—that of Caddy up in a tree looking at her grandmother's funeral while her brothers remain below, seeing only her muddy drawers. Here is the pertinent passage:

We stopped under the tree by the parlor window. Versh set me down in the wet grass. It was cold. There were lights in all the windows.

"That's where Damuddy is." Caddy said. "She's sick every day now. When she gets well we're going to have a picnic."

"I knows what I knows." Frony said.

The trees were buzzing and the grass.

"The one next to it is where we have the measles." Caddy said. "Where do you and T.P. have the measles, Frony."

"Has them wherever we is, I reckon." Frony said.

"They haven't started yet." Caddy said.

They getting ready to start, T.P. said. You stand right here now while I get that box so we can see in the window. Here, les finish drinking this here sassprilluh. It make me feel like a squinch owl inside.

We drank the sassprilluh and T.P. pushed the bottle through the lattice, under the house, and went away. I could hear them in the parlor and I clawed my hands against the wall. T.P. dragged the box. He fell down, and he began to laugh. He lay there, laughing into the grass. He got up and dragged the box under the window, trying not to laugh.

"I skeered I going to holler." T.P. said. "Git on the box and see is they started."

"They haven't started because the band hasn't come yet." Caddy said.

"They aint going to have no band." Frony said.

"How do you know." Caddy said.

"I knows what I knows." Frony said.

"You dont know anything." Caddy said. She went to the tree. "Push me up, Versh."

"Your paw told you to stay out that tree." Versh said.

"That was a long time ago." Caddy said. "I expect he's forgotten about it. Besides, he said to mind me tonight. Didn't he say to mind me tonight."

"I'm not going to mind you." Jason said. "Frony and T.P. are not going to either."

"Push me up, Versh." Caddy said.

"All right." Versh said. "You the one going to get whipped. I aint." He went and pushed Caddy up into the tree to the first limb. We watched the muddy bottom of her drawers. Then we couldn't see her. We could hear the tree thrashing.

"Mr Jason said if you break that tree he whip you." Versh said.

"I'm going to tell on her too." Jason said.

The tree quit thrashing. We looked up into the still branches.

"What you seeing." Frony whispered.

I saw them. Then I saw Caddy, with flowers in her hair, and a long veil like shining wind. Caddy Caddy. (SF 906–7)

This vignette rehearses the novel's earliest scene—the funeral (in 1898) of the children's grandmother Damuddy. That funeral takes place inside the house; the children are kept outside so as to be spared the experience of grief and death. The young Caddy knows her grandmother is ill, but believes she'll soon be well and there will be a celebratory party. Frony, one of the younger blacks among the Compson helpers—but not so young as to be unaware of what is happening inside—insists, refrain-like, that she knows what she knows. The innocence of childhood—Caddy's wondering in what rooms black children have the measles—is before us, as Caddy waits impatiently for the party to begin. These games and childlike maneuvers, however, hardly remain in the sun-drenched territory of Twain-like childhood. Enter Faulkner's italics, launching his time-contortions. Pivoting on "getting ready to start," the narrative suddenly shifts from the 1898 funeral scene to the 1910 wedding scene. Seven-year-old Caddy in the tree is now nineteen-year-old Caddy in her wedding dress. This time, only Benjy is kept away from the ritual. The Compsons know that her wedding will distress him; they fear that his bellowing will ruin the ceremony. They have ordered T.P. (another of the black retainers, older than Luster) to keep Benjy entertained outside. They have not guessed that T.P. will do this by getting the two of them drunk on the "sassprilluh" that is for the reception.

The intoxicated T.P. urges Benjy to climb on a box and look through the window at the wedding inside. At just this juncture (and without the italics that ought to announce it), the narrative shifts back to the 1898 funeral scene, with Caddy waiting for the party to begin. It is the same scene as before, yet not the same: the later wedding puts intense pressure on the earlier funeral. The tensions begin to sink in for the reader—death inside and play outside, knowing and not-knowing, parental injunction and children's transgression. As the child Caddy climbs the forbidden tree, the novel arrives at an extraordinary moment of coalescence. Caddy looks out from the tree and sees her grandmother dead. The innocent brothers down below look up and see Caddy's muddy drawers. Then, in a sudden return to the 1910 wedding scene, Benjy sees his sister Caddy decked out like a bride "with flowers in her hair, and a long veil like shining wind." Seeing her thus dressed, Benjy glimpses his coming abandonment: "Caddy Caddy."

Each of the scenes retains its integrity, yet they mesh with the most provocative implications. Faulkner returned throughout his life to this moment, even seeing it as "the only thing in literature which would ever move me very much: Caddy climbing the pear tree" (NOR 227). As Caddy looks on her grandmother's death, her mud-stained drawers imply—to us, not to her—the menses that have not arrived, but that will eventually launch her on the path of maturation: bleeding, sexual activity, marriage, reproduction, and death. Her whole blood-carried life in time is implicitly before us in this crystallized moment. ("I saw that peaceful glinting of that branch [the stream]," Faulkner wrote of this scene a few years later, "was to become the dark harsh flowing of time sweeping her to where she could not return to comfort him, but that just separation, division, would not be enough, not far enough. It must sweep her into dishonor and shame too" [NOR 230].) More, Faulkner writes this scene so as to make Frony's question to Caddy—"what you seeing"—appear to receive its answer from Benjy in the next line: "*I saw them. Then I saw Caddy.*" Pressing Caddy's vision of the dead Damuddy in 1898 onto Benjy's vision of the bride Caddy in 1910, Faulkner makes the juxtaposed funeral and wedding suddenly merge. The overcharged image becomes telescopic, hallucinatory, prophetic. The decked-out bride with "a long veil like shining wind" is darkly suggestive of the flower-strewn and bedecked corpse of Damuddy. The two seeings (funeral and wedding) and the two seers (Caddy and Benjy) become one. The effect is stunning: Caddy seems to see, all at once, her dead grandmother, her own wedding, and her own corpse many years later, stretched out on a bier, dressed with flowers and the long veil of the dead. A moment harbors a lifetime: blind-sighted yet intolerably full. Faulkner writes the scene so as to challenge the ongoingness of linear time itself. He provides the closest of close-up zooms and the widest of wide-angle lenses all at once. Time explodes in its assaulting nowness, even as it intimates its long-gathering, ultimate patterns.

More broadly, the wedding *is* a funeral. Caddy's marrying enacts a desperate departure from the suffocating Compson home, one that breaks Benjy's heart and condemns Quentin to suicide two months later. Neither brother survives Caddy's defection, though Benjy will live out his abandonment for the next twenty years, clinging to his fence while he waits for Caddy to come home from school. More broadly yet, the Compson family is immured in archaic Southern rituals that deform its children's bodies and minds. The radiant Caddy, taught by her mother to feel guilt for any expression of her sexuality, rebels, and becomes illicitly pregnant. She is hurriedly made to choose another man for husband before her altering body reveals its secret. This marriage is likewise doomed. Weddings double as funerals. Penetrated by her mother's shrill insistence on virginity-as-honor, Caddy judges herself incompetent to raise her own child. She gives the baby up to its vindictive grandmother, where it will grow up doomed as well. Named after the brother, Quentin, whose suicide Caddy understood all too well, that little girl passes her childhood as a perpetual reminder of her mother's shame and her brother's torment. Eventually, she too will flee the Compson home, with no better prospects than her mother had. Nothing fructifies. A microcosm of Southern dysfunction, this ailing home reveals antebellum values prevailing in the only form possible fifty years after 1865: as shame-producing, life-denying injunctions. Such values constitute a ghostly, impossible "*might have been*" (as he would put it in *Absalom,* emphasis in the original) that tarnishes everything that is.

Can all of these reverberations be "there" in the childhood passage cited? Yes and no: not for the children themselves, yet available to us as readers revisiting the scene. On revisiting, the vignette takes on its extraordinary resonance. Faulkner insists on our *first* experiencing it as incoherent shards of assault in present time. We are made to share the children's uncomprehending. Faulkner thus enacts his signature move: he keeps his readers in the dark for much of their initial encounter with his overcharged materials. He makes his reader experience assault as one does experience assault: uncomprehendingly, one's ordering resources overrun, trouble pouring in from causes not yet identified. Benjy introduces the reader to a world suffered rather than understood. Terrifyingly innocent of the orientations that bind experience into manageable cultural pattern, Benjy stumbles as a figure of pure exposure.

For Faulkner to entrust the first quarter of his novel to Benjy's consciousness was to run an enormous risk. How can you *write* the illegibility of idiocy without making it legible? If you somehow succeed in writing idiocy as illegible, how can you make it readable? Dostoevsky's idiot, by contrast to Faulkner's, never ceases to be readable. We access Dostoevsky's Myshkin like all the other characters in *The Idiot,* realizing that his difference is spiritual—not a matter of the language Dostoevsky used to "say" him. Benjy, however, is mind-damaged. He cannot speak (out of his mouth comes only drooling or bellowing). Thus Faulkner took on the task of generating a language for Benjy's interiority that would be (immediately) foreign yet (eventually) familiar. To do this, he created Benjy from within. (It is disquieting to see him later from the outside, as one does in the final chapter narrated in the third person. One has come to know him otherwise.)

Created from within: the breakthrough in *The Sound and the Fury* is Faulkner's new rhetoric for writing interiority. Homing in on inner trouble, Faulkner's novel *speaks* the distressed mind's babbling, its indifference to linear time and fixed locations. For his first three novels, he had remained safely on the outside of such distress. Inside, but unsayable, had been Donald Mahon's fatal wound. Outside, all too sayable, had been the endless speechifying of *Mosquitoes*. Wordless depth or surface logorrhea. How to get words to say what was deeper than words? "It's my damned head," young Bayard had murmured, that's where the trouble was. But Faulkner had not yet learned to articulate the wreckage coiling in that wordless space. In writing Benjy and Quentin Compson, he figured it out:

> *I have committed incest I said Father it was I it was not Dalton Ames* And when he put Dalton Ames. Dalton Ames. Dalton Ames. When he put the pistol in my hand I didn't. That's why I didn't. He would be there and she would and I would. Dalton Ames. Dalton Ames. Dalton Ames. If we could have just done something so dreadful and Father said That's sad too people cannot do anything that dreadful they cannot do anything very dreadful at all they cannot even remember tomorrow what seemed dreadful today and I said, You can shirk all things and he said, Ah can you. And I will look down and see my murmuring bones and the deep water like wind, like a roof of wind, and after a long time they cannot distinguish even bones upon the lonely and inviolate sand. Until on the day when He says Rise only the flat-iron would come floating up. It's not when you realise that nothing can help you—religion, pride, anything—it's when you realise that you dont need any aid. Dalton Ames. Dalton Ames. Dalton Ames. If I could have been his mother lying with open body lifted laughing, holding his father with my hand refraining, seeing, watching him die before he lived. *One minute she was standing in the door.* (SF 937–8)

To find his way thus into Quentin's distress, Faulkner had to break with an entire tradition's way of writing inner trouble. That tradition—as countless novels reveal, as *Flags* reveals as well—insisted on proper syntax and grammar. It bound its materials into the decorum of complete sentences: a subject, a verb, and a predicate. Such sentences—the bread and butter of fiction—represented the human being as a discrete doer performing a discrete deed. The bare bones of such sentences enacted a little parable of potency. They said by their very form: *I can do this.* All of which is absent here. Quentin's clauses either lack verbs or mix their tenses indiscriminately—present perfect, past, conditional, conditional perfect, present, future. The nineteenth-century tools Faulkner inherited could represent a figure in distress only as someone seen from a certain distance and clothed in appropriate syntax. Such a figure appeared—proper syntax makes this happen—as something stable, gathered into presence in black and white. By contrast, Faulkner knew that a figure in distress was someone moved and moving, penetrated by absent forces, his mind hurtling through multiple spaces and times—a figure of desire and lack—alive and in color. It's as though the rhetorical palette he had inherited had no pigments for rendering Mahon's living wound, or the silent misery lying somewhere beneath the endless speechifying of *Mosquitoes*.

To articulate the color of distress, Faulkner had to reposition Quentin—to place him differently in space, time, and the field of others. More, Faulkner had to articulate—as though it were happening without anyone telling it—the drama of Quentin careening through his life, drowning in the emotional force-field of absent others. Space in the quoted passage loses its coherence. The reader is swallowed up in Quentin's place-shifting interiority, as his frantic mind darts to the scene the previous summer with Caddy's first lover, Dalton Ames, then to his dark conversations with Father, then to his fantasy of looking down on himself as a suicide so deep in the waters of the Charles River that even Christ's call for resurrection will fail to make him stir, and then to the even stranger fantasy of being secretly present at Ames's conceiving, himself becoming Ames's mother who removes Ames's father's penis just before ejaculation, thus killing Ames before Ames can be born. Faulkner's new way of representing time is equally deranged. The Dalton Ames moment, the Caddy at the door moment, and the moment with Father are pressed together while remaining apart—not fused but confused. The passage eclipses time's cleanly forward motion from A to B to C (perhaps the deepest assumption our sanity requires and that conventional narrative blessedly respects). Finally, absent others lodged inside the self—Ames, Father, Caddy—speak in a deafening roar. Often silent in the presence of friends or acquaintances, Quentin is bedlam inside. His mind is a defective transformer through which human voices pass like so many electric charges. He is in pain and going down. Faulkner has learned how to make Quentin's hurt not only transparent but radioactive. In his demise we see the failure of once-aristocratic Southern culture to pass on to its young the filters necessary for screening and negotiating experience, for surviving.

Where might Faulkner's own distress figure in the many-peopled song of pain that is *The Sound and the Fury?* One can answer only speculatively. This novel focuses, from start to finish, on a nightmarishly dysfunctional family—told from the perspectives of the children who most suffer the fallout. Neither *Soldiers' Pay* nor *Mosquitoes* even approached family distress, and *Flags* dealt with it only in passing. The house of Sartoris was ailing—that was clear enough—but the trouble seemed to locate elsewhere. Young Bayard's agony attached to a war that had ended, a car heading out of control, a mustang too ferocious to ride, a defective plane all but guaranteed to crash during test flight. The big house—the emblematic Sartoris plantation—remained imperturbably frozen, immured in stately Southern rhythms that had long ago lost their vitality. Not so for the house of Compson. Approached close up, it transmogrified into a prison patrolled by the widowed Mrs. Compson and her chain of oversized keys. It served, no less, as traumatic origin for the sensitive eldest son Quentin, a little kingdom for the despotic middle son Jason (once he became in charge), a space of unchanging rituals for the idiotic younger son Benjy, and a setting of emotional suffocation for the vibrant daughter Caddy—and later for her daughter Quentin.

Something of Faulkner's own imaginary lodges in them all. The mind-damaged Benjy houses most radically his creator's sense of home as doom. Incurably needy, abandoned by his mother and later by his sister, incapable of getting beyond the fence, Benjy radiates the pathos of disorientation, the punishment of being terminally misunderstood. He is Faulkner wordless, trapped, impotent, and alien. Quentin—narrated in a sort of infrared distress—suffers, no less than Benjy, from an inability to outlive childhood. His precocious brilliance serves him naught. Harvard operates as unavailing sanctuary for this eldest son who never left home emotionally, whose suicide was launched from the place of (apparent) departure. Both brothers negotiate their mother's orphaning of them—"If I could say Mother," Quentin murmurs—by way of an insupportable emotional investment in their sister, Caddy. As for Jason, he seems to embody Faulkner's sardonic reflection on what might have transpired had he remained an obedient son—and become a version of his own father. Not for nothing did Maud Falkner recognize in Jason a portrait of her husband Murry: "his way of

talking was just like Jason's, same words and same style" (F 217). Murry
Falkner: the embittered husband forever blaming others for his own failed
life. Finally, Caddy and her daughter Quentin: eros gone off the rails, desire
deformed by parentally instilled guilt and repression, and then turned self-
destructive by the urge to hurt those who had hurt you. The portraits are
indelible—unjudged yet unforgivable. It is as though once Faulkner managed to get all the way into these battered psyches—to grasp their trouble
in its stubborn complexity—there was nothing to do but *see*.

But Faulkner's personal investment may lodge most deeply in his style,
not in characterological echoes. The *gesture* of *The Sound and the Fury*
emerges in its use of interior monologue. Critics have noted that without the interior monologue in *Ulysses* six years earlier, Faulkner might
never have deployed that technique in *The Sound and the Fury*. For his
part, Faulkner always minimized indebtedness, even denying that he had
read *Ulysses*.[5] Yet Faulkner's denial has its truth. Though Joyce helped him
to interior monologue, Faulkner's deployment was his own. A technique
that in *Ulysses* renders the moment-by-moment cohesion of the mind
delivers, in *The Sound and the Fury*, a traumatic uncohering—the unprepared psyche under assault. The inner wound Faulkner had repeatedly
implied but never articulated—from *The Marble Faun* through Donald
Mahon and Bayard Sartoris—was finally located. It lodged at home, and
it could be made to speak.

Childhood was not Faulkner's only locus for interior monologue. But
it cannot be accidental that he moved to this locus and that technique
at the same moment in his career. Faulkner used the technique to gather
together, as though magnetically, troubles that had been accumulating over
time—and to speak those troubles as they tumbled into each other in a
moment of distress. The unpreparedness that marked childhood, children's
vulnerability to forces and facts they experienced (on their bodies as well
as their minds) but did not comprehend: these realities now exploded onto
the page. Refusing the decorum of fixed space and linear time, rejecting
the propriety of classic syntax (no shaping subject/verb/predicate here),
interior monologue gave Faulkner's breakthrough novel its pathos and
power. Articulating the naked moment of *is*, such monologue first spoke
Faulkner's supreme insight. We are not masters in the present moment,
we do not see our way as we move through it. Mastery and insight come
later, thanks to a retrospective take on experience: what we call wisdom.
But in the assault of ongoing life itself we are often not ready, usually not
wise. All the novels Faulkner had read proceeded otherwise, toward insight,

recognition, resolution. They sought, and eventually reached, the calm that follows the storm. That seemed to be the unspoken mission of fiction itself, the core story it was devised to deliver. By contrast, his task, he seems to have recognized, was to find words to say the storm before the calm. This storm, which we use all our resources to see beyond, is life in the present moment whenever habit or expectation fails: sound and fury.

Pride and Nakedness: As I Lay Dying

As though riding an interior commotion he had just begun to tap, Faulkner moved in 1929 from summer's immersion in the proofs of *The Sound and the Fury* to autumn's immersion in *As I Lay Dying*. The darker *Sanctuary*, written in the prenuptial months of 1929, had been put on hold. His new bride, on reading it in typescript, had recoiled in disgust. "It's horrible" (F 239), she told him—a response with which he concurred, thinking the novel might be profitable nonetheless. But Hal Smith of Cape and Smith—friend and partner in the new firm that would bring out *The Sound and the Fury* later that year—reacted no less vehemently. "Good God," he told Faulkner, "I can't publish this. We'd both be in jail" (ibid.). The deck was cleared for the book-in-progress, and *As I Lay Dying* proceeded with unprecedented swiftness.

Perhaps the new book's effortless gestation made Faulkner a touch dismissive in his later remarks. In writing it he missed what *The Sound and the Fury* had given him: "that eager and joyous faith and anticipation of surprise which the unmarred sheets beneath my hand held inviolate and unfailing"—the exhilarating sense of not knowing what comes next, but trusting it will come right. With this follow-up book, however, "I set out deliberately to write a tour-de-force. Before I ever put pen to paper and set down the first word, I knew what the last word would be and almost where the last period would fall" (NOR 226). He liked to say that it took only six weeks to compose this book from opening word to closing sentence, adding that he wrote it during the night shift he had taken at the Oxford power plant (using the hours from midnight until four in the morning, free from distracting noises). He was exaggerating only slightly; the book was completed in forty-seven days, and the revisions it underwent were minor. What had enabled its swift and painless birth?

One answer is that *The Sound and the Fury* and *As I Lay Dying* are fused as a pair of gorgeous twins (both proceeding by way of interior monologues) that would have no equal among the other novels he would write.

The sustained creative work and intricate revision that produced the older twin—this was no easy labor—made the delivery of the younger one more relaxed and predictable. The impetus behind them both was singular—one sperm fertilizing two eggs. They share an unwavering attention to devastating family dynamics. Both novels trace the helpless dependency of children on their parents and the frustration that occurs when that dependency is betrayed. *As I Lay Dying* turns the screw yet further, capturing the children's anguish when the mother dies and their dependency is ruptured altogether. None of Faulkner's other novels would mine interior monologue so extensively or brood on family tensions so provocatively. These are his two lyrical masterpieces, both of them staging the drama of orphaned children's exposed hearts and minds.

The Sound and the Fury burrowed massively into the three Compson brothers' minds; all of its chapters are over forty pages long. *As I Lay Dying*, by contrast, distills its portraiture into fifty-nine jagged monologues (running from a sentence to several pages). More, it narrates its materials by way of fifteen characters' reflections. At the center are Anse and Addie Bundren and their five children. On the periphery stand the bemused or horrified neighbors and bystanders who, chorus-like, comment on their journey. The novel's fictional time takes only a few days, as the family make their tragicomic trek to Jefferson, in order to bury their dead mother in her own family's plot. Getting there proves to be an ordeal; they must pass through flood and fire. Further, a corpse exposed for several days in August to the Mississippi sun occasions not just an ordeal but a scandal. The deceased mother had exacted from her husband a promise to bury her in Jefferson. The living Bundrens carry out this pledge with their own mix of incompatible motives.

Faulkner gives Addie—about one hundred pages after her death—the most powerful monologue in the novel. Her haunting speech occurs in some nebulous space and time, as though it rose from the coffin itself. Or maybe not so nebulous, since the deeper move of the book is to show that Addie's biological death hardly puts an end to her life. Death is "only a state in which the others are left," as Mr. Compson had mused in *The Sound and the Fury* (SF 936–7). Its reality explodes only in the living. The book's seemingly awkward title is unerringly exact: its 175 pages enact the entire family's experience of one woman's dying, through the distress of the others who are left. Addie's dying releases in her offspring an anguish that each seeks to deflect in his own way. Jewel, the love child secretly fathered by the preacher Whitfield, cannot bear his carpenter brother Cash's relentlessly crafting

Addie's coffin outside her window as she lies dying. "If you'd just let her along. Sawing and knocking, and keeping the air always moving so fast on her face that...you can't breathe it, and that goddamn adze going One lick less. One lick less" (11). He fantasizes erasing his father and brothers from the scene: "It would just be me and her on a high hill and me rolling the rocks down the hill at their faces, picking them up and throwing them down the hill faces and teeth and all by God until she was quiet and not that goddamn adze going One lick less" (11). Jewel's other strategy (the term is too conscious) involves replacing Addie with a wild mustang whose untamable viciousness he passionately embraces, leading Darl (the all-seeing brother and hence the insane one) to muse: "Jewel's mother is a horse" (61).

The youngest child, Vardaman, least able to manage the fact of his mother's dying, attempts the most outrageous counter-strategy. First, he bores holes into the coffin Cash has prepared for her: "'Are you going to nail her up in it, Cash? Cash? Cash?' I got shut up in the crib the new door it was too heavy for me it went shut I couldn't breathe because the rat was breathing up all the air. I said 'Are you going to nail it shut, Cash? Nail it? *Nail* it?'" (AILD 43). Vardaman next thinks his way clear by fantasizing her transformation into a rabbit; then, more satisfyingly, into the large fish that he has just caught, cut up, and prepared for dinner. His logic is impeccable: "Then it [the fish] wasn't and she was, and now it is and she wasn't. And tomorrow it will be cooked and et and she will be him and pa and Cash and Dewey Dell and there wont be anything in the box and so she can breathe" (44). Later, this primitive ritual of psychic displacements is complete, permitting Vardaman's temporary evasion of his wound. In a one-sentence chapter, the shortest and strangest in the novel, he thinks, "My mother is a fish" (54).

Not that these children are sentimentally bonded with their mother, nor she with them. This lyrical novel is also Faulkner's most severe, as it explores "that pride, that furious desire to hide that abject nakedness which we bring here with us...carry stubbornly with us into the earth again" (AILD 31). Pride and nakedness: *As I Lay Dying* probes the all but unrelinquishable barriers we require to conceal our psychic nakedness from others, the distress that occurs when those barriers are breached. Many of the book's fifty-nine sections articulate the self's inwardness—at once fiercely maintained yet imprisoning—even as this is silently experienced in the presence of vocal others. Addie Bundren had felt her imprisonment inside selfhood the most keenly. Her awareness (earlier, as a teacher) of her students "each with his and her secret and selfish thought" drove her wild. She would whip them with a switch, thinking with each blow, "Now you are aware of me!

Now I am something in your secret and selfish life, who have marked your blood with my own for ever and ever" (114). Mere words, Addie knew, were incapable of crossing this divide:

> we had had to use one another by words like spiders dangling by their mouths from a beam, swinging and twisting and never touching, and that only through the blows of the switch could my blood and their blood flow as one stream...I would think how words go straight up in a thin line, quick and harmless, and how terribly doing goes along the earth. (115–7)

Words that swing and twist and never touch—reminiscent of Faulkner's earlier poetry, that "cocktail of words" that substitutes for the real—are no good. They fail to penetrate the pride-installed boundaries that protect the self's exposure, conceal its lifelong nakedness. What is needed are words that wound, words that break through the self's defenses. Addie's intact husband Anse will go to his grave unmarked and virginal (despite his having fathered four children), having remained cushioned throughout his life, thanks to the cottony insulation of the words he lives within and takes to be real. *The Sound and the Fury* was Faulkner's first novel to hew its way into "wordless" territory. He twisted its syntax and procedures with such violence that the conventional word-parade ceased, and the released word-image escaped its familiar boundaries. Released, it enacted, "terribly," not a saying but a doing that "goes along the earth." It sought not to entertain, not even to deliver truths, but to penetrate the reader's heart.

Halfway through *As I Lay Dying*, an intimate moment occurs in which Cash and Darl reminisce over their brother Jewel's earlier strange behavior. They believe that he has been spending his evenings "rutting" with some-one else's wife, and Cash muses: "A young boy. A fellow kind of hates to see...wallowing in somebody else's mire." Darl reflects,

> That's what he [Cash] was trying to say. When something is new and hard and bright, there ought to be something a little better for it than just being safe, since the safe things are just the things that folks have been doing so long they have worn the edges off and there's nothing to the doing of them that leaves a man to say, That was not done before and it cannot be done again. (AILD 85–6)

The passage's personal connection seems undeniable. Several months earlier, while writing *Sanctuary*, the recently wedded Faulkner had envisaged himself starting off from someone else's scratch and scratching. Here he sees himself wallowing in a previous man's mire.

More suggestively, Darl's thoughts point to an artistic project that had long been Faulkner's own. Only now, though, did Faulkner see what the project required of *him;* only thus did he fulfill it in these two lyrical novels. "You've got too much talent," Anderson had warned. "If you're not careful, you'll never write anything." Until he risked himself—found experimental techniques for breaking through his own defensive pride and articulating the formless nakedness within—his work would never penetrate anyone's "damn head." He might have gone on to write a dozen novels, yet (in Anderson's sense) never have written anything, his words just "swinging and twisting and never touching." Until *The Sound and the Fury,* he had not accessed what lay speechless inside. He had not pressured words so strenuously that they made that silence speak. The "doing" had been too easy. If he were candid, he could not have said about any of his earlier writing: "That was not done before and it cannot be done again."

But what exactly had he done? What new territory had he found his way into in these two books? Perhaps it involved going not further on land but deeper into water, going underwater. The most hallucinatory sequence in *As I Lay Dying* narrates the family's crossing of the flooded Yoknapatawpha River. They do not manage this crossing intact, their pride and privacy safeguarded. The wagon bearing Addie's corpse plunges into the swollen waters, and Cash breaks again a leg that had not healed from an earlier breaking. On the other side of the river, finally, Darl surveys the quietly treacherous water: "It looks peaceful, like machinery does after you have watched it and listened to it for a long time. As though the clotting which is you had dissolved into the myriad original motion" (AILD 110). Did Faulkner realize that in writing *The Sound and the Fury* and *As I Lay Dying* he had submitted the nakedness of his inner being to something like "the myriad original motion"? That in seeking to word and thus expose to others the wordless psyche—by shedding the masks, attitudes, and judgments that protect the self and provide it sanctuary—he had run the risk of unclotting, of self-dissolving? *The Sound and the Fury* and *As I Lay Dying* make their way beyond all masks and attitudes. They plunge deeper than judgment. "It's like there was a fellow in every man," Cash thinks at the end of the journey, "that's done a-past the sanity or the insanity, that watches the sane and the insane doings of that man with the same horror and the same astonishment" (161).

CHAPTER 2

UNTIMELY

Because the tragedy of life is, it must be premature, inconclusive and inconcludable, in order to be life; it must be before itself, in advance of itself, to have been at all.

—*The Town*

A FAILED ELOPEMENT

They both were desperate as 1918 arrived and the likelihood of Estelle's marriage with Cornell Franklin loomed unavoidable. Neither wanted it to happen, but it seemed to approach with a logic and momentum they could not counter. To the outward eye, Franklin was as appealing a candidate for marriage as Faulkner was not. Handsome, ambitious, the son of an established Southern family, he had graduated from the University of Mississippi in 1913, covered with honors. President of his class, captain of the track team, he was the most notable of the suitors the precocious Estelle attracted. He took her to the glamorous college parties she was otherwise too young to attend, and he may have spoken of a future they might share. Since older boys had been buzzing around her and saying similar things for years now, she knew that such chatter went with the pleasures of the chase. It augured little. When her parents sent her off to Mary Baldwin College that same year—to get a proper "finishing" to her education—she hardly thought of Franklin as a future husband. Her bond with Faulkner was deeper—something she unthinkingly drew on as a talisman that would protect her from the consequences of her own flirtations. For his part, Franklin hardly knew that Faulkner existed. Finishing law school at the university in 1914, Franklin headed to Honolulu, where family connections had secured him the post of collector of the port. His career was all before him and already on the rise. He knew that when the time came, Estelle would be the right partner to share it with him.

Mary Baldwin had been at best a mixed blessing—too Presbyterian and restrictive to accommodate Estelle's energies. Within a year, she was back in

Oxford, enrolled as a special student at the university, continuing to attract suitors. Yet she never ceased to wear Faulkner's gold ring. She must have believed that—somehow—the intimacy they had shared over the years would serve as a keel to take her through whatever turbulence lay ahead. Franklin, meanwhile, had prospered as anticipated. By December 1917, he had become assistant district attorney in Honolulu, with the prospect of a federal judgeship. Three years had passed; it was time for the next step. He instructed his mother to send Estelle a double diamond ring, and he wrote her to say that it meant their engagement. He was returning to Oxford in April, so that they could marry.

She was both unsurprised and dumbfounded. Her friends and family had been expecting nothing less; they congratulated her on the catch of the year. Franklin's mother, a close friend of her own mother, shared her delight with the Oldhams. Elaborate wedding plans were set in motion. Only Estelle resisted, in a silent way that indicated a desire to escape but no plan for doing so. Rather than openly rebel, she appeared at social functions without Franklin's impressive ring on her finger. When her mother pushed for an explanation, she allowed that the ring had been lost. Intensive searching discovered it at the bottom of one of her dresser drawers. She was caught in a trap—one she could not free herself from, since it took the shape of her own social identity. Franklin was approaching with an offer of marriage because she had always encouraged his pursuit.

Desperate, she turned to Faulkner for a way out, but he felt as hemmed in as she did. It had taken him, also, a lifetime of becoming who he was to find himself in this trap. The trap of who he was: a brooding poet yet to publish poems, a young man without a high school diploma, a frustrated cashier in his grandfather's bank, someone easily identified as one of the town's aimless and heavy-drinking youths; in short, a bad bet. He had no prospects, no counter-argument to propose. What he wanted most not to happen was getting ready to happen—not despite who they were, but because of who they were. She could not bear it. "I suppose I *am* engaged to Cornell now," she told him, "but I'm ready to elope with you." "No," he answered, "we'll have to get your father's consent" (F 54).

Was he determined, like Sutpen in *Absalom,* to have the big wedding or no union at all? Was he paralyzed by his own contradictoriness—the solitary genius on the one hand, the son and citizen and family man on the other? Could he have realized that his answer, by guaranteeing her marriage to Franklin, would wreck his life? That a moment's eight-word utterance could have a lifetime's consequences? He was not ready for this crisis. Did he glimpse that this is what a crisis is—what you are not ready for? Almost thirty years later, one of his narrators would brood: "Because the tragedy of life is, it must be premature, inconclusive and inconcludable, in order to be life; it must be before itself, in advance of itself, to have been at all" (TN 279). There is something awry about our insertion in time itself. We get hold of our experience only in its wake. Untimely: the events that define us are in advance of themselves. They register now as violence; they get their definition only later. Too late, we see that we have been—defined. It would take him another ten years to understand how fatally he had been defined by saying no to her proposal to elope. This awful life-moment did not reveal its portent when it occurred. It would take "tomorrow and tomorrow and tomorrow" for him to realize what was at stake today, in a moment's utterance.[1]

Her parents of course refused their consent; so did his. No one else was about to authorize his union with Estelle. In the quick of the moment, he did not find it possible to do so on his own. Defeated, they bowed before the separation seemingly decreed on them. She withdrew into a silent grief, even as she entered the circle of nuptial activities: the bridge and breakfast and bridal parties before the big event. The night before the wedding, staying with her great-aunt, she wept for hours, inconsolable. "I'm going to go to your father and make him call this wedding off," her alarmed great-aunt declared. "No, you mustn't do that," she responded: "Daddy will be furious. It's too late" (F2 1:204). "Its not even time until it was," Quentin muses in *The Sound and the Fury*. By the time you firm up your sense of what you must not do, you are already immersed in its doing. It was too late. She would marry Cornell Franklin. On that fateful April 18, 1918, Faulkner's brother Johncy served as the chauffeur who drove them to the church.

As for Faulkner, unable to shape his fate in the moment called for, he relapsed into the care of others, something he would do often in the years ahead. Weeks before the wedding—once he was sure nothing could prevent it—he had accepted Phil Stone's offer of lodgings in New Haven, as well as Stone's plan to negotiate their entry into the war before it ended. The war: nothing less than that would have the weight and substance to free him from the pain of his love loss. Much later, in *Absalom*, Faulkner would have Mr. Compson articulate the same spurious hope that "the War would settle the matter…since it would not be the first time that youth has taken catastrophe as a direct act of Providence for the sole purpose of solving a personal problem which youth itself could not solve" (AA 99). But Phil Stone could—if anyone could—arrange a way out.

Stone had been arranging ways out for the past four years. Ever since Stone's return to Oxford in 1914, Yale degree in hand to match the Mississippi one obtained earlier, he had found in Faulkner a focus for his own energies and ambitions. Stone was the sort of man who needed someone else for this release. "I'm like an elaborate intricate piece of machinery which doesn't quite work," he once described himself.[2] In Faulkner he recognized a different kind of machinery—one that might work. Lending the budding teenaged poet book after book from his own library, introducing him to both the classics in English literature and the latest in modern poetry, Stone provided Faulkner with the education he failed to get either in high school or (as a special student) in college. "Provided" is too gentle a term: "To say that Phil 'encouraged' Bill, as so many biographers do," recalled a university acquaintance later, "is gross understatement. He cajoled, browbeat, and swore at him; he threatened and pleaded. Encouragement came later."[3]

Stone seemed connected to everyone. It was Stone who introduced Faulkner to elegant Stark Young (Mississippi's early twentieth-century claim to literary fame). This introduction led, in 1921, to Faulkner meeting Young's friend Elizabeth Prall in New York. She in turn would procure for the impecunious Faulkner a clerk job at Lord and Taylor's bookstore that fall. Later, in 1924, she would marry Sherwood Anderson and move to New Orleans with him. There Faulkner would renew his acquaintance, and through her he would become, in 1925, a friend of Anderson as well. Stone's circle of acquaintances hardly stopped there. He was familiar with underworld communities as well as those above ground—gambling clubs, brothels and speakeasies, suppliers of bootleg liquor—in Clarksdale, Memphis, and New Orleans. These, too, he generously introduced Faulkner to, furnishing materials of character and plot that Faulkner would draw on exhaustively in the fiction to come. All told, the unstinting Stone made available to Faulkner books to read, ideas to probe, money to finance *The Marble Faun*, and keys to both illicit underworlds and respectable centers of culture. Most deeply perhaps, Stone furnished, this time unawares, the resonant image of his own complex failure. A talented and sensitive son of the planterly Old South, Stone was unable to deal with the New South's rising tide of rednecks—the Vardamans and Bilbos who were coming to power. He revealed in himself more than himself. Looked at aright, he radiated the larger plight of Faulkner's once-aristocratic Compsons and Sartorises, as they struggled against the multipronged invasion of carpetbagger and white trash Snopeses.

Stone would make all of this available to Faulkner over time. Right now, in the spring of 1918, he promised to secure a way into the war. He had his reasons for wanting to lead Faulkner in that direction. He, too, was disappointed in love; the two young men had for some time made common cause as spurned lovers. Did their bond go further than that? Do the often overwrought and quasi-erotic relations between young men in Faulkner's novels owe something to an ambiguous intimacy between mentor and pupil? It seems clear that Stone was not only Faulkner's closest friend during Faulkner's late teens but also a guide who saw Estelle as a dangerous competitor. She could lead his budding genius astray. Stone had already done what he could to dampen Faulkner's ardor; talk of elopement only made him more apprehensive. Then, shortly before Estelle's marriage, Stone learned that Faulkner had secretly tried to enlist with the air division of the U.S. army. Stuffing himself with bananas and drinking as much water as he could swallow, Faulkner had presented himself at the recruiting station—and been rejected: too short (five feet five and a half inches) and too light (125 pounds). Startled by this reckless attempt, and alarmed that his prodigy might reconsider the elopement option, Stone went into action. He telephoned Maud Falkner from New Haven and told her of her son's attempt to enlist. He then urged her to support his move to get Faulkner up to New Haven instead. There, under his guidance, the two of them would find the right way to join the war. Maud must have assented, for Faulkner boarded the train in Oxford at the end of March, bound for New Haven and a world elsewhere.

"THEY HAD STOPPED THE WAR ON HIM"

Faulkner was already modestly known as a player of roles. His expensive, tight-fitting Memphis clothes had earned him the sobriquet "the Count." More, his storytelling and poetic activities made him widely recognizable as "literary." In addition, he enjoyed already a reputation for undue silence and undue drinking. Such role-playing is as naught, however, when compared to the array of performances that began with his boarding that train to New Haven. Staying in Stone's rooms, he began in earnest to plot his masquerade. The two of them decided that their most likely entry into the war would be Canadian, not American—by way of the Canadian RAF. To accomplish this, they reasoned, it would be necessary to pass themselves off as British. To that end, they enlisted one of Stone's British friends at Yale to tutor them in British pronunciations. According to Stone, they then determined that an English accent might not suffice to persuade the Canadian recruiters: they might need "documents" to prove their British provenance.

So they prevailed on a Yale student's friend in London to mail back to them a British-stamped letter of reference—signed by an invented vicar named "Reverend Mr. Edward Twimberly-Thorndike." Their reverend stoutly testified to their standing as "god-fearing young Christian gentlemen" (F2 1:206–7). Evidently, it worked—if it was needed at all, since Canadian RAF recruiters in New York were not all that picky in 1918 about accepting volunteers. Stone never pursued the plan any further, but Faulkner got himself accepted into a Canadian RAF program in Toronto. On July 19, he began training to become a fighter pilot.

The letters he wrote home from Canada, during the last five months of 1918, are revealing. He tells his mother: "A young fellow named Bushell whom I knew very well" suddenly died in a football game "and was given a military funeral, the same as an officer would have been. It was very unusual for a private soldier to get" (TH 125). No reflections about the sudden death of Bushell ("whom I knew very well") but emphatic attention to the status accorded to the funeral. Faulkner seems to have been desperate to gain such status himself. A vignette one of his biographers heard from another cadet in Faulkner's camp speaks to this desire: "On one occasion, when Faulkner received a check from home, he bought drinks for his four roommates and wound up conducting a one-man drill on the sidewalk, calling out commands loudly and then executing them smartly" (F 62–3). His role-playing is patently on display in this piece of psychodrama. As though entranced, Faulkner performed both the giving and receiving of commands, himself a one-man theater of war.

The photographs taken of him during this period tell a collaborative story. The earliest one of "cadet Faulkner" shows him in all his inadequacy—a slight, unsmiling young man, shapelessly immersed in the standard uniform issued to all cadets. Tellingly, he refused to send his mother this undistinguished photo. Instead, he spoke of, and drew for her, the officer's uniform he would soon be entitled to wear—a drawing replete with officer's belted tunic, garrison cap, breeches, putties, and stick. In November, he wrote her that his old uniform was wearing out, and that the new trousers he bought had led to his being mistaken for "a flying officer in mufti" (TH 130). On the December day he was demobilized, he replaced his cadet overcoat (apparently "stolen" from him) with one he bought "from an officer who was hard up" (138). The sartorial result: Faulkner returned to Oxford at the end of 1918 decked out in an officer's resplendent garb, just as he had drawn it. He was proudly wearing the wings of a flying officer and a hat of the kind permitted only to soldiers who had seen action. For the next several weeks, as demobilized soldiers streamed back to Oxford in early 1919, he wore this uniform around town, sometimes "carrying a swagger stick and taking salutes from returning soldiers who had not achieved officer status" (WFSH 183).[4]

The role-playing did not stop with the wearing of unearned uniforms. He had peppered the Canadian letters to his mother with references to the progress he was making as a pilot. For the next twenty years he would jauntily recount solo flights he had undertaken and mishaps he had suffered. Often he would go further, speaking of military action high over France, of war-inflicted wounds requiring surgically installed plates in his head and in his knee. To enhance the role, he took to limping with a cane once he returned to Oxford. Later, he would inform his stepson Malcolm that his nose had been broken in a wartime plane crash (rather than in a high school football accident). The claims he made to others who knew him less well were often more embroidered; many of these would be dispelled only after his death in 1962. Examining his Canadian RAF discharge papers in the 1970s, his official biographer found the word "Nil" written in the column headed "Casualties, Wounds, Campaigns, Medals, Clasps, Decorations, Mentions, Etc" (F 66). There is likewise no official record of the flight mishaps he reported during those days of training. Indeed, he would have had to go to another training camp to do any solo flying at all. The facts are unambiguous. The war ended in November, while he was still in flight training school. He saw no action, flew no planes, did not even know how to fly them. What is going on in this egregious gap between role and reality?

As James G. Watson has proposed, Faulkner's assiduous self-presentation is here on display, a claim Watson buttresses by pointing to the difference between that unflattering first flight-training photo and the ones Faulkner later had taken of him at Oxford, after the war. In the first photo Faulkner just accepted the verdict of the camera lens. He was passively "captured" by this picture rather than actively on display in it. His refusing to relinquish the photo to his mother suggests that he somehow understood this distinction. Thereafter, as in the famous 1930s photos taken by his Oxford friend J. R. Cofield, Faulkner carefully arranged how he would appear. The amused Cofield called him "a devout camera fiend." Faulkner would meticulously arrange the attitude of his body and clothing so as to signal the performance he had in mind. The camera would obey, capturing and communicating the stance of identity he was seeking to perform—this to the point of elaborate invention, of out-and-out lies.

Why would he engage in such deception? In *Flags in the Dust* (written in 1927) Faulkner allowed Horace Benbow to answer that question: "You forget that lying is a struggle for survival…little puny man's way of dragging circumstance about to fit his preconception of himself as a figure in the world. Revenge on the sinister gods" (FD 710).

The recollected self, like the preconceived self, is a figure in the world, a figure of consequence. This is how we project identity, as well as how—over time—we want to remember it. This is what we look like in the beneficent light of *was* or *might be*. But life occurs as neither before nor after; it erupts as *is*, an often nasty assault by the sinister gods. Puny and exposed, one encounters unanticipated circumstance, and one's self-image as a figure in the world suffers grievously. Lying is how one makes up, later, for what one was unprepared for earlier. As another of Faulkner's biographers puts it, his strenuous investment in lying "corrects" reality by supplying it with the rich subjective coherence denied by the events themselves.[5] He strides later, to make up for earlier stumbling. Faulkner was not ready when the moment to keep or lose Estelle occurred. He was not ready when the Great War occurred. He would find ways, later, to "correct" both mistakes. He would marry her later—even as he already glimpsed it was too late to make good on the first defection. And he would get into the war the only way he could, later. He would perform the role—in his dress, his words, and his gestures—of one who had experienced it.

Why was it so important to have seen military action? The painfully close answer is that his brother, Jack, had indeed experienced the war that Faulkner pretended to know. Joining the Marines in May of 1918, Jack did make it to scenes of action in France. He encountered the enemy in Belleau Woods and Soissons, as well as St-Mihiel and Epinal. He was gassed in Champagne, and on November 1—ten days before Armistice— he was badly wounded in the Argonne. Shrapnel tore open his right knee and penetrated his skull, miraculously lodging there without doing further damage. (With characteristic modesty, Jack later viewed the Purple Heart he was awarded "as everlasting evidence that I forgot to duck" [FOM 103].) Jack knew only too well—and had surgically installed plates to prove it— the war to which his brother pretended.

THE RESONANCE OF *U*

The distant, more indirect answer is no less revealing. It is well known that Faulkner chose to insert the letter *u* into the spelling of his name, thus

distinguishing himself from the Falkners who preceded him. As in Freud-
ian family romance, those earlier Falkners had birthed his body but not his
soul. He first announced soul birth by his assertion of the *u*—at the time of
his recruitment into the Canadian RAF. There he lied about his birthplace
(England), his birth date (1898), and the spelling of his name (Faulkner).
The last of these lies stuck with him. His letters home during those months
of 1918 inconsistently addressed his parents as sometimes Falkner and
sometimes Faulkner. When asked later why he spelled his name differently
from his parents or grandparents, his answers varied but returned often to
the same grounds: that was the way his legendary great-grandfather, Colonel W. C. Falkner, had originally spelled the name. He would explain that
the Colonel later removed the *u* because he had heard of some no-good
folks nearby who spelled it with a *u*. On this account, the great-grandson
was restoring an earlier reality, not inventing a new one. More tacitly, he
was disinheriting two generations of Falkners who stood between him and
his mythic progenitor. What did this larger-than-life figure of nineteenth-
century exploits, a man dead eight years before Faulkner was born, mean to
a little boy growing up in the twentieth century? Why, when a third grade
teacher asked him what he wanted to be when he grew up, did Faulkner
answer, "I want to be a writer like my great-granddaddy"? (F 23).

W. C. Falkner, the young loner who showed up on his uncle's Ripley
doorstep in 1841 seeking asylum, began soon to better his position. By the
mid-1840s he was reading law. When the Mexican War broke out in 1846,
he joined it and saw action—including the loss of three fingers, thanks to
a musket ball coming his way. On his discharge papers, issued in 1847, his
name was indeed spelled "Faulkner"; at some later point he removed the *u*.
He married Holland Pierce in 1849 and fathered a son whom he named
John Wesley Thompson ("J.W.T") Falkner. Soon thereafter he became
embroiled in another scene of violence. A certain Robert Hindman (a com-
rade in the Mexican War) accused Falkner of blocking his membership in
the Knights of Temperance. Hindman pulled a revolver, they fought, the
gun misfired. Falkner killed Hindman with his knife in self-defense—a
verdict the jury upheld. The Hindman family would long view it as pure
and simple murder. Two years later, a friend of the Hindmans quarreled
with Falkner, the two men fought, and Falkner shot him dead. He was
again tried and acquitted. By then he was widowed. Soon he remarried
and began to produce a second family, while continuing to practice law
and extend his land investments. When Mississippi seceded in early 1861
(the second state to do so, after South Carolina), Falkner became captain

(he had sought a brigadier generalship) in a company he helped to form, the Magnolia Rifles. Swiftly promoted to colonel, he fought daringly, even recklessly, during the battle of First Manassas. His imperious manner made him unpopular, however, and his troops did not reelect him the following spring as regimental commander. Piqued, he quit the Confederate army a few months later, in the summer of 1862. For the next two years, he organized and led a group of several hundred guerrilla fighters—the First Mississippi Partisan Rangers—who impeded where possible Grant's invasion south. In 1864, he was probably running the blockade around Memphis, stealing Yankee supplies that were sorely needed back home.

Official violence ceased after Appomattox in 1865, but personal violence was never far from the Colonel. In the postwar years his law practice continued to prosper, and he became obsessed with railroad possibilities in northwest Mississippi. To that end, he made a business alliance with one Richard Thurmond. They became successful, and eventually—in typical Falkner fashion—he forced Thurmond out in order to control the railroad himself. By 1889, he had written several books (including *The White Rose of Memphis,* a popular yarn that went through several editions), had become wealthy through real estate and railroad investments, and was seeking to enter the Mississippi state legislature. His political opponent was Thurmond; there had been angry words between them. On the November afternoon when he was overwhelmingly elected to the seat, Falkner walked into Ripley's town square. He had made a new will and was no longer carrying a gun. He walked toward the entry of Thurmond's law office; within minutes Thurmond came out, carrying a .44 pistol in his hand. "Dick, what are you doing?" Falkner said, as Thurmond fired at point-blank range. His throat pierced, the Colonel died the next day. Thurmond was later acquitted in a drawn-out, acrimonious, and contested trial. The jury, it seemed, was not ready to find the Colonel innocent of the violence that had once more erupted around him. In time, a huge monument—fourteen-feet high and made of Carrara marble, with an eight-foot statue of the Colonel mounted on it—was erected over his grave in the Ripley cemetery. He had commissioned it many years earlier, hoping, it was said, that grateful townsfolk would put it up in the square after his death. They never chose to do so, and the weather-stained monument stands to this day atop his plot in the deserted Ripley graveyard. One hand of the giant marble man is hidden, protecting from view the three fingers shot off during the Mexican War. At an unknown later date, someone chose to "balance" matters by shooting off the same three fingers in the visible other hand as well.

Throughout his life, Faulkner would return to the legendary figure of his great-grandfather, reborn in his fiction as Colonel Sartoris. His brooding statue presides over *Flags in the Dust*. Later, he would stir Faulkner's imagination further as the ruthless progenitor Carothers McCaslin in *Go Down, Moses*. Between Colonel W. C. Falkner's violent death in 1889 and Faulkner's own childhood in the first decade of the twentieth century, there grew around the storied ancestor an irremovable patina of grandeur and violence. Decisive, ambitious, talented, murderous, he was above all unstoppable. It is not too much to say that Colonel Falkner incarnated for his young great-grandson the force that underlay Southern masculinity and achievement. Like the railroad he fostered, his life signaled unambiguously the release of power. So to address the question why Faulkner might have lied as he did about his participation in the war, we listen again to Horace in *Flags:* "lying is a struggle for survival...little puny man's way of dragging circumstance about to fit his preconception of himself as a figure in the world." Men serve in war—especially, perhaps, Southern men do. That is their obligatory figure in the world. His own great-grandfather had served sublimely. Faulkner would go on to view this ancestor in the most intricately critical ways, but surely the first response was captivation. His earliest statement of the bond with his legendary great-grandfather occurs in the biographical sketch he submitted to the editors at Four Seasons Press, as they prepared to bring out *The Marble Faun* (1924):

> Born in Mississippi in 1897. Great-grandson of Col. W. C. Faulkner, C.S.A., author of "The White Rose of Memphis," "Rapid Ramblings in Europe," etc. Boyhood and youth were spent in Mississippi, since then has been (1) undergraduate (2) house painter (3) tramp, day laborer, dishwasher in various New England cities (4) Clerk in Lord and Taylor's book shop in New York City (5) bank- and postal clerk. Served during the war in the British Royal Air force. A member of Sigma Alpha Epsilon Fraternity. Present temporary address, Oxford, Miss. "The Marble Faun" was written in the spring of 1919. (SL 7)

Faulkner here reconfigures his own genealogy. Such a performance cleanly deletes Murry Falkner, and J. W. T. Falkner before him, as though the descent of the family *u* were a ceremony that took place only once every four generations. Anxiety about the unimpressiveness of his first twenty-six years may show as well in the cavalier details. Faulkner was an "undergraduate" at the University of Mississippi for only three terms (and even then thanks to a postwar law classifying him as "special" along with other demobilized men who were allowed to attend university without a high school diploma). The other activities he mentions seem deliberately whimsical, and his claim of service in the war is downright mendacious. His identifying Oxford as a "temporary" address almost suggests that he sees his real (but as yet undeclarable) address as Mount Parnassus.

Off-balance, uncertain—"they had stopped the war on him"—the range of roles he affected during the immediate postwar years implied Parnassus more than Oxford. With Phil Stone he continued his sorties—to Clarksdale, Memphis, and New Orleans—to engage in gambling, bootleg drinking, and other activities unavailable in Oxford. At Stone's instigation, he also actively submitted for publication the poems he was writing. Once he got a lucky break. The *New Republic* accepted his reworking of Mallarmé's "L'Après-Midi d'un Faune," offering him $15 for it. They would publish it in their August 6, 1919, issue. Enchanted, he and Stone redoubled their efforts, only to find each subsequent submission rejected. They then copied out "Lines from a Northampton Asylum," by the early nineteenth-century English poet John Clare, and submitted it to the same magazine. It, too, was rejected. Finally they copied out a widely known masterpiece—"Kublai Khan"—and submitted that to the *New Republic* under the name of its real author, Samuel T. Coleridge. Another rejection soon arrived, along with—according to Stone—this editorial note "We like your poem, Mr. Coleridge, but we don't think it gets anywhere much" (F 72).

ADVENTURES OF COUNT NO 'COUNT

During the postwar years in Oxford, Faulkner remained in aggressively role-playing mode. Following the initial season of sporting his unearned war uniform—worn not just on ceremonial occasions but at dances and on the golf course as well—he settled into an equally self-conscious role as special student at the university. He took courses in English, Spanish, and French, but he was better remembered for his cultural and sartorial pretensions. Earlier, his expensively tailored suits had earned him the title "the Count." Now his more elaborate costuming—replete with cane, limp, and swagger—elicited from his university peers the derisive term "Count No 'Count." Seemingly descended from Parnassus and returned from war-torn France, Faulkner maintained his façade of imperturbability. He published poems in the university literary magazine, the *Mississippian,* as well as contributing elegant, Beardsley-inspired drawings. Annoyed classmates eventually refused to take his cultural pretensions lying down. The title of one of his poems—a translation of Paul Verlaine's "Fantoches"—was misprinted in the *Mississippian* as "Fantouches." That title and the poem's most famous line—"la lune ne garde aucune rancune"—soon generated a satiric response. There appeared in the same magazine a counter-poem—"Whotouches," described as "Just a Parody on Count's 'Fantouches' by Count Jr."—and it ended thus: "how long the old aucune raccoon" (F 81). Journalistic ripple effects continued, and a month later the *Mississippian* published "Cane de Looney," written by one "Peruney Prune."

By the fall of 1921, having quit his desultory studies at the university, Faulkner found himself at loose ends. His poems, though occasionally accepted by the *Mississippian,* were turned down by national journals. Estelle's periodic returns to Oxford—her married status blazoned in the figure of her accompanying daughter, Victoria—stimulated him and frustrated him in equal measure. Neither the stimulation nor the frustration was welcome. Finally, there was no job he could conceive of in Oxford that remotely appealed. Played out, he turned once more to the man who had bailed him out in the past and would, he hoped, do so again. Once contacted, Stone proposed the same path of escape that had worked earlier; he urged Faulkner to come north, offering to share his rooms in New Haven. So Faulkner packed his bags and headed to the Northeast for the second time in his life—to New Haven at first, preparatory to a more protracted stay in New York. He was determined to become an artist; attempting to perform that role in Oxford had become too burdensome to continue. New Haven would at least not object to his artistic striving, and Greenwich Village was widely fantasized as the sort of place that might actually abet it.

New Haven did accommodate him, and Greenwich Village amazed him. Of his first subway trip in the big city, he wrote his mother:

> The experience showed me that we are not descended from monkeys, as some say, but from lice....Great crowds of people cramming underground, and pretty soon here comes a train, and I swear I believe the things are going a mile a minute when they stop. Well, everybody crowds on, the guards bawling and shoving, then off again, top speed. Its like being shot through a long piece of garden hose. (TH 157–8)

Amusing, but also latently horrifying: as always, Faulkner was attuned to the speed of things. The machine-fueled rush and roar of New York penetrated his nerves. Later, in *Sanctuary,* his most disturbing images would circulate around unstoppable entities hurtling at inhuman speed underground, as well as the menace of an encroaching "little rubber tube wrong side outward" (SAN 331). Nevertheless, the generosity of Stark Young (thanks to Stone) and Elizabeth Prall took care of basic needs. Young gave him lodging until he could find a place of his own; Prall found him the Lord and Taylor job. He could look into the mirror every morning and say to himself that he was holding his own, even supporting himself in the bohemian capital of America. Yet he knew that this was hardly a sustainable life rhythm; he would never be a New Yorker. When Stone reached him, late that fall, with another proposal—this one a homecoming—it was hard to say no.

If Stone's proposal had not been so outlandish, he might have accepted it at the outset. But the proposition was incredible. With the help of Lem Oldham (Estelle's politically influential father), the entrepreneurial Stone had somehow persuaded U.S. senator Byron Harrison to offer Faulkner the position of postmaster of the University of Mississippi post office. Faulkner turned it down immediately. When Stone pressed again, and yet a third time (with Maud Falkner's secret collusion to get her boy back home), he at last relented. He did so against his better judgment, which told him—even in the brevity of the moment—that this was no job for him. But what were his other options? The post office would pay $1,500 a year, more than double his salary at Lord and Taylor's. Why not give it a try?

During the next three years, in Stone's often-quoted words, Faulkner "made the damndest postmaster the world has ever seen" (F 109). He could not take the job seriously. His favorite activities—when he was in the office and ostensibly at work—seem to have been bridge and mah-jongg. If the weather was fair, he liked to close shop and join others for a game of golf. Eventually he set up his working quarters so as to indulge in tea with his friends, or, if alone, to do some private reading in "the Reading Room." Reading materials were not hard to come by. He developed the habit of casually "borrowing" any journals that crossed his desk and appealed to his eye—journals intended for their Oxford recipients. Taciturn as ever in conventional situations, he saw no need to carry on conversations with his customers. He hardly knew most of them and never did care for small talk. He seemed to consider them lucky to get their mail at all; many complained that they did not get their mail at all. Discontent mounted, and eventually, in September 1924, it boiled over. Mississippi's postal inspector, Mark Webster, sent him a three-page letter laying out seven categories of dereliction of duty alleged against him. Apparently he felt no need to read that letter either, so he was surprised when—in the midst of a bridge game in the office—Webster appeared at his door. The game was over, Faulkner immediately realized. Silently walking away with his bridge buddies, he turned and said, "I reckon I'll be at the beck and call of folks with money all my life, but thank God I won't ever again have to be at the beck and call of every son of a bitch who's got two cents to buy a stamp" (118).

The years between 1918 and 1924 testify to a wide range of sustained performances. In addition to the preposterous postmaster, there was the frustrated lover—still writing poems for his beloved Estelle, still arrested in his desire for her. There was also Count No 'Count, University of Mississippi poseur par excellence, as well as the weary, war-wounded veteran who had flown planes and seen action overseas. No less, we find the vagabond Faulkner whose gambling and boozing trips increased as he moved into his midtwenties, with many of his friends married off and in domestic arrangements. There is as well Faulkner the scoutmaster, remembered with something close to adoration by his younger charges. (He occupied this position until one of the local ministers objected to a well-known boozer sullying that sacrosanct post.) Placed next to each other, all these Faulkners appear as performances. Although each role being performed expresses some abiding dimension of the same human being, they add up to make a troubling portrait. The man who mishandles his postmaster job to that spectacular degree seems both to lack any unifying core and to be willing to make others pay for it—a man given to colorful performances yet obscurely in flight from himself. It was not only Estelle's parents who considered him a bad bet, some six years earlier. He might have struck himself as a bad bet even now. Such self-criticism would have been sharpened by the all-but-public assessment of him leveled by his uncle John at about the same time. Standing on the central square in Oxford, his uncle had told a group of listeners, "that damn Billy is not worth a Mississippi goddam—and never will be....He's a Falkner and I hate to say it about my own nephew, but, hell, there's a black sheep in everybody's family and Billy's ours. Not worth a cent" (F 117–8).

Not worth a cent. To what extent did this unforgiving assessment roil inside the young man who made his way to New Orleans a few months after the Post Office debacle? Did the newcomer to Sherwood Anderson's literary circle harbor a set of doubts about himself—more as a human being than as a fledgling writer—that functioned as an unwanted secret sharer? Does Elmer's bumbling helplessness, written while Faulkner lodged in Paris later the same year (1925), testify to something still unformed, exposed, and damaged inside him—a defective "clotting which is you" that would unclot if not protected by carefully maintained posturing? Did the published author of *Soldiers' Pay* and *Mosquitoes* recognize in Liveright's harsh verdict on *Flags* an inner incoherence that nothing was likely to straighten out, least of all marriage to a just-divorced Estelle? Whatever the answers to these questions, the man who wrote a trio of masterpieces between 1928 and 1930—*The Sound and the Fury, As I Lay Dying,* and *Sanctuary*—was someone in trouble, a man who was stumbling. And writing masterpieces inseparable from it.

"I HAVE CREATED QUITE A SENSATION"

He was too busy doing it to realize what he had done. He would later look back in amazement at that "one matchless time" when almost everything he put on paper took on incandescent form.[6] Decades later, in Manila in 1955, he would say "The writer's got to add the gift of his talent; he has got to take the truth and set it on fire" (LG 201). At that time he might, on looking back, have been unable to see in *Sanctuary* any embodiment of "the truth." But he could not have denied that in *Sanctuary* he had set something on fire—his career itself. "I have created quite a sensation," he would write Estelle from New York in November 1931 (SL 53). Prospective publishers were buzzing about him like bees about honey, competing with each other to sign the next book. How had this sudden courtship come about?

It started with the publication of *The Sound and the Fury.* Only a modest popular success, the book made professional critics sit up and take notice. He would never receive a more penetrating encomium than that penned in 1929 by Evelyn Scott—a contemporary novelist whose review was included in a special edition (a thousand copies) of the book: "Here is beauty sprung from the perfect *realization* of what a more limiting morality would describe as ugliness," she wrote. "Here is a humanity stripped of most of what was claimed for it by the Victorians, and the spectacle is moving as no sugar-coated drama ever could be" (CH 78). Even though baffled by his procedures, critics recognized that Faulkner was breaking new ground—that no American novelist had written like this before.

One critic even grasped that the book's experimental procedures placed on its reader an extraordinary burden: "This is not an easy book," the *Nashville Tennessean* reviewer conceded. "It cannot be read objectively; the reader, if he is to savor the best in this book, must surrender himself entirely" (CH 84). "You can do it too easy," Anderson had warned. Beginning with *The Sound and the Fury,* Faulkner would henceforth rarely be easy—not on himself, not on his reader. To inhabit Benjy and Quentin, Darl and Vardaman, to get inside their "damn heads," he had had to yield up his own defenses—his masks of superiority and pose of indifference. He had had to write them as if wholly inside them, seeing and feeling what they saw and felt, judging as they judged—but never judging them. To savor the best in this and his subsequent masterpieces, readers would likewise have to forego defensive judgment—and plunge. Some were beginning to do so.

The Sound and the Fury began it, *As I Lay Dying* expanded on it, and *Sanctuary* set it into juggernaut motion. What contributed most to the Faulkner "sensation" was perhaps not so much the brilliance of any of these novels, nor even that of the three of them together. It was the astonishing pace at which they had appeared, meteorically, between October 1929 and February 1931—in less than sixteen months. Almost overnight, he had become a literary phenomenon, a name in every serious fiction reader's face. For a decade, he had been dreaming of such recognition, but it had taken the fantasy form of *might-be*. When it finally hit—in 1931—he was unprepared. Encountering the arrival of his own fame—a reality, like other realities, "in advance of itself"—the best he could muster was a bewildered acceptance. Like the young Joe Christmas (in *Light in August*), he was being catapulted into experiences that escaped his ordering framework. Like Joe as well, he might have glimpsed that he would never understand what was happening. At most, he might develop practices to make it manageable. These would only "come later, when life had begun to go so fast that accepting would take the place of knowing and believing.... The accepting was to come later, along with the whole sum of entire outrage to credulity" (LA 530). He stumbled into fame.

If recognition was what he wanted, it was no less something that, after June 20, 1929, he would have little time to ponder. Married now, the honeymoon over, he had to start performing as a husband and eventual father and home owner—lifetime roles that, unlike his earlier ones, he would neither abandon nor master. To take on these latest roles properly, he knew he would need money—regularly and in substantial amounts. This had never been his forte. Beginning in early 1930, with several published novels now under his belt, he targeted more aggressively the short story market: the national journals such as *Scribner's, Harper's, Collier's,* the *American Mercury,* and especially the *Saturday Evening Post.* These paid dramatically better than the advances he received for his novels (as much as $750 per story), and he could write the stories swiftly. In turn, they exacted something from him that he was loath to provide: a simplification of plot and character lines, such that the finished product be swiftly recognizable as salable. He thought of this quid pro quo, even then, as the whoring required by his new marital status. He could hardly know that such compromises would barely count as a peck on the cheek compared to Hollywood assignments he would soon be carrying out. *Sanctuary* was too spectacular for its author to escape the movie moguls' notice for long. In less than two years, his need of funds and their desire to trade on his name would come together as an agreement legally executed above ground but fiendishly conceived in hell.

Faulkner both married a family and in time produced his own. Estelle's two children (at least at first) lived with them; he chafed at their doing this together in rented rooms. He was thirty-two, and Oxford, after all, was his town. He knew that he had begun to demonstrate the fallacy of his Uncle John's contemptuous judgment. Not worth a cent. Well, four published novels didn't bring in much money, but they revealed—to anyone willing to notice—that this vagabond was not to be dismissed. Ownership of a house would further demonstrate his mounting respectability. Not any house though: he wanted a significant house—one that already spoke of his region and would signal his rightful place within it. The old Shegog place on Taylor Road, just outside town, fit the bill. An antebellum two-story colonial with a once-elegant portico, Georgian doors, a wide gallery, and a curved, cedar-lined drive, situated on four wooded acres: it was redolent of nineteenth-century Southern tradition. Badly dilapidated, it was also—just barely—affordable. For $6,000 at 6 percent interest, with no down payment, it could be his. Estelle, he hoped, would soon be pregnant with his own child. This was the right place for all of them, and he signed the papers for it in April 1930. It needed a new name for its new lease on life. Having read in Frazer's *Golden Bough* of the rowan tree as a Scottish symbol of domestic protection against witches, he decided to call it Rowan Oak. He would need all the help he could get.

Luckily, his vagabond years had included a good deal of amateur carpentering. He required those resources and more, as he set about repairing beams, putting in a new roof, installing screens, attending to the plumbing, and painting the walls. This labor would continue not for months but for years, as he moved on to more intricate improvements. Like Sutpen in *Absalom*, once he began to get his new home's material needs under control, he started to manage its cultural ones. Mammy Callie and Uncle Ned—black domestics intimately associated with his own upbringing and going back even further, to the Young Colonel—soon joined, unbidden but welcome, the new home owner and his wife. Uncle Ned took over butlering duties, as well as caring for the yard. Mammy Callie would help Estelle bring up the children not yet born, as she had helped bring him up earlier. A powerful rhythm older than he was began to assert itself, as Rowan Oak came into symbolic plantation focus, gathering to itself its modest but obligatory retinue of servants. Centuries of black/white Southern relations, passively encoded in these arrangements, were being renewed. He was now the master. Uncle Ned and Mammy Callie asked for no wages; they did not need to. They knew without speaking, as he did, that he would be responsible for their food, shelter, clothing, and health care. He would do the right thing.[7]

The man who not long ago had spent three years in his university post office job deliberately doing the wrong thing had not undergone a change of heart. Rather than change his identity, he took on these new responsibilities as unavoidable overlay to his earlier, still unrelinquished commitment to bohemianism and vagabondage. His pride in his house and his resentment toward its demands—like his acceptance of his marriage and his resistance toward it—silently competed with each other. He would complain about mortgages, taxes, insurance, and domestic outlays for the rest of his life, even as he insisted on—took pride in—shouldering these burdens.

Within two months of moving into Rowan Oak, Estelle became pregnant, and this pregnancy was difficult—like Estelle's earlier ones. The new baby was born at an inopportune time: an icy night in January 1931, some eight weeks before expected. They named her Alabama, in honor of his beloved great-aunt, but the name bestowed no protection. The baby's health began bad and quickly got worse. Unprepared for life outside her mother's body, she probably needed an incubator, but none was available nearer than Memphis. Faulkner took her home to Rowan Oak, the obstetrician made visits every day, but the child was sinking. Ten days after her birth, Alabama died, without her weakened and hospitalized mother having ever seen her alive. Once more, Faulkner recognized his impotence before the assault of *is*—as though his baby's irreversible decline stayed mockingly in advance of any counter-measures he could cobble together. He watched her death approach inexorably—a coming reality he viewed with horror but could not prevent. Her fate seemed sealed by the sinister gods. Alabama would haunt him later, and her unlived possibilities would appear to him as uncannily prefigured in the earlier genesis of his heart's darling, Caddy Compson. "So I, who never had a sister," he would write in an unpublished 1933 preface to *The Sound and the Fury*, "and was fated to lose my daughter in infancy, set out to make myself a beautiful and tragic little girl" (NOR 228). The peace of *was*, the turmoil of *is*. Unable to save his daughter during the assault of present time, he repossessed her imaginatively, retrospectively yet in advance of her actual birth. Aligning his dead baby with his immortal Caddy, he bestowed on her a fullness of meaning she could not have possessed that dark day in January 1931—bestowed it later.

Estelle remained weak that entire spring and into the summer as well. He urgently needed money to keep his household intact; he had already missed the March mortgage payment. In droves, he began to submit short stories to the national journals, trying to remedy the situation. Despite a number of acceptances, the rejection letters came back, also in droves. Then something quite different arrived in the mail. Professor James Wilson of the University of Virginia wrote to invite him to a conference of Southern writers, to be held in Charlottesville. Instigated by Ellen Glasgow and supported by notables such as James Branch Cabell, Thomas Wolfe, Paul Green, Donald Davidson, Sherwood Anderson, and Allen Tate, the conference would seek to shed light on the recent flourishing of Southern letters. *Sanctuary* had been published in February 1931, to a hailstorm of critical response. *The Sound and the Fury* and *As I Lay Dying* had appeared shortly before that, and the latter was now lined up for translation into French. Faulkner had become unignorable, and they wanted him to be among the thirty-four conference attendees. The letter he wrote in response reveals his misgivings even as he said yes:

> Dear Mr Wilson—
> Thank you for your invitation. I would like very much to avail myself of it, what with your letter's pleasing assurance that loopholes will be supplied to them who have peculiarities about social gambits. You have seen a country wagon come into town, with a hound dog under the wagon. It stops on the Square and the folks get out, but that hound never gets very far from that wagon. He might be cajoled or scared out for a short distance, but first thing you know he has scuttled back under the wagon; maybe he growls at you a little. Well, that's me. (SL 51)

He arrived in Charlottesville apprehensive, and apparently his first words to the reporter-host awaiting him were "Know where I can get a drink?" The host took him to his own bootleg supplier, and, cushioned by a bottle of corn whiskey, the two of them spent an amiable evening together. As the conference got under way, things went from bad to worse. He appeared at the first meeting wearing what the playwright Paul Green took to be an aviator's cap, and he swiftly became the focal point of the conference. His response to this unwonted attention was to hit the booze more aggressively. "Bill Faulkner had arrived and got drunk," Sherwood Anderson later reported. "From time to time he appeared, got drunk again immediately and disappeared. He kept asking everyone for drinks" (F 286). Allen Tate recalled Faulkner asking Tate's wife where he could get another drink, then vomiting all over her dress (WFSH 233). The situation had gotten out of hand. Hal Smith, Faulkner's friend and publisher, finally reacted. With the help of Paul Green, they got him into a car and drove to New York. Faulkner seems to have been steadily drinking the whole time. As they drove through Washington, D.C., he jovially invited a policeman they passed on the street to join them for yet another. On October 26, they arrived in New York.

A virtual firebomb of attention was waiting for him there. Harold Guinzburg of Viking and Alfred Knopf of Knopf and Bennett Cerf of Random House were already lined up, impatiently expecting his arrival, each determined to sign him up. The presence of such figures of power stridently bidding for his attention increased Faulkner's anxiety, and he stepped up the drinking. Hal Smith became alarmed again and once more got him away, this time on a boat trip to Jacksonville and other Southern cities, before returning to New York a week later. Throughout this side trip, Faulkner drank heavily, rashly promising manuscripts to young admirers who were there to help manage him. Once back in New York, he started to career out of control again. When Tallulah Bankhead, on meeting him, begged him to do a screenplay for her, he wrote Estelle excitedly: "The contract is to be signed today, for about $10,000" (F 289). (Nothing ever came of this project.) A couple of days later, he wrote to Estelle again, still more excitedly: "I have created quite a sensation....In fact, I have learned with astonishment that I am now the most important figure in American letters" (291).

"With astonishment": astonishment and inebriation seem to have characterized the six weeks of his frenetic stay in New York. He was more or less continually sprung. Pressed in an interview by a New York journalist, he claimed that Southern Negroes were childlike and would be better off "under the conditions of slavery...because they'd have someone to look after them" (F 292). He would later make race remarks more offensive than that, typically when under the influence. Once he met Lillian Hellman, Dashiell Hammett, and Nathaniel West, that same fall, he had available a peerless New York crew of fellow drinkers. He was now passing out in public places frequently enough for Hal Smith to contact Ben Wasson for help. Wasson urged Estelle to come up quickly to New York and rescue her high-flying husband; she took the train and arrived by the beginning of

December. Her presence, however, seemed to add fuel to the fire. Cerf later remembered her standing at the window of his apartment on Central Park South, during one of his parties. She turned to him, remarked on the beauty of the view outside, and said: "I feel just like throwing myself out the window" (295). Alarmed, Cerf responded, "Oh, Estelle, you don't mean that." She stared back and said, "*Of course I do*" (295, emphasis in the original). Dorothy Parker spoke as well of scenes of hysteria, of Estelle ripping her dress and attempting to leap out the window of one of Parker's Algonquin Hotel rooms. Another of their new acquaintances, Marc Connelly, recalled her slipping out of control at a social gathering one night. Faulkner was standing next to her, engaged in conversation, when he noticed what was happening. With no expression on his face, Connelly said, Faulkner quietly reached out and slapped her, very hard. She returned immediately to normal, and he continued his conversation.

What was going on during this astonishing outburst of manic behavior that lasted from late October to mid-December 1931? He had long been a heavy drinker, but something newly disturbing seemed to emerge during the University of Virginia fiasco. Faulkner knew that no other American writer could have produced that trio of masterpieces, but somehow this knowledge was private, his alone. *The Sound and the Fury,* he would later say, was a book he wrote for himself. *As I Lay Dying* followed hard upon it, composed in a power plant during night hours with no other company than that of an unlettered black coworker. *Sanctuary* was indeed written with a larger audience in mind—as a potboiler, as he would repeatedly characterize it in later interviews. But we know that it, too, was conceived and drafted during the ominous days of his last five months of bachelorhood—one of the most brooding and incommunicable periods of his life. Suddenly, all three books were no longer his but the property of an aroused and clamorous literary world. He was under siege, in the hands of strangers, and he did not know how to handle it. If this was fame, it was violent, dizzying, impossible to manage. Moreover, it left a bad taste in the mouth the next morning.

"You know that state I seem to get into when people come to see me and I begin to visualize a kind of jail corridor of literary talk," he wrote Ben Wasson about the Southern conference debacle (SL 56). "Jail corridor": so he had viewed the marital prison he was preparing to enter in June 1929. But the reasons for this later feeling of claustrophobia were different. He could not forget that—no matter how deliberately—he had not pursued his education past the eleventh grade. He had no business speaking to these literary people. He wrote novels but despised "literary talk." That was the province of university professors who loved to hear the words coming out of their mouths. He required silence—for his sanity and to get his work done. His intense bond with his books was speechlessly enacted in writing them, not in talking about them later. He was a hound dog who sought the widest recognition, but more than that, viscerally, he wanted to stay scuttled under that wagon. Is it any wonder that his greatest fiction—including the three novels that launched the New York frenzy—centers on the unpreparedness experienced during moments of sudden exposure? That his signature work involves a risking of "the clotting which is you" to the dissolving force of "the myriad original motion"? Or, as he put it in *Sanctuary*, those moments when "the flatulent monotony of…sheltered lives [is] snatched up without warning by an incomprehensible moment of terror" (287)? Crisis: the assault of what you are not ready for. This rhythm of untimeliness marked his life. It marks his greatest fiction as well.

"ITS NOT EVEN TIME UNTIL IT WAS": *THE SOUND AND THE FURY*

Quentin's chapter in *The Sound and the Fury* closes not on his suicide (which is never narrated) but on a remembered conversation with his father. Mr Compson insists that ongoing time mocks all values. Disbelieving, Quentin counters by telling his father of his desire to do "something so dreadful" that time itself—shocked—would come to a halt. "That's sad too," Mr. Compson responds, "people cannot do anything that dreadful they cannot do anything very dreadful at all they cannot even remember tomorrow what seemed dreadful today" (SF 938). Nothing endures. Even Christ was not crucified for all time but gradually "worn away by a minute clicking of little wheels" (935)—entrapped and pulverized within the ceaseless ticking of a clock. Personally disempowered, Mr. Compson cannot protect his daughter or console his son. His impotence is more than personal. Nothing in the set of Old South values he learned as a child is of any use in the New South of 1910. His daughter's lost virginity may be breaking her brother Quentin's heart, but this loss centers on a value Mr. Compson has come to regard as illusory. At the same time, he sees it as tragic beyond accommodation. Mr. Compson soaks such contradictory responses into manageability by quietly drinking himself to death. Having compressed his gathered nihilism into a single word, he passes it on to his son: "temporary." Quentin chokes on the word: "and i temporary and he was the saddest word of all there is nothing else in the world its not despair until time its not even time until it was" (1014).

"Its not even time until it was." Moving forward through unrepeat-ing time, we make sense of experience only in the condition of its having already passed. "Excrement Father said like sweating" (SF 935–6)—this is another of Mr. Compson's cryptic remarks that circulate in Quentin's mind. The phrasing figures time as a medium that flows out of our bodies—some-thing we pass through our pores. Time emerges only as already used up and excreted. This is time as belatedness, as the too-late-ness that creatures caught up in temporariness—which means all human beings—experience. The Marble Faun "who would a god become" sought to bestride ongoing time, to dominate it. This desire cannot be fulfilled. *The Sound and the Fury* elaborates the fallout of that condition. Virtually every character in the book suffers from untimeliness.

Mrs. Compson, for reasons the novel assumes but never explains, has refused to mother her own children. Clinging belatedly to the courtship phase of her own youth, she cannot spiritually consummate—endorse as real—the marriage whose physical consequences are all around her. Her three sons, emotionally disowned, turn to their sister Caddy. For each of them, she must serve as a belated replacement of the missing mother. Mrs. Compson had originally named her youngest son Maury, in honor of her Bascomb brother Maury. Once she realized he would never be normal, she renamed him Benjamin. This symbolic move silently declares: there is no precious Bascomb blood (which she shares with Maury) inside that child's body. Her renaming him transforms the infant that lodged for nine months in her womb into an unlucky accident that befell her. Inside her own mind, she is still intact, virginal. At a level deeper than thought, Benjy realizes that he has been orphaned, and he clings to Caddy to make up for it.

The eldest son, Quentin, is likewise orphaned: "If I could say mother," he thinks. No less than Benjy, he turns belatedly to Caddy for sustenance, fantasizing an incestuous relation with her that would cast the two of them into the remotest corner of hell: "*Only you and me then amid the pointing and the horror walled by the clean flame*" (SF 966, emphasis in the original). When he encounters a little girl outside Cambridge (his chapter takes place at the end of his freshman year at Harvard), he can see her only as a rep-etition of Caddy. "Sister," he obsessively calls her. The episode concludes with his being arrested for attempted molestation of the girl: a verdict poi-gnantly false and true. Later that day, he suddenly—and, to all those around him, inexplicably—attacks his handsome classmate Gerald Bland. In his own mind he is hitting out at Dalton Ames, Caddy's first seducer, of a year earlier. Traumatized, he is physically here and now, but more deeply he is still there and then, in that earlier scene of his sister's deflowering.

The middle son Jason might appear the least damaged by his mother's absence, but he suffers from belatedness as much as his brothers. Caddy's fiancé had promised to provide Jason with a bank job, a way out of this decaying family, but the failure of that marriage led to Herbert's withdrawing the offer. Caddy herself—shamed, disowned—has long since fled home. So Jason has available only her illegitimate daughter, yet another Quentin, as an object for the revenge he cannot exact on his sister. Untimely like the others, he strikes, today, at proxies for yesterday's humiliations.

Caddy may be banished into absence, but she careens in memory across the paths of her hapless brothers. Her idiot brother Benjy remains immovably attached; her younger brother Jason still thirsts for revenge; her older brother Quentin wanted both to take and to safeguard her virginity. Her first lover, Dalton Ames, was a traveling salesman who appeared casually, did his damage, then departed for good. Except in Quentin's mind, where he lives on belatedly, immortal—the past one can neither erase nor accept. Once the family learned that she was pregnant, they secured a husband—who left her as soon as he realized that he was a replacement for others who had been there earlier. If one were to map the emotional tangle Faulkner explores in this novel, Mrs. Compson and Caddy would be at its center. She is physically present but emotionally absent, while Caddy is physically absent but emotionally encompassing. Both radiate damage into others surrounding them. Pressed to make up for all her mother did not provide, the overburdened Caddy cannot but fail at her subsequent relationships. A figure of the richest emotional possibilities, she is no less a figure of waste—suggestive of what Faulkner will call in *Absalom* "*a might-have-been that is more true than truth*" (emphasis in the original).

Caddy's daughter, Quentin, is the novel's purest embodiment of untimeliness. Beginning with her name—imposed on her by her fleeing mother, in honor of the baby's suicidal uncle Quentin—this single representative of the next generation is doomed. She has no choice but to stand in for her uncle and mother who—wounded by others and wounding in return—have long since departed. Faulkner brilliantly makes the reader complicit in this misrecognition. We first hear her called Quentin in the early pages of Benjy's opening chapter. At that point we do not know that Benjy's sister Caddy later gave birth to an illegitimate child whom she named Quentin. All first-time readers therefore assume that Benjy is referring to his own brother Quentin (who has already appeared in the central remembered scene in the novel, the Compson children playing by the stream at the time of Damuddy's funeral). Faulkner thereby ensures that we get her gender and her generation wrong. Indeed, her gender and her generation *are* wrong. Both her grandmother Mrs. Compson and her uncle Jason see her, and abuse her, as a belated stand-in for her dead uncle and departed mother—there to receive the long-simmering resentment they can no longer levy on Quentin and Caddy.

Nothing concludes in this novel. "If things just finished themselves," Quentin silently reflects. Nothing begins either. Events have already been launched and are fatally in train before one enters the scene and becomes aware of them. Not only is this true for the characters—their prehistory trumps their history—but Faulkner makes it true for the reader as well. His astonishing technique in *The Sound and the Fury* keeps us immersed in the barrage of present moments, makes us feel them *as* assault, thanks to his refusing to provide the temporal overview that would put people and events in perspective. Lacking that overview and the objectivity it would seem to bring, we suffer the characters' lives rather than judge them. We become immersed in a time that is "premature, inconclusive and inconcludable." Such time is experienced, subjectively, as outrage—"in order to be life; it must be before itself, in advance of itself, to have been at all."

Need it be said that novels do not normally proceed this way? That most novels silently transform the stumbling that is ongoing life into the purposefulness that is recollected life—life as gathered together and represented in narrative? Long before 1929, Soren Kierkegaard had grasped the same truth. "It is perfectly true, as philosophers say, that life must be understood backwards," Kierkegaard wrote in his 1840s journals. "But they forget the other proposition, that it must be lived forwards."[8] Life as a something stumblingly lived forward: what is that but unpreparedness in the present moment, the quandary of not knowing what to do? Like everyone, Faulkner knew what this felt like. Like few others, he managed, as a writer, to make his fictions know it too. His way of doing so transforms him from a regional to a world-class writer. Caddy and her brothers stumble through *The Sound and the Fury* as no earlier characters had stumbled. But they look like dancers, next to Temple Drake in *Sanctuary*.

"THE FAINT, FURIOUS UPROAR OF THE SHUCKS": *SANCTUARY*

From 1931 on, Faulkner would be known by untold numbers of people, derisively, as the "corncob man." Most of them would never read *Sanctuary*.

Those who did may have been surprised by how difficult it is to locate the infamous scene of the rape, done with a corncob. Even today, few critics can briefly synopsize the novel without mentioning the corncob. The word instantly summons up a bestial image of rape, arousing repulsion. Faulkner himself would later speak only rarely of *Sanctuary,* and when he did so, his stance was not far from repulsion. Hal Smith—who had earlier been horrified by the book in draft form—reversed himself without explanation a year later and sent *Sanctuary* on to Faulkner at Rowan Oak. He had put it in galleys so that it might be proofed. On reading it over, Faulkner found himself in a dilemma. In the wake of *The Sound and the Fury* and *As I Lay Dying,* he did not like what he was looking at. Though he could ill afford it, he chose to revise *Sanctuary* at considerable cost to himself. He would not allow it to shame its magnificent predecessors.

The corncob has a prehistory in Faulkner's life and art. As teenagers, the three older Falkner boys engaged in their share of neighborhood fights. Johncy remembered most vividly the ones conducted with corncobs: "Getting hit with one of them [a wet corncob] is like getting hit with a wet brickbat" (MBB 118). In *Flags,* the fleeing young Bayard (he has caused his grandfather's death in an automobile accident and cannot face his family) retreats to the home of a backcountry family named MacCallum. At night, he is offered one of their old beds "filled with corn shucks: it rattled beneath him, drily sibilant" (FD 822). He has trouble sleeping, dreams vividly that he is already dead, then turns over on his back: "the shucks whispered beneath him with dry derision" (822).

Childhood violence, displacement, nightmare, insomnia: the figure of corncob and corn shucks already possessed a number of meanings for Faulkner. Cheap country mattresses were often stuffed with corn shucks; nothing could be more familiar. But such mattresses were uncomfortable and noisy, disturbing for a man who slept badly much of his life. The nightmare on the shucks experienced by young Bayard becomes, in *Sanctuary,* exponentially more deranging. In ways that make one think of Kafka, familiar images of normal life—a corncob or corn shucks—take on a sinister life of their own. A shuck-filled bed Temple Drake is supposed to lie on comes alive with motion, a throwaway corncob transforms into a weapon of primitive assault. Temple finds herself in an uncanny space where no arrangement remains docile. At Frenchman's Bend (a bootleggers' hideaway in the country she has now stumbled into, after a car accident), objects that are normally manageable transmogrify. The verb Faulkner uses again and again to narrate Temple's frantic motion in this house is "sprang."

She snatched it [her hand] up with a wailing shriek, clapping it against her mouth, and turned and ran toward the door. The woman caught her arm...and Temple sprang back into the kitchen.... "Let go," she whispered, "let go! Let go!" She surged and plunged, grinding the woman's hand against the door jamb until she was free. She sprang from the porch and ran toward the barn.... Then suddenly she ran upside down in a rushing interval; she could see her legs still running in space, and she struck lightly and solidly on her back and lay still.... Her hand moved in the substance in which she lay, then she remembered the rat.... Her whole body surged in an involuted spurning movement...so that she flung her hands out and caught herself upright...her face not twelve inches from the cross beam on which the rat crouched. For an instant they stared eye to eye, then its eyes glowed suddenly like two tiny electric bulbs and it leaped at her head just as she sprang backward, treading again on something that rolled under her foot. She fell toward the opposite corner, on her face in the hulls and a few scattered corn-cobs gnawed bone-clean.... Then she got to her feet and sprang at the door...rasping at the planks with her bare hands. (SAN 243–4)

The corncob man: this entire passage conveys the ongoing rape of Temple, hours before the actual rape occurs. None of the material surfaces near her accommodates her body. Kitchen door and barn door, the other woman's hand, her own hand, her own legs, the scattered corncobs (for the moment harmless): these entities seem wired, gone awry, capable of "rasping" her. Charged with hostility, they align with the rat. As in a nightmare, the rat that is remembered in one sentence will within a few more be only twelve inches from her face. It stares at her eye to eye as though it knows her; then it leaps. As in a nightmare, she can escape nothing that approaches.

The power of *Sanctuary* lodges in passages such as this. Critics have long contended that such focused hostility must be Faulkner's own. Nowhere else in his fictional universe is a protagonist subjected to the physical abuse inflicted on Temple. As in the foregoing passage, her legs stop functioning as her own—"'I'd look at my legs and I'd think how much I had done for them...and now they'd gotten me into this,'" she whines to Horace later (SAN 329). Popeye picks her up by the back of the neck repeatedly—the pressure making her eyes bulge—and that is the least of his aggressions. Faulkner cannot take his eye off what is being done to her at Frenchman's Bend. Layer after layer, the sanctuaries that protect her identity are stripped away; the assault is at once bodily and psychic. "My father's a judge," she wails, as she seeks to smile, cringe, or fantasize her way back into security.

Her defenses ripped from her, her identity—as molded by "my father the Judge" and the protocols of Southern gentility—ends by collapsing on itself. She becomes, for the last third of the book, a denizen of the Memphis underworld, hooked on booze and riddled with lust, caught up in that other scene. She has traded Daddy for "Daddy" (Popeye), who—impotent himself—makes orgasmic, whinnying noises as he stands by her bed, watching her writhe in intercourse with his surrogate Red. Here is Temple waiting for Red: "she felt long shuddering waves of physical desire going over her, draining the color from her mouth, drawing her eyeballs back into her skull in a shuddering swoon" (343). Her shuddering eyeballs recall the rat's glowing ones. Living creatures are here accessed as body parts propelled by instinct. They surge and glow. "She could tell all of them by the way they breathed" (234). The human world, if stripped of its sanctuaries and pressured sufficiently, transforms into a feral barnyard.

We may remember that Faulkner liked to describe *As I Lay Dying* in terms that suggest a wager with himself. "I took this family," he said at the University of Virginia in 1957, "and subjected them to the two greatest catastrophes man can suffer—flood and fire, that's all. That was simple *tour de force*" (FIU 87). *Tour de force: Sanctuary* joins *As I Lay Dying* as a sort of narrative experiment in how much pressure people can bear. In both novels, he submits the habits and pieties (the sanctuaries) of his central figures to an all-but-apocalyptic assault—flood and fire in the one, the underworld of Frenchman's Bend and Memphis in the other—in order to discover what, under the impress of that assault, those figures will become. He exposes "the clotting which is you" to "the myriad original motion." With almost inhuman detachment, he experiments with his materials, pushing them past the conditions that sustain their coherence. Fascinated, he keeps his eye on the "unclotting" that ensues.

It is a short step from "inhuman" and "fascinated" to "misogynistic," and many readers—offended by the abuse inflicted on Temple—take that interpretive step. Some of the abuse supports such a reading. The novel indulges in recurrent sneers about Temple's protectedness, her ignorance of everything outside her family's world of genteel privilege. To that extent *Sanctuary* can be seen as committed to "teaching her a lesson." Yet Temple learns no lesson; the book is darker than any pedagogic purpose can illuminate. The spectacle produced by these two tour de force novels may lack the heartbreaking emotional depth of *The Sound and the Fury* and *Absalom, Absalom!* That notwithstanding, *As I Lay Dying* and *Sanctuary* remain focused—comically, terrifyingly, unforgettably—on what happens when the pressure mounted on identity ends by overwhelming identity itself. "It's like there was a fellow in every man," Cash thinks at the conclusion of *As I Lay Dying*, "that's done a-past the sanity or the insanity, that watches the sane and the insane doings of that man with the same horror and the same astonishment" (AILD 228). Temple reveals such sanity/insanity when the pressure on her reaches that point, as she is being raped:

> "Then I said That wont do. I ought to be a man. So I was an old man, with a long white beard, and then the little black man got littler and littler and I was saying Now. You see now. I'm a man now. Then I thought about being a man, and as soon as I thought it, it happened. It made a kind of plopping sound, like blowing a little rubber tube wrong-side outward. It felt cold, like the inside of your mouth when you hold it open. I could feel it, and I lay right still to keep from laughing about how surprised he was going to be. I could feel the jerking going inside my knickers ahead of his hand and me lying there trying not to laugh about how surprised and mad he was going to be in a minute." (331)

In this passage we encounter Temple's traumatic wound itself; Faulkner makes it speak. The fantasy-narrative it speaks articulates and conceals the assault she has undergone. We see everything materially relevant—the corncob, the invaded body, the jerking flesh—but we see it fantastically reconfigured. That is, we see the crazily crossgendered scenario that her defenses have summoned into being for psychic survival. In *The Sound and the Fury*, Quentin imagined himself as Dalton Ames's mother, withdrawing her husband's penis before ejaculation, killing Ames before he lived. No less bizarrely, Temple has fantasized herself onto an impossible stage. Faulkner narrates less what is done to Temple than what she does with what is done to her. Her doing is psychic alone because there is no way of escaping Popeye except by fantasy. Popeye co-opts reality; she absents herself through fantasy. The poetry of this passage is the poetry of Temple's outraged system of defenses. Inasmuch as the purpose of defenses is to forestall such outrage, Faulkner's prose finds its way to Temple's very core. With horror and astonishment, we hear her psyche speak. What it speaks is no feral barnyard, no release of animal instinct, but a kind of pain that only human beings, on the rack, are capable of.

I began this discussion of *Sanctuary* with "the faint furious uproar of the shucks," and I shall end there. Brilliant as is Faulkner's making Temple's wound speak for itself, he is no less attentive to the psychic transfers that fill this novel. Characters obsessively watch others who may or may not know they are being watched, a silent transfer moving across the gaze. *Sanctuary* opens on the edge of a spring in the woods—a mirroring body of water whose Narcissus echoes go all the way back to *The Marble Faun*. The self sees no alluring image of itself in that mirror, however. Instead, the bookish Horace—who is leaving his marriage and has stopped en route to get a drink of water—stares into the reflection of the criminal Popeye. Squatting, they silently "face one another across the spring, for two hours" (SAN 5). What is passing between them? Faulkner does not say, yet he launches *Sanctuary* on that note. He thus prepares us to envisage Horace—who by way of gender, morality, and education is Temple's opposite—as, unspeakably, her secret sharer. Over two-thirds of the way through the novel, Horace finally comes upon Temple, holed up in a Memphis brothel. She has become corrupted by Popeye, sexually besotted with Red. Only now do we hear what has actually happened to her, as (in the passage just quoted) she tells Horace of her rape. Stunned, silent, he makes his way back to Jefferson. Once home, he picks up a photo of his stepdaughter, the sexually alluring Little Belle. Staring at it, entering her swooning gaze, he becomes enveloped in the voluptuous odor of honeysuckle. His entire physical economy buckles, unable to bear the contradictory impulses surging through him. He rushes to the bathroom and plunges toward the toilet bowl:

> [he] leaned upon his braced arms while the shucks set up a terrific uproar beneath her thighs. Lying with her head lifted slightly . . . she watched something black and furious go roaring out of her pale body. She was bound naked on her back on a flat car moving at speed through a black tunnel, the blackness streaming in rigid threads overhead, a roar of iron wheels in her ears. The car shot bodily from the tunnel in a long upward slant . . . toward a crescendo. . . . Far beneath her she could hear the faint, furious uproar of the shucks. (333)

The corncob man. Nowhere in the novel do we get a more powerful image of the assault Temple undergoes. Drawing on that 1921 New York subway experience, Faulkner renders the bound, naked body of Temple as undergoing a subterranean ordeal at inhuman speed. The pervasive blackness suggests Popeye in his unchanging black suits, suggests evil and the underworld more broadly. The corn shucks are both all around her and far beneath her, faintly audible. She is both penetrated and detached, a sacrificial victim. Most tellingly, however, this passage does not begin with Temple at all. For three pages, the text has been following Horace, as he shakily makes his way home past midnight and picks up the photo of Little

Belle. Then it becomes hallucinatory, a nightmarish scene of unspeakable transfers. Horace becomes Temple, it is happening to him. More disturbing yet, Horace's helpless attraction to his nubile stepdaughter transfers to his attraction to Temple (the two young women are the same age, and neither of them is innocent despite their pretense). His body erupts at the signs of his arousal. About to retch, he rushes to the toilet bowl—which now becomes the bed of "furious" shucks. Leaning on his braced arms over that uproar beneath her thighs, it is Horace who, aghast, seems to be both raping her and suffering her rape.

Faulkner called this book a cheap idea, a potboiler. His critics saw deeper and glimpsed Dostoevsky. Svidrigaylov in *Crime and Punishment* both protects and violates children. At the end of that novel, he dreams of doing the first and finds—in the dream—that he is doing the second. Abruptly awakened by what he has glimpsed in the nighttime theater of himself, he rises from bed, wanders to the seediest part of St. Petersburg, and commits suicide. Faulkner claimed not to have read Dostoevsky, but he said that about a number of writers he was familiar with. Secret sharers—the term is Conrad's, a writer Faulkner never disowned—were his imaginative familiars. His great work penetrates beneath the sanctuaries of identity—those conceptual bulwarks within which we can claim that we are thus and so, and not otherwise. Exerting unbearable pressure, these novels come upon unspeakable transformations—as though, deep down, human being itself were shapeless plasma rather than fixed essence. The clotting that is you can unclot. At awful times it does unclot. The one who writes a misogynistic potboiler—a man who sees his difference from a woman as absolute, who abuses her and believes she deserves what she gets—is the corncob man. But the one who writes the nightmarish transferences that stalk our daytime identities is a genius. They are both Faulkner, and it took them both to write *Sanctuary*.

"SOMETHING IS GOING TO HAPPEN TO ME": *LIGHT IN AUGUST*

Light in August is perhaps Faulkner's most piercing narrative of race, and I shall attend to it in that light in the next chapter. Appearing in the fall of 1932, it is the fourth of the masterpieces he produced within a time frame of less than thirty-six months. By then, thanks to *Sanctuary*'s corncob, Faulkner had become notorious, and by then he had experienced his first bout of Hollywood glitz. *Light in August* points in two directions. It announces his newfound concern with his region's most abiding trouble—race relations—a concern he would return to repeatedly during the next sixteen years. It reprises, as well, the signature interests of his three previous novels: the unpreparedness of childhood and the assault of the present moment.

The sequencing of events in *Light in August* was not easy for Faulkner to get right, and the novel communicates to its reader a growing anxiety about what follows what, and why. It opens in the present tense, on the road. Pregnant Lena Grove, swollen and on the verge of labor, is walking toward Jefferson, catching wagon rides as she can. Actually, she is trying to find her departed lover, Lucas Burch, who left her about six months earlier, when certain bodily events revealed their meaning. Nothing in the book is easier to decode than her belly and the plight it announces. So every reader settles down, after the first thirty pages, to read the developing story of abandoned Lena Grove.

Chapter 2, however, opens on "Byron Bunch knows this" (LA 421). The next twenty pages recount a pair of matters from the perspective of hereto-fore unannounced Byron. First, he recalls the earlier arrival in Jefferson of two strangers—one of them sinister and rootless (named Joe Christmas), the other loudmouthed and shiftless (named Joe Brown). They both took jobs at the sawmill where Byron works. Second, he recalls the arrival of Lena Grove at the sawmill on Saturday afternoon—just a day earlier— when he was the only one still at work. Byron's interest in Lena becomes swiftly transparent to the reader. For her part, inquiring about Burch, she had been told of Bunch. She thought—hoped—that maybe it was a mis-pronunciation and that Bunch would turn out to be Burch; she headed to the mill to find him. We are entering a rural comedy of manners, and we now expect to get the rest of Bunch's story.

Chapter 3 opens, instead, in the dark household of a man whom Bunch tends to visit a few times each week—a former preacher named Hightower. It dilates for the next fifteen pages on Hightower's painful history in this town. He is not just a former minister but a defrocked one. His house is not just dark but is deliberately avoided by the community of Jefferson. With chapter 4 we finally get a sequence we expect: twenty pages of conversa-tion between Byron and Hightower, in Hightower's house. They speak of Christmas and Brown, and of Lena and her quest for Burch. It is clear to them both that Joe Brown is the Lucas Burch she is seeking. It is clear to us as well that Byron is falling for this heavily pregnant woman, even as he feels the responsibility to join her to her fleeing and worthless lover.

With this as background, Chapter 5 opens after midnight, on an unidentified date. It focuses wholly on Joe Christmas's thoughts, feelings, and actions during the next twenty-four hours. These sixteen pages are as brilliant as anything Faulkner ever wrote. Cryptically—in the present moment of consciousness—they convey Joe's mounting anger toward Brown (they share the same cabin), his increasing frustration over previous actions unknown to us and only alluded to here, his aimless postmidnight wandering outside the cabin in his underclothes and with his knife, and his suffocating walk through Freedman's Town (the black neighborhood of Jefferson). The chapter closes with him sitting outside a dark house at midnight:

> He was not thinking *Maybe she is not asleep either* tonight. He was not thinking at all; thinking had not begun now; the voices had not begun now either. He just sat there, not moving, until after a while he heard the clock two miles away strike twelve. Then he rose and moved toward the house. He didn't go fast. He didn't think even then *Something is going to happen. Something is going to happen to me.* (LA 486, emphasis in the original)

The prose is lean, sharp as Joe's knife. The italics suggest a sort of mental reflection deeper than conscious thought. There, lodged in this subterranean territory, the woman who occupies the dark house moves raging inside him. He is waiting for something, but he does not know what, as he sits listening to the clock strike midnight. When he rises and heads toward the house, he is at once wholly focused yet unaware of what he intends to do. The last clause in italics—"*something is going to happen to me*"—is eerily disturbing. The syntax may tell us why. The subject of the sentence is "something." Joe himself is relegated to the subordinate position of the object of the preposition: "to me." All our practice as speakers of English tells us that the clause, if healthy, would read otherwise: "I am going to do something." But Faulkner has it exactly right. *Something* has priority. Whatever it is, he will not *do* it: it will *happen to* him. As we learn much later, he is only moments away from murderous violence. But he does not seem to know that. He does not even name—in this sentence—the other person on whom the violence will be released. In his roiling mind, it is all happening *to him*. The chapter ends teetering on the verge of an approaching climax.

Chapter 6 begins by ignoring everything that has preceded it: "Memory believes before knowing remembers. Believes longer than recollects, longer than knowing even wonders. Knows remembers believes a corridor in a big long garbled cold echoing building" (LA 487). No first-time reader is prepared to recognize the time as thirty years earlier, the place as an orphanage in Memphis, and the consciousness as that of Joe Christmas,

a young child now. A first-time reader is especially unprepared to coordi-
nate these cryptic data because the ending of the fifth chapter has all but
promised something else. Instead of delivering on that promise, chapter 6
and the three subsequent ones unfold the events of Christmas's childhood,
concluding seventy-five pages later in another scene of violence. By this
time Joe is eighteen.

Chapter 10 then summarizes, in under ten pages, the next fifteen years
of Joe's life. It ends by delivering him, now thirty-three years old, at the
doorstep of the same dark house he sat outside of, six chapters ago. The time
is two years earlier than the time of chapter 5. Entering the house stealthily
at night, he meets its owner, a middle-aged woman named Joanna Burden.
She thought she had heard a thief breaking in, and they confront each
other in the kitchen. The next three chapters (we are at this point 170 pages
into the novel) narrate their developing relationship. It is a liaison at once
intimate and violent, and we watch it move toward a moment of pending
violence that we have *already* witnessed, but not understood:

> And so as he sat in the shadow of the ruined garden on that August night
> three months later and heard the clock in the courthouse two miles away
> strike ten and then eleven, he believed with calm paradox that he was the
> volitionless servant of the fatality in which he believed that he did not believe.
> He was saying to himself *I had to do it* already in the past tense; *I had to do it.*
> *She said so herself.* (LA 605, emphasis in the original)

We are with Joe again, outside that dark house, and he is about to perform
what, so many pages earlier, he was on the edge of performing. He hears the
same clock striking the same hours. Since this is not for him a repetition, he
still does not know what he's going to do. But for us it is a repetition, and,
unlike him, we are now positioned—thanks to the intervening pages—to
understand what is happening. We know that Joanna Burden lives—lived—
inside that house. We also know that someone—almost certainly Christmas—slit her throat with a knife and fled the scene. Because Faulkner deploys
time in such a way that later chapters introduce earlier materials heretofore
unknown, a moment like the one above sets off remarkable reverberations.
We experience simultaneously both our knowing what he has done and his
not-knowing what he will do.

More, Faulkner has by now prepared us to decode those phrases about
"volitionless servant" and "fatality" and belief or disbelief. We have witnessed (in preceding chapters) Joe's adoption by an abusive foster father,
the Calvinist McEachern. McEachern tried brutally to beat the doctrine

of predestination into the little boy. Joe silently endured the beatings, refusing to learn his catechism. This passage suggests that he has been penetrated by it nevertheless. Like a ghostly secret sharer, McEachern's fatalistic teachings lodge inside Joe, cohabiting there unacknowledged, alongside Joanna's Presbyterian gloom. Marked by both McEachern and Joanna, even as he thinks he shares none of their beliefs, Joe envisages the act he is about to do as already done. "*I had to do it* already in the past tense." He is a Calvinist despite his repudiation of Calvinist doctrine. Faulkner arranges for us to recognize—as insight—a contradiction that his character lives as blindness.

Why would Faulkner present Christmas in this intricately recursive manner? What is Faulkner up to as he challenges our normal ways of reading events? Why does he refuse to supply the simpler temporal sequencing that is the bread and butter of narrative? As veteran readers of fiction, we not only anticipate such sequencing but virtually demand it. Faulkner's great work does not provide it, and this is a major reason that he is difficult to read. The anticipated sequence is of course linear—a move from trouble seeded in the past to present complications arising from that trouble, and finally, satisfyingly, to later resolutions of what came before. A move of steadily increasing enlightenment, in the sense that usually the protagonist—and always the narrator (and therefore the reader)—remains abreast of what is developing. Almost all novels supply that linearity—and the gradual illumination that accompanies it—in their ordering of materials. Why does Faulkner refuse to do so?

This entire book is an attempt to answer that question with the fullness it deserves. For now, let us consider the following. We do not in reality make sense of our lives by moving in that empowering way from past through present and into the future. As Kierkegaard noted, we *live* life forward, gropingly, even as we *understand* it backward, retrospectively. Or as Faulkner has Mr. Compson put it, "Its not even time until it was." Only later, in looking back, do things already done become clear—often too late to intervene upon them. It is later that we find (impose) those demarcations that announce beginnings, middles, and endings in experience that has passed (been "excreted").

But a "middle" is legible as a "middle" only if we know the beginning it follows and the ending it precedes. Until we know what comes before and after, a middle is—a muddle. Narrative fiction delights in muddles, but only to the extent that it satisfyingly turns them into middles. It then turns middles into precursors of endings. Narrative fiction *exists* to do this.

Going from muddle to meaning—trouble to illumination—is how novels make sense of life. This is what it means to *plot* human behavior. You start off (if you are a novelist) with a compelling idea about how things will turn out (or have turned out: you might start with the end itself). This idea can be and often is revised while the narrative is being written, but for the narrative to reach a satisfying conclusion, it must reveal—to retrospective hindsight—a gathered sense of beginning, middle, and end. Such emergent coherence—of lives shown, at the end, to have taken on shape and meaning—is the province, precisely, of narrative. No human being starts off or continues that way, however. Because we are in life, not in narrative, the end—our end—cannot yet be known.

If we press on the familiar verb *recognize*, it breaks apart into *re-cognize*. We must cognize twice before we recognize once. Until it happens the second time, we do not know what the first happening has meant. Faulkner is peerless in his capacity to dramatize the difference between cognizing and re-cognizing. His deployment of repetitions allows his readers, later, to move from the former to the latter. More than perhaps any other novelist, Faulkner invents procedures that pass on to us the turmoil of present time when seeing is not yet *seeing*. The insight we eventually arrive at is ours alone. Faulkner scrupulously keeps it from his characters because they—unlike us—are caught up in the blindness of their ongoing lives. They rarely are granted the privilege of becoming readers of their own lives, permitted to recognize themselves. In making us inhabit (for quite a while) their darkness, Faulkner generates in us a powerful sense of the stumbling of present moments not yet shaped into recognition.

These four masterpieces reconceive prior novelistic conventions for managing time (for making sure it delivers recognition). Benjy, Quentin, Temple, Joe: these characters' lives are caught up in trouble that refuses to take on satisfying focus over time. The issue is *time*, how humans actually move through it. Faulkner astonishingly restores something of the living messiness of that motion. For instance, as he suggests when he writes "Memory believes before knowing remembers," he immerses Joe Christmas in time in ways that escape Christmas's own understanding. Joe unconsciously believes what he no longer remembers. Worse, what he has forgotten has not forgotten him. If you asked Christmas what his troubled life was all about, at most he might reflect: "*All I wanted was peace*" (LA 481, emphasis in the original). But there is no peace in his life, and no understanding of why it is missing. He lives his life not as retrospective understanding but as a sequence of violent missteps in the present. It took all of Faulkner's genius to make narrative *say* such missteps, to make readers experience the blindness of the present *as* blindness. Stumbling is likewise how Temple experiences the nightmare at Frenchman's Bend—as well as how the idiot Benjy lives at the mercy of a time scheme whose logic forever escapes him.

Faulkner's great work, in showing how we inhabit ongoing time differently from narrative conventions for representing life in time, sustains within us, longer than we might like, a state of unpreparedness for what comes next and why. This is why *Light in August* "begins" five different times. No given moment is the beginning. Each is saturated in what went earlier, resonant with what will come later—but none of this is clear from the start, or even soon thereafter. Joe's moments are difficult to decipher because they contain so much more—diffusely, even unconsciously—than he knows to be in them when they actually occur. McEachern and Joanna Burden live inside him in ways he will never decipher. So he falters, and his creator makes us falter in reading him—makes us pause at cryptic thoughts or memories, start over again on hypotheses about what is happening and why. Light does eventually arrive in *Light in August*—unbearable light—but no character in the book is in possession of it. No reader gets to that light very quickly either. So let me say it again. Faulkner is hard to read—and at the same time supremely worth reading—because he makes his great work express the challenge of being in time. He had to reinvent novelistic form to get his fiction to do this. By 1928 he somehow grasped that this was the work before him. His muddled life had opened up the path.

"I BARE HIM ON EAGLES' WINGS"

The romance of flight began perhaps in childhood, as one of the brothers' escapades. Under Faulkner's guidance, the three of them (Dean would have been too little) had labored for weeks—with rotten wood, rusty nails, grocery bags, wrapping paper, and a design taken from a boys' magazine—to build their own plane. Eventually he was satisfied with the results and determined to give their craft its trial run. He would be at the controls. The collapse that followed that comic enterprise eerily foreshadows a number of subsequent attempts to rise into the air.

At about the same time during their childhood, his brother Johncy would recall, there was another airborne adventure—one they witnessed rather than participated in. At one of the local fairs, the most spectacular stunt involved the exploits of a scruffy and drunken airman. This fellow would arrive on the scene already deep into booze, carrying a parachute and a huge, shapeless, canvas bag. The plan was to fill the bag with hot air to the point where, with him attached below, it would rise as a sort of huge balloon off the ground. It took most of the day for the coal-supplied fire to produce enough hot air to launch the project. The boys watched, mesmerized, as the bag would slowly start to billow. During this time, the airman steadily cursed and clamored for more booze, his eyes red and streaming, thanks to the unremitting smoke and flames. Eventually the gigantic inflated balloon showed signs of imminent departure. Its inebriated passenger-pilot, still cursing, began to fasten his parachute harness and strap himself in. By the time the contraption rose into the air, the boys' excitement would be beyond containing. They would run at full speed, following the airborne craft, hoping to see the pilot make his exit. They would come upon him minutes later, already on the ground and fumbling with the harness straps. He would be so intoxicated that he hardly felt the violence of his clumsy landing. Drink, grease, cursing, and desperate risk: did Faulkner always carry these associations with human attempts at flight? Or did he remember them only later, during the 1930s? These were the years when he avidly watched barnstorming flyers perform their daredevil stunts at county fairs—the years prior to his writing *Pylon*.

The only countermove to Estelle's marriage to Franklin that Faulkner had been able to conceive of that might be weighty and engrossing enough to take him out of his grief was entry into the war. Whether that entry would take place by way of Canada or America, he insisted that it be in the air. The acronym *RAF* would remain a precious one he never tired of mentioning. His five months of flight training in Canada would not only give him material for a number of stories and at least four novels but also nurture his fascination with the mechanics of flight, with the fragile and murderous beauty of aircraft. He could not get enough of the planes, and his sketches—as one of his biographers has noted—"were almost as precise as manufacturers' schematic drawings" (F 63). Whatever else drew him, one irresistible aspect was the planes' seeming weightlessness: mere "kites" constructed of wood and canvas and wire, powered by unreliable engines. Soon he could distinguish expertly among the different military craft at the Canadian air base, and he was writing home to Maud of solo flights. These vignettes would later expand, balloonistically, into the higher regions of fantasy—flights, crashes, and injuries—all unsupported by evidence.

As early as September 1919, he acted—in secret—on the real state of affairs. He had learned that one of his University of Mississippi gambling buddies, Robert Buntin, was a trained pilot; and he confided in Buntin:

"Everybody thinks I can fly, but I can't" (F 79). At Faulkner's instigation, they sneaked away to practice flying. Soon he began to realize that one crucial dimension of flying resisted mastery. He had trouble landing his craft safely—trouble that, when he took up flying later, he would never fully surmount. During the 1920s, when he was too strapped for cash and caught up in other roles perhaps, the love of flying went underground. But once *Sanctuary* hit big, money—at least the promise of it—started to arrive, and new opportunities arose. Hollywood had entered his life in 1932, and MGM wanted their famous RAF veteran to work on scripts about flying.

In early 1933, he decided it was time to renew his infatuation. He contacted Vernon Omlie, a professional instructor who ran a flying school in Memphis, to set up a series of lessons. "He said he wanted to get his nerve back," Omlie recalled, "and learn to fly all over again before anybody knew what he was doing" (F 314). Omlie agreed to support Faulkner's elaborate fiction of himself as the fighter-pilot who had become gun-shy as a consequence of two crashes during the war. He needed lessons to overcome his anxiety, and Omlie was an ideal instructor. In addition, Omlie served as portal to a larger world of barnstorming pilots performing daredevil stunts in the 1930s. Faulkner required some seventeen hours of dual control training with Omlie before he was ready in April 1933 to solo in Omlie's big Waco.

The rest of that year he would continue to fly the Waco, sometimes taking Johncy's boys with him. His three brothers were not long in sharing his fascination with flight, and he encouraged them to do so. He was not only hooked; his delight in flying seemed close to manic. When Estelle delivered her next baby, in June 1933, he waited only eleven weeks before taking the infant Jill and her mother up on joy rides. Later, the four brothers would do some modest barnstorming together; they would even be advertised as "The Flying Faulkners." In the fall of 1933 he took the plunge and purchased Omlie's Waco. The plane was not cheap; it cost him $6,000. If we consider that he had paid the same amount three years earlier for Rowan Oak and its four acres, we get a measure of how far he went to indulge his obsession. As his most recent biographer has noted, a 1933 photo of him standing in front of the Waco possesses a unique feature. Like virtually no other picture, this one shows him smiling broadly, his relaxed face beaming with the pride of ownership.[9]

His father Murry had been in bad health for some time now, and his heart condition had worsened during the hot summer of 1932. After suffering a major attack on August 11, Murry succumbed ten days later. Faulkner was in Hollywood at the time, working for Howard Hawks on a screenplay of his own story "Turn About." The only reference to his father's passing I know of occurs in a letter he wrote a month later to Ben Wasson: "I had to leave Cal. before I finished it [the script] because of my father's death." The letter continues: "I hope to hell Paramount takes Sanctuary. Dad left mother solvent for only about 1 year. Then it is me" (SL 65). A father's dying, so few words from the son in response to it. The rest of the letter is concerned with his screenplay activities and financial woes. Faulkner's brevity is mutely revealing, though none of his biographers explores its resonance. Murry Falkner is eclipsed (by Faulkner himself, as well as his biographers) in the bigger narrative of his famous son. As though to rub it in, the local obituary spelled Murry's surname "Faulkner," furthering his erasure as one Murry Falkner who had tried, and failed, to make his life make sense. Many years later, as Maud neared her own death, she asked her oldest son about the afterlife: "Will I have to see your father there?" "No," he said, "not if you don't want to." "That's good," she said. "I never did like him" (F 679). Faulkner would laugh when he repeated this vignette, just as he would smile when he repeated the earlier cigar-and-pipe one. Both vignettes contributed to the ongoing erasure of Murry Falkner. Together, Faulkner and his mother completed his eclipse.

After his father's death, Faulkner felt it incumbent on himself to offer Dean whatever measure he could of the paternal support that was no longer there. The widowed Maud was growing increasingly—and, Faulkner suspected, unhealthily—dependent on Dean. For his part, Dean—though likable and well-adjusted—floundered from job to job. Faulkner thought he needed help, and determined to provide it. Dean welcomed this renewed attention. He had long adored his brilliant oldest brother, going so far as to cultivate a thin mustache that resembled Faulkner's, and even adding a *u* to his name so as to tighten their intimacy.

Perhaps the air, Faulkner might have pondered, would offer Dean a space for flourishing that the land had not. Since Dean already loved to fly, why shouldn't he consider doing so professionally? Of the four brothers, Dean showed signs of becoming far and away the most gifted pilot. It made good sense, Faulkner decided, to put up the money to pay for Dean's further flight instruction with Omlie. Omlie found Dean to be a star student, and by the spring of 1934, Dean had actually moved in with Omlie and his wife. He was getting a professional education in flying, en route to becoming a sort of junior partner in Omlie's aviation business. So Faulkner took the logical next step and worked out an agreement to transfer ownership of his

Waco to Dean. With the Waco, Dean and Vernon could do air shows in the nearby states—Tennessee and Missouri as well as Mississippi. It seemed a good plan, and Dean's life was taking on focus. The previous fall, he had met an adventurous young woman named Louise Hale. She liked him immediately, and she enjoyed the scruffily glamorous world that went with him: Vernon and his wife, the other aviators, the airports and barnstorming flights. Within weeks, Dean proposed marriage, and Louise accepted, despite his having warned her: "Mother and Bill will always come first" (F 338). Soon after their marriage, to Dean and Louise's delight, she learned that she was pregnant.

During the years following *Light in August,* Faulkner's letters spoke of materials that would find their place in some six more novels: *Absalom, Absalom!, The Unvanquished, Requiem for a Nun,* and the Snopes trilogy (*The Hamlet, The Town,* and *The Mansion*). It would take him twenty-five years to deliver all the books gestating in his mind in the early 1930s. Not mentioned in that group, however, is the novel Faulkner suddenly, at breakneck speed, wrote in two months during the fall of 1934—*Pylon.* He had probably been conceiving *Pylon* unawares for some time; perhaps it had been simmering ever since the balloon episodes of childhood. At the least, Faulkner's fascination with flying—rekindled in early 1933—made the writing of this novel virtually effortless. "He has got to take the truth and set it on fire," Faulkner would claim in that 1955 interview in Manila. What in the drama of flying set Faulkner's imagination aflame? *Pylon* lets us approach that question.

As his most recent biographer has noted, *Pylon* is neither the most audacious nor the most experimental of Faulkner's novels. But it is the most extravagant. Only an intermittent intellectual rigor keeps its prose from appearing alarmingly overheated. One need not go far to find the cause of the overheating: the spectacle of the planes themselves and—by extension—of the men who fly them:

> creatures imbued with motion though not with life and incomprehensible
> to the puny crawling painwebbed globe, incapable of suffering, wombed and
> born complete and instantaneous, cunning intricate and deadly, from out
> some blind iron batcave of the earth's prime foundation. (PYL 793)

The fascination of the planes shimmers in this passage. They pulse with a form of being that mocks all human structures (protective sanctuaries) erected to make life safely livable, organized, mutual. Free from the messiness of human attachment ("painwebbed"), these murderous objects exist unto themselves. Immune to development over time, they beam forth a primitive cohesion eons older than the interdependency of later human arrangements. Another description extends this resonance: "Waspwaisted, wasplight, still, trim, vicious, small and immobile, they seemed to poise without weight, as though made of paper for the sole purpose of resting upon the shoulders of the dungareeclad men about them" (787). The passage emphasizes the most incredible dimension of the planes. Nothing so frail should be able to move so fast and do so much damage in so little time. Led out onto the tarmac, they seem docile, obeying the men who service and fly them, as they seem to balance poised on their keepers' shoulders. But they can unexpectedly sting: "waspwaisted" may also recall Faulkner's earlier "mosquitoes"—those winged creatures capable of diving down and deranging the lives of those they suddenly attack.

Speed is the common element, speed that exceeds survivable frequencies. Faulkner's prose strains—in its verbal pressing of words together ("pain-webbed," "wasplight," "dungareeclad"), as well as its relentless deployment of adjective upon adjective—to "say" such objects (and their world) outside the range of conventional ways of saying. As though—to be faithful to these extraordinary machines and the lives that circulate recklessly, obsessively, around them—convention must be stood on its head. Marital convention is jettisoned, in the anarchic arrangement of two flyers sharing the same woman (none of the three knows who has fathered the child resulting from their promiscuous intercourse). Likewise, capitalist convention dictating prudence, hard work, calculation, and eventual profit has little purchase on them. *Pylon* pointedly pits its nonchalant yet desperate flyers against the manipulative, moneyed bosses who run the airport and advertise the races. These men are ultimately concerned with profit; their behavior is based on a cost/benefit model. On that model, one moves through time by establishing procedures for arriving at the anticipated bottom line. Not so for the pilots. Their time line has little to do with a calculated increase in profit. "Because they aint human like us; they couldn't turn those pylons like they do if they had human blood and senses and they wouldn't want to or dare to if they just had human brains" (PYL 804).

As the quoted passage shows, Faulkner does not sentimentalize the pilots. Yet they escape the withering critique the narrative levies on the money men. Colonel Feinman, patron and financier of the new airport that sponsors these races, comes in for especially virulent narrative treatment. Feinman—or "Behindman," as the flyers scornfully refer to him—has made his pile in the sewer business. The text delights in juxtaposing his disgusting, but profitable, traffic in human shit against the flyers' transcendent risking of their lives in the air. "It aint the money" recurs as a refrain for understanding the flyers' economically irrational behavior. Does Faulkner's life-long tenderness toward vagabondage—his frequent references to himself as a bum, as one who spent his prolonged youth refusing or savaging the jobs that came his way—insinuate itself here?

The pilots who compete for the prizes are both desperate for the money and cavalierly dismissive of it. Mere cash is beneath contempt as a motive for directing behavior. Yet *Pylon* is rife with monetary transactions (one critic has counted some sixty-seven of them). The unnamed Reporter (through whose mesmerized eyes Faulkner narrates this novel) is a spendthrift—with others' money. Borrowing gobs of cash from his inexplicably generous boss, the Reporter takes dozens of cab rides, throwing dollar bills at the drivers as he rushes away from their vehicles. One is reminded of Faulkner's similarly conflicted stance toward money. He would borrow—casually and extravagantly—from his publishers (sometimes not asking permission in advance). In letters to his agents and editors, he would also obsess endlessly over his need for money. Whenever he was in temporary possession of it, it poured out of him. He would have liked to be Maecenas. To allow one's life to be ruled by money appeared to him as a form of thralldom. "I reckon I'll be at the beck and call of folks with money all my life," he had fumed in 1924, "but thank God I won't ever again have to be at the beck and call of every son of a bitch who's got two cents to buy a stamp." Being fired from that job had liberated him from a routine he detested to the point of scandalous inattention. Scheming to make one's money appreciate—in and of itself—struck him as no less despicable. It signaled a slavish devotion to incrementally paced hoarding—a sort of Yankee-inspired tiptoeing through life, always checking the credit-debit sheet. It plotted life in an anal and unworthy fashion.

By contrast, the flyers risked their lives utterly, each time they rose into the air. "They had escaped the compulsion of accepting a past and a future" (FIU 36), Faulkner would say of them later, at the University of Virginia. In *Pylon* itself, the same point emerges starkly: "And the ship is all right," one of them says, "except you wont know until you are in the air whether or not you can take it off and you wont know until you are back on the ground and standing up again whether or not you can land it" (906). So much for plans for mastering life in advance, for calculating before and after. To fly those "kites" is to experience time as pure presence. We will know what is happening when it has happened; no prior preparation is any good. Or rather, prepare as we can, such preparation is puny and futile. Once we leave the sanctuary of the earth, we are flaunting the sinister gods—the unknowable force that Mr. Compson calls the "dark diceman" (SF 1013). Or, as Faulkner would later (in *The Hamlet*) describe the time-model implicit in the flyers' behavior: "Breathing is a sight-draft dated yesterday" (HAM 313). As though our breath itself had an unappealable liquidation date of yesterday written on it, collectible on sight. The encounter could come at any moment; it will give no prior notice. No experience brought this more powerfully home to Faulkner than flying planes.

Pylon enacts these convictions by its way of representing the human body. Characters rarely eat in this novel, though they frequently remind themselves or each other to do so. Instead, they smoke and drink; they vomit too. Even that is closer to their core identity than eating. Consider this passage in which one of the pilots, Shumann, has browbeaten his crewman, Jiggs, into eating a sandwich:

> Chewing, Jiggs looked full at Shumann, holding the bitten sandwich in both grimed hands before his breast as though it were a crucifix, chewing with his mouth open, looking full at Shumann until Shumann realized that Jiggs was not looking at him at all, that the one good eye was merely open and filled with a profound and hopeless abnegation…and that Jiggs' face was now slicked over with something which in the faint light resembled oil in the instant before Jiggs began to vomit. (PYL 902)

That sandwich will never get eaten. Eating—the basic function enabling self-sustaining over time—is as revoked within him as swallowing will be for Faulkner's intoxicated characters. Locked into his present moment, Jiggs smokes, drinks, and vomits. He does not eat; that practical activity is transcended in *Pylon*.

Does it follow that what is being pursued—in the antics of the flyers and of the Reporter obsessively following them—is something opposed to all practicality? Does the risking of life constitute flight's core fascination? Fatal accidents grimly accumulated during the barnstorming events Faulkner witnessed during the early 1930s. Did he grasp that what hypnotized him in this activity was the dance of death? It is hardly coincidental that after hearing in June 1934 of the famous pilot Jimmy Wedell's fatal crash, he deemed the moment right for executing his own last will and testament. Wedell had gone down while giving a beginner flight lessons. Surely the all-risking encounter with death is what Faulkner had seen eight years earlier in young John Sartoris in *Flags*. With his warplane riddled with German bullets, John swung his feet out of the cockpit, seconds before taking the plunge. He thumbed his nose at his brother Bayard—helplessly watching from another plane—then "flipped his hand at the hun...and jumped" (FD 765), mocking the death he hurtled toward. For John's epitaph, Faulkner had chosen a text from Exodus: "I bare him on eagles' wings and brought him unto me." When Faulkner wrote those words in 1927, he surely cognized their meaning. At the end of 1935—suddenly, awfully off course—he would recognize in them a different meaning.

In a fury of composition, he completed *Pylon* in December 1934. Three months later, Dean received his transport license; he was flying the newly acquired Waco regularly. In November 1935, he flew it to an air show in Pontotoc, Mississippi, where he would give flying lessons. Louise was four months pregnant; when the baby came, they would need the money. Dean took up one last group of passengers that afternoon, but the Waco failed to return to the airfield. Rumors of a crash soon began to spread. Late in the afternoon, Faulkner got the phone call at Rowan Oak: Dean was dead. The Waco had been found, buried six feet into the earth; all of the bodies were mutilated beyond recognition.

Faulkner would not allow other family members to approach the mangled corpse. He carried a photo of Dean with him, and he worked all that night with the undertaker, using the photo to help recompose a face that might passably resemble Dean's. The motives driving this nightmarish act are unknowable, but one can hazard some grotesque mix of family piety (make Dean presentable again), self-inflicted torture (his Waco: his fault), and the engraving of a life-long memory (Dean's mangled face to remain forever inside him). The next morning, they transported the body back to Oxford. Faulkner's grieving cousin Sally Murry persuaded him to keep the coffin closed; neither Maud nor Louise ever saw Dean again. The accident would never be fully explained, though expert witnesses—after studying the position of instruments on the destroyed Waco—believed they knew what might have happened. They speculated that one of the passengers, with some flight training already under his belt, had been offered the controls by Dean, had panicked, and had suddenly put the Waco into a plummeting spin that Dean had no time to prevent. "Don't reproach yourself," Jack consoled his older brother. "What happened wasn't your fault. You weren't responsible for it" (F 356).

That was the official verdict, but Faulkner's private one was different. He had actively encouraged Dean's fascination with flight, paid for Dean's instruction, and sold Dean (at reduced cost) the plane in which he went down. How could the Waco he had proudly displayed in that earlier photo be the plane that killed his brother? The dreams that had attached to that craft, the horror that now replaced them. Dean's death set off in him a self-indictment that would remain beyond pacifying. He started to drink again sometime after the accident, and he reached a point—talking with Louise—when his anguish suddenly mounted and spilled over. Tears welled up and his body shook, as he said to her, "I've ruined your life. It's all my fault" (F 356). When he made the arrangements for the funeral, he chose for his youngest brother the same epitaph he had bestowed on young John Sartoris: "I bare him on eagles' wings and brought him to me." Maud resisted this repetition, perhaps seeing in it an excessive marker of Faulkner's own grief. What he saw in it we can never know, but one thing is likely: that the assault of life has nothing in common with the dreams and aspirations we draw on to imagine it before it arrives.

The three of them lived together for the next few weeks in Maud's house: mother, son, and widow. Maud would survive this disaster, but something in her was permanently broken. She kept sleeping pills by her bedside, wondering when the moment would come to take them all. "I've lived too long," her sister-in-law remembered her saying. During these days of grief, Faulkner would help Louise as he could—run her bath, bring her a glass of milk. One morning at breakfast she said, "I can't eat. I dreamed the whole accident last night." He was silent, then replied, "You're lucky to have dreamed it only once. I dream it every night" (F 356). Untimely: our lives are premature, inconclusive, and inconcludable. "*Maybe happen is never once,*" Quentin Compson would muse in *Absalom*. We play and replay the events that give us identity. In advance of themselves when they first arrive, they come up different, later. The woman he had not eloped with, the war he had not entered, the plane he had secretly been incapable of flying: each of these had multiple, incompatible lives over time. Each had escaped him at first. Each had then become an intricate part of his life. The first and the last would break his heart. Along with Estelle's marriage to Cornell Franklin, Dean's death was the worst thing that ever happened to him. Its subterranean half-life would last as long as he did.

At the end of 1935, Faulkner was finding himself once more embroiled in money troubles. His financial responsibilities badly exceeded his capacity to meet them on the proceeds brought in by his writing. He was now committed to supporting Louise and her not yet born daughter (who would be named Dean). He would of course continue to take care of both his widowed mother and his recently increased family (his daughter Jill was by then two years old). His other brothers recurrently needed his help as well. In addition, Estelle's parents had fallen into precarious financial straits, not to mention Faulkner's continuing responsibility for Estelle's older offspring, Victoria and Malcolm. It went without saying that he would not cease to be answerable for the needs of Uncle Ned and Mammy Callie. All told, he was paying taxes and insurance on two houses—his own and his mother's—and helping meet the expenses of the several other households of his extended family. As home owner and inheritor of traditional ideas about a Southern master's duties, he accepted all of these obligations. But he was under greater monetary stress than ever before. The emotional stress was perhaps even keener; it was certainly more intricate.

Reaching him from several sources, guilt was ravaging Faulkner. For the rest of his life he would feel guilt for the death of Dean. More, Hollywood provided the only solution he knew for his money troubles—an ambivalent solution composed of temporary release and habit-forming entrapment. Some four years earlier, he had first embraced that solution. In December 1931, Sam Marx of Twentieth-Century Fox sent Leland Hayward (Ben Wasson's boss at the time) the following telegram: "DID YOU MENTION WILLIAM FAULKNER TO ME ON YOUR LAST TRIP HERE. IF SO IS HE AVAILABLE AND HOW MUCH" (F 296). How much would it cost to buy him? For the next twenty years, Faulkner would be a purchasable Hollywood property, assessed wholly in monetary terms. He knew this and hated it. He disapproved of the tinselly glitter of the place. Worse, he always remained disdainful toward the film medium itself. He had found, however, a consolation there that could only have deepened his feelings of guilt. He had met and fallen hard for Meta Carpenter, a Southern-born woman who was divorced, attractive, and eleven years younger. She worked for Howard Hawks, typing scripts among her other duties. Faulkner pursued her intently, and soon they were lovers.

I shall return in chapter 4 to both Meta Carpenter and Hollywood. Before us now—and the subject of the following chapter—is a final, more impersonal and pervasive source of the guilt surrounding him throughout his life but assailing his imagination only in the 1930s. This source derived from racial experience all Southerners shared, few acknowledged, and none would explore as he did—to the point of nightmarish recognitions: white abuse of blacks. Centuries of socially sanctioned racism tarnished his country's proudest claim of liberty and justice for all. Faulkner believed in that claim, had tried seventeen years earlier to go to war in defense of it, and would try again during World War II.

In *Light in August*, he had first broached the brutality of his region's race relations. Soon he was writing gentler stories of whites and blacks at the time of the Civil War. He would later reconfigure and assemble these as *The Unvanquished*. Most of all, though, he was trying to think his way through the recalcitrance of a bigger book—one that would seek to articulate the comprehensive tragedy of race in America. He hardly knew, as he was struggling with *Absalom*, that he would eventually produce—in the trio composed of *Light in August, Absalom, Absalom!* and *Go Down, Moses*—the most resonant exploration of the national trauma of race that any white novelist has yet written. How could he have known? He was at the time riddled with competing calls on his conscience. Writing the final chapters of *Absalom*, he was trying to keep his head above water, as an inner chorus continued silently to indict him. There was no lack of relevant charges: his failed marriage, his role in Dean's death, his increasing alcoholism, his bargain with Hollywood, his affair with Meta, his participation in his region's deep-rooted abuse of blacks. All of these missteps clamored inside, as he wrote his way into Thomas Sutpen's appalling innocence and Quentin Compson's even more appalling inheritance. *Light in August* had implicitly launched a rendezvous with race in America. Half deliberately, half unthinkingly—his talents now at their high-water mark—he would take on the encounter.

CHAPTER 3

DARK TWINS

The problem of the twentieth century is the problem of the color-line.

—*W. E. B. Du Bois*

"GO SLOW NOW"

He had apparently been drinking fairly heavily, and the outrageous words tumbled out: "If I have to choose between the United States government and Mississippi, then I'll choose Mississippi....[I]f it came to fighting I'd fight for Mississippi against the United States even if it meant going out into the street and shooting Negroes" (LG 261). So spoke Faulkner in a New York interview with Russell Howe. It was early 1956; civil rights turmoil was approaching a boiling point. A young black woman named Autherine Lucy had been accepted into the University of Alabama. Southerners were already rioting at the prospect, but a federal court ordered the university to admit her nevertheless. Faulkner desperately wanted Lucy and the integrationists who stood behind her to back off. He was certain she would not enter the university alive. Word of his desire to speak got out, and the *Reporter* magazine set up an interview. Howe might been amazed to hear America's foremost novelist—however intoxicated—speak as he did. When the interview appeared in print (in the London Sunday *Times* as well), Faulkner was horrified by his own words. He had seen no prior draft. He immediately wrote a letter to the *Reporter* explaining that the statements attributed to him were ones "which no sober man would make, nor...any sane man believe" (ESPL 225). Off-balance in that charged interview moment, he felt betrayed by the mirror image of his own quoted voice. A month later, he would claim that Howe's interview was "more a misconstruction than a misquotation" (F 618). Even though accurately reported (as Howe strenuously insisted), the views expressed in that interview were not his. Faulkner's words, but not his thoughts. Not really Faulkner. Something more than incoherence is at work here.

Dark twins—the title of this chapter—is a phrase Faulkner used in *Mosquitoes* to characterize the intricate bond between an author's life and his work: "A book is a writer's secret life, the dark twin of a man: you can't reconcile them" (MOS 461). The phrase conveys a pairing that is intimate and inalienable, yet foreign and alienated. The two entities are bonded by way of a commonality that estranges the one from the other. With respect to race (a realm already implied by "dark") the phrase may suggest a similar vexed bonding—Faulkner's abiding twinship with blacks and his no less abiding difference from them, by way of his whiteness. The dark face he sees—as a Southerner—in the mirror proposed by race cannot be his own, yet he fleetingly glimpses himself there as well. More broadly, for several centuries in the South, the two races have been intertwined and cordoned off— at once inseparable and unreconcilable, scandalously connected by blood though segregated by law. Most of his fellow white Southerners denied the twinship, insisting instead on the unbridgeable difference between whiteness and darkness. But Faulkner—caught in a weave of racial realities he could neither master nor escape—moved through this uncertain territory like a man careening between the poles of blindness and insight. Deeply fissured within, he found himself making incompatible utterances, each true to incompatible experiences. Recurrently he appeared—and heard himself as—not-Faulkner. He knew at once too much and not enough. His lifelong immersion in the sea of race enacts this paradox in a range of ways.

The default pole in Faulkner's paradoxical racial stance is disidentification. He is not his dark twin. "Shooting Negroes" is an utterance, however accidental and unintended, whose hostility cannot be explained away. It is hard to imagine his saying "shooting whites," no matter how much he had been drinking. Somewhere inside his psyche, inculcated there and confirmed by his region's truisms, he *could* envisage shooting Negroes. His words to Howe further reveal his incapacity to enter black lives. "I have known Negroes all my life," he proclaimed, "and Negroes work my land for me. I know how they feel." Warming to his theme, he added that, if it came to violence, "My Negro boys down on the plantation would fight against the North with me. If I say to them, 'Go get your shotguns, boys,' they'll come" (LG 262). The master/slave model is patent. He is the master of the plantation, they its obedient workers; he is the man, they the boys; he owns the guns and gives the orders, they follow suit. He is the active subject, they the docile object. This widely shared fantasy failed the South in the Civil War, when black slaves—given the chance—fled in huge numbers from their astonished Southern masters. The fantasy is all the more outrageous when sounded in 1956. Even intoxicated, he had to have known that neither his home (Rowan Oak) nor his farm (Greenfield Farm) was a plantation. Or is it that in foundational matters, the passage of time itself seems illusory? That beneath and behind the twentieth-century Southerner's home and farm there lurks the destroyed yet indestructible antebellum plantation? Untimely: remnants of antebellum identity remain embedded, shardlike, in this anguished Southerner caught up in mid-1950s racial turmoil. In crucial moments, such as this unrehearsed New York interview, these remnants rise troublingly to the surface. Dark twins is also a notion about identity over time. The living Faulkner harbors inside himself the unaltered convictions of his dead fellow white Southerners of 1865.

Mississippi/land/plantation: the Howe interview reveals that in matters of race, Faulkner thought in terms of place. Race released in him a primordial tenderness toward his region—in Faulkner's imaginary, a white region in need of protection. As racial turmoil intensified, his image of his region under attack transformed predictably, returning magnetically to the crisis of 1860. He imagined a (white) South sanctified once more by menace and separate (once again) from the country to which it belonged. More than a century of regional custom and memory could be heard in particular utterances. Shortly before the Howe interview, Faulkner had made another widely quoted racial statement—this one also soaked in the sanctity of his region's history. "Go slow now," he had appealed to black leaders, in an article appearing in *Life*. "Stop now for a time, a moment," he urged them. *Brown v. Board of Education,* decided by the Supreme Court in 1954, had given the black leaders leverage; Autherine Lucy's admission to the University of Alabama was legally unstoppable. "You have the power now," he wrote, but it is a power to be restrained. Other race-focused statements made during the mid-1950s intimated that when he said "go slow," he meant *really* slow. Questioned in a 1955 interview in Japan, he glossed the change sanctioned by *Brown* as follows: "That will take a little time…the Negro himself has got to be patient and sensible. But it will come, as I see it, and maybe in three hundred years" (LG 90). Three hundred years; elsewhere he would speak of five hundred years. He was urging blacks to adopt a pace of political change that could only appear to them as glacial.

Abstractly, he wanted black emancipation. He knew, and publicly proclaimed, that Jefferson's 1776 Declaration of Independence, followed by Lincoln's 1863 Emancipation Proclamation, meant no less. But on the ground in the South, such emancipation was unimaginable. "Go slow" actually meant: *don't*—not yet, not until we are ready. He knew his region's (white) people too well to believe that they were anywhere near ready. In speech after speech, letter after letter, during the 1950s, he urged patience on blacks and a change of mind on whites. Not a change of heart. He had spent his life paying attention to and making sense of white hearts in the South; he knew the anger and frustration seething there. An outburst of uncontrollable racial violence was what he feared. Forcibly admitting Autherine Lucy into the University of Alabama would release it. The white South, he was sure, was about to explode.

At heart, for him, it was the white South at risk, not its black people. At a Southern Historical Association conference in Memphis in 1955, he said the following: "We will not sit quietly by and see our native land, the South, not just Mississippi but all the South, wreck and ruin itself twice in less than a hundred years, over the Negro question" (ESPL 151). In private correspondence he was more colloquial, his stance more forthright. He wrote a concerned fellow Mississippian of his fear that "for the second time in a hundred years, we Southerners will have destroyed our native land just because of niggers" (SL 391). "Just because of niggers": the phrase resonates with centuries of inculcated racism. Why won't they be patient, wait out a change in Southern behavior and politics that is admittedly overdue but that will in time arrive?

White hearts could not be forced to change, but black hearts—again, one hears his regional disidentification with blacks—could be made to alter more swiftly. He soon came to believe that integration would become possible only if Negroes ceased to be—Negro. During his year of teaching at the University of Virginia (1957–58), he pronounced:

> Perhaps the Negro is not yet capable of more than second-class citizenship. His tragedy may be that so far he is competent for equality only in the ratio of his white blood....He must learn to cease forever more thinking like a Negro and acting like a Negro....His burden will be that, because of his race and color, it will not suffice him to think and act like just any white man: he must think and act like the best among white men. (ESPL 157)

Even granting that Faulkner was speaking to white organizations at a white university, this speech bizarrely distorts the realities it backhandedly recognizes. Faulkner granted a history of miscegenation only to imagine its (unintended) benefits for blacks. He focused not on the scandal of white abuse but on the fantasized potential that the resulting fraction of white blood in black veins would in time enable. More, just as white brutality was erased in this vision of miscegenation, so was it erased in his insistence that black behavior be equal to the *best* of white behavior.

The same distortions had appeared a year earlier in his "Letter to the Leaders of the Negro Race." There he urged those leaders to say to their followers: "We must learn to deserve equality so that we can hold and keep it after we get it" (ESPL 111). *Deserve equality*: Faulkner's phrasing rejected Jefferson's insistence on equality as a self-evident truth in need of no prior deserving. Not so for blacks: Faulkner was willing to mortgage their equality to demonstrated proofs of merit. Missing from these utterances was the capacity to enter empathically into black lives, to envisage those lives as already precious and in need of support on their own terms. He had trouble accessing the human reality of blacks as something other than abstracted material potentially reshapable into familiar white forms. For him, in pronouncements such as this one, no equality for blacks until they looked like whites. And smelled like whites too: "But always," he advised black leaders to tell their people, "let us practices cleanliness…in our contacts with" the white man (111). If such obtuseness about racial turmoil were the last word concerning Faulkner's dark twinship, it would be mainly a matter of much darkness and little twinning. The pole of disidentification would be triumphant. Most black leaders and white radicals read him thus, and they ended by expecting little from this famous Southerner. A man whose concern led to proposals offering several more centuries of waiting had little to contribute to the solution they were urgently seeking.

How could he have contributed further to their solution? His entire life, saturated in the regional history that had shaped his identity, oriented him toward a good deal of racial blindness. Some twenty-five years before civil rights agitation, at the time of his much celebrated arrival on the New York literary scene (following the publication of *Sanctuary*), he had been interviewed about race. At that time, he casually allowed that Southern Negroes were childlike and would be better off "under the conditions of slavery…because they'd have someone to look after them" (F 292). Blacks as obedient children when enslaved, potential beasts when emancipated: this binary articulated the South's abiding racist cliché. The racial imaginary in Faulkner's greatest novels far transcends this demeaning opposition, yet the racial otherness encoded in the opposition recurs as a sort of default position. Something permanent in his mindset participated in his region's dominant discourse of race. He would always remain, whatever his anguish, "a native of our land and a sharer in its errors" (ESPL 205).

"THIS THING OF KILLING NEGROES WITHOUT CAUSE"

"Even if it means going out into the street and shooting Negroes," Faulkner had found himself saying in 1956. It may be hard in the twenty-first century to recall the pervasive race-fueled violence that blanketed the Southern landscape like immovable summer heat during the first half of the twentieth century. One of Faulkner's finest stories, "Dry September," opens on a note that bonds implacable weather with inexorable violence: "Through the bloody September twilight, aftermath of sixty-two rainless days, it had gone like a fire in dry grass—the rumor, the story, whatever it was. Something about Miss Minnie Cooper and a Negro" [CS 169]. Faulkner wrote that story in 1931. Twenty-five years earlier, Memphis (some eighty miles northwest of Oxford) was widely recognized as the "Murder Capital" of America. So much of Memphis's routine violence was racial that the city's leading paper, the *Commercial Appeal*, thought fit (in 1906) to exhort its readership as follows: "This thing of killing negroes without cause…[is being] overdone…white men who kill negroes as a pastime…usually end up killing white men" (cited in F2 1:302). The norms running through this editorial—and newspapers live and die by shared norms—testify to the casual entrenchment of Southern racism. The editorial assumes that all readers of the paper are white; that whites killing blacks is being "overdone" as a "pastime" (like irresponsibly killing game beyond the limits of the hunting season); and that the disturbing consequence of such a foolish practice—the reason for the editorial—is that white men could end up getting killed.

What racial arrangements explain the stunning callousness of these norms? To approach this question fully would require consideration of a history beginning four centuries ago with the Middle Passage and New World slavery. A much shortened version can start with the quietly racist organization of social space in the twentieth-century South. Quietly: this ordering system, imposed by whites and more or less tolerated by blacks, often functioned smoothly. I grew up in a quietly segregated Memphis fifty years after it was dubbed the "Murder Capital" of America. In the mid-1950s, Memphis proudly sported a different title (won in nationwide competition): "cleanest city in America." That appellation would become searingly ironic a decade later, when Martin Luther King—intervening in a protracted garbage collectors' strike—was assassinated at the Lorraine Motel in downtown Memphis. Killing Negroes continued unabated, though this time the cause was not in doubt.

Ever since *Plessy v. Ferguson* (the landmark Supreme Court decision upholding segregation in 1896: the doctrine of "separate but equal"), white and blacks had lived in elaborately stratified worlds. As C. Vann Woodward noted, the proliferation of Jim Crow laws throughout the South (following *Plessy*) underwrote a racial barrier extending to "virtually all forms of public transportation, to sports and recreations, to hospitals, orphanages, prisons, and asylums, and ultimately to funeral homes, morgues, and cemeteries"—from cradle to grave.[1] Yet the two races so kept apart also rubbed shoulders constantly. Restaurants, trains, buses, drinking fountains, swimming pools, and public toilets might be quarantined into segregated spaces. But in country stores, at Saturday markets, and in private homes—not to mention other territories devoted to commerce (such as Murry Falkner's livery stable)—whites and blacks shared social space. Faulkner was born into a world that confidently organized his experience of blacks: how he would engage them, when and where he would see them. A glance at four "innocent" childhood passages from John Faulkner's *My Brother Bill* reveals (all unawares) the principles guiding that organization.

"Mother said when she came to the door and saw us [covered in dust], she could not tell us from Jessie's children" (MBB 23). "Mother came out and told us to leave [the lost kite] alone and when the Negroes came in that night she would have one of them get a ladder and haul the kite down for us" (29). "Dad flung the reins to Mother and jumped to the ground yelling for the Negroes" (42). "You could get most any Negro to take charge of the butchering [of hogs] for the chitterlings" (51). All innocent, all revealing: the comic pseudoconfusion between white Falkner kids and Jesse's black ones; the secure dependence on hired black help to retrieve a kite from a tree (there is no doubt that "one of them" would do that: they are here for these purposes); the immediate "yelling for the Negroes" to put out a fire caused by a steam engine (they are always nearby, a group without individualizing distinctions, with nothing more important to do and no need to be politely asked); the shared conviction that "most any Negro" would be available to butcher hogs for chitterlings. (The rank odor of chitterlings repelled most white sensibilities, but not black ones.) In these passages, John was focusing on the Falkner boys' childhood shenanigans. But he also lets us see how extensively a white childhood in the early twentieth-century South assumed the subordinate presence of useful, obedient blacks. A sanctioned racial hierarchy functions so smoothly in these vignettes as apparently to operate by itself, with no one needed at the wheel.

Something like these unthinking racial norms surfaces in a 1921 letter Faulkner wrote from New Haven to his father back home. This was his second experience out of the South (the first—his attempt to enter World War I—had occurred three years earlier). He may have been deliberately catering to his father's unapologetic racism, or the letter might signal a racial naïveté genuinely his own: "You cant tell me these niggers are as happy and contented as ours are," he wrote Murry; "all this freedom does is make them miserable because they are not white" (TH 149). Blacks as childlike, happier with someone to take care of them (as during the peaceful time of slavery): little in Faulkner's extensive dealing with black people, early and late, would radically undermine this regional frame of racial understanding.[2]

By 1930, Mammy Callie and Uncle Ned had entered his household and come under his care. That such care was generous and loving does not keep it from being paternalistic at its core. These people were not-white. He did not typically see himself when he looked into the mirror of their faces. Some fifteen years later, he wrote Bob Haas (his editor at Random House), complaining about the slowness of his writing: "One reason it goes slow," he wrote, "maybe the main one, is conditions here. Negro servants in this country have all quit....For two years now I have had no house servants except a doddering old man and a 12 year old boy who must go to school too" (SL 256). How different is this from his brother John's casual assumption of where blacks figured on the social map and what they were expected to do? In neither case did the white man wonder who those helpers were, what they were like apart from their (meagerly recompensed) relation to him. Faulkner showed no interest in why they might be leaving the South in great numbers (the letter was written in 1947, just after World War II: the time of the great migration north). He could understand their departure only by way of the dismissive verb "quit."

The scene of racial segregation did not always operate smoothly. From the 1890s through the 1930s, the Mississippi politicians James Vardaman and Theodore Bilbo powerfully exploited white anxieties that liberated blacks would be dangerous blacks. These two men channeled and rode a wave of racial anger often referred to as "the rise of the Rednecks." Plantation patricians—men who had to be careful in their treatment of blacks, however contemptuous their thoughts about them, since black workers were required to make their cotton profitable—increasingly gave way to populist leaders exploiting the incensed thoughts and fears of poor whites. The latter, as Faulkner recognized in the mid-1950s, stood to lose the most from black emancipation. Soon after Vardaman became governor in 1903, he declared, "Six thousand years ago, the Negro was the same in his native jungle that he is today" (WFSH 157). A year later, Vardaman expanded on his subject: "You can scarcely pick up a newspaper whose pages are not blackened with the account of an unmentionable crime committed by a negro brute, and this crime, I want to impress upon you, is but the manifestation of the negro's aspiration for social equality, encouraged largely by the character of free education in vogue" (157). "The rumor, the story, whatever it was. Something about Miss Minnie Cooper and a Negro": decades of postbellum Southern racial practice had made such rumors commonplace, their credibility immediately to be granted. When Faulkner tried, many years later, to make the case for a single system of public education—for whites and blacks alike—he was up against an almost impenetrable thicket of long-nurtured apprehension and resistance.

Fanned to its most vicious form of expression, such hostility would flare into the ritual violence of lynchings. Faulkner claimed he had never witnessed one, and there is little reason to doubt him. But Mississippi led the nation in lynchings during this period: "In the twenty years from 1889 to 1909, at least 293 blacks were lynched there, more than in any other state in the nation" (WFSH 157). One of the most notorious lynchings—that of Nelse Patton—occurred in Oxford in 1908. Patton was thought to have murdered a woman named Mattie McMillan with a razor blade. He fled the scene but was soon caught by outraged whites. Historian Joel Williamson has shown how journalists and politicians fed the flames of the ensuing racial fury. First reported as "a white woman," Mattie was within hours referred to as "a white lady"; at first she was "killed," but within hours the papers reported her as "assaulted and killed." Furious Oxford whites caught Patton and stubbornly refused to let the law take its course. Brick by brick, for many hours and with many hands, they tore down the symbolically charged courthouse to get at Patton and extricate him from the protections guaranteed by the law. They riddled his body with bullets and strung him up naked and mutilated on a telephone pole, where his body remained on display all night. Ten-year-old William Faulkner slept only one thousand yards from the courthouse that night. He didn't have to have seen that ritual dismembering to remember its impact for the rest of his life.

ANCESTRAL SHADOWS

I have stressed so far the pole of disidentification—the ways in which Faulkner, when looking into the mirror posed by blacks, managed not to see himself reflected in their lives. This is the Faulkner who casually

spoke (all his life) about blacks as "niggers," who saw civil rights agitation
as essentially the menace of his beloved South being destroyed yet again
(thanks to their impatience), and who envisaged their emancipation only
by way of their ceasing to be black. This Faulkner was helped to such views
by regional ideas and arrangements of race that long preceded his birth
and would remain after his death. This Faulkner had little to say of use to
civil rights activists who wanted to address centuries of racial abuse, and
soon. But this is not the Faulkner who—within the less fettered space of
his speculative imagination—wrote *Light in August* and *Absalom, Absalom!*
and *Go Down, Moses.* The writer of those novels managed powerfully to
escape the blindness attached to being "a native of our land and a sharer in
its errors." And not only the writer saw beyond racial stereotype. The man
himself may have been privy to genealogical vignettes—ancestral shadows—that would deepen, if not reorient, his racial thinking. He may have
heard of a family history different from the normative one passed down
the generations—involving illicit acts of miscegenation and their consequences. His great-grandfather's turbulent life was rumored to have been
racially reckless as well. It was averred that he had spawned a shadowy black
line, blood-joined to yet officially separated from the white line. If this
were so, then the fictional dark twins of *Mosquitoes,* products of imaginative
invention, might have harbored behind them actual Falkners—mulattos
who were not imaginary at all, but the mistresses and offspring of the progenitor's matings. If Faulkner had such knowledge, it would have prompted
him to reconsider not just the meaning of the legendary Colonel's life. It
would have more troublingly implicated him in the racial images he saw in
his region's mirror.

To return once more to the progenitor, following Williamson's account of
him, via courthouse and census records: two years after the death in 1849 of
his first wife, Holland Pearce, W. C. Falkner married Lizzie Vance. Though
never a large slaveholder, W. C. did alter the "complexion" of his holdings
during the following decade: "in 1850 all of the slaves in the yard were black;
in 1860 they were all mulatto" (WFSH 23)—findings noted by the census taker. These mulattos consisted of two adults—a twenty-seven-year-old
woman and a twenty-one-year-old man—and four children, aged from one
to eight. Williamson argues that the father of those offspring was possibly
the younger black male but more plausibly W. C. himself.

That situation...was not at all unusual in the slaveholding South at large. In
virtually every community there was at least one white man, or sometimes an

entire family of white men, who mixed. Almost invariably, these men chose young women who were mulatto rather than black, and household servants rather than field hands. (24–5)

The pattern of such couplings typically took one of three forms: an unmarried slaveholder would choose as de facto wife a mulatto slave and would beget children upon her; or a widowed slaveholder would—in his deceased wife's stead—take a household slave (often the wife's maid, as in the case of Thomas Jefferson and Sally Hemmings); or a slaveholder would sustain two families: the white one living in the main house and the black one kept in the slave quarters. Williamson considers the other men who might have fathered these mulatto children—W. C.'s younger brother James or other Ripley bachelors or widowers—and concludes that the most likely figure was "the most powerful person in this woman's life, namely, the master" (WFSH 26). As a strong-willed, impetuous man, W. C. Falkner's psychological profile also fits the bill. A grieving widower in 1849, responsible for a sickly infant and five slaves inherited from his deceased wife, he might have taken as consolation a mulatto mistress during the two years before he met and fell in love with Lizzie Vance. Might have: this—the end of chapter 1 of the Colonel's "shadow family"—can only be speculation.

For chapter 2, fast-forward many years later to that isolated Ripley cemetery where the Old Colonel lies interred. Visiting there in the late twentieth century, Williamson came upon—as anticipated—the Colonel's huge marble monument rising over his plot, signaling to the absent world his significance. Few of his white family lie near him, not even his wife Lizzie (though there is ample room in his plot). But three members of that mulatto family group of 1860 are in the Ripley cemetery: Emeline Falkner (the mother) and two of her daughters, Delia and Hellen. His curiosity piqued, Williamson unearthed a good deal of Emeline's family circumstances. Born a light-skinned slave to a wealthy family in eastern Virginia, she was sold in her midteens to a carpenter named Benjamin Harris. Within a few years, she gave birth to Delia and Hellen; both girls believed that Harris had sired them, even as he also maintained a white family. A man of few business skills, Harris increasingly used his slaves as collateral for loans. In that way, his unpaid debt to W. C. Falkner led in 1858 to Emeline and her two daughters moving into W.C.'s yard. At some point in the mid-1860s, Emeline gave birth to another child, Fannie Forrest Falkner. Emeline's descendants, according to Williamson, "have always maintained that Colonel Falkner—not Ben Harris—was Fannie's father" (WFSH 65).

There is some circumstantial evidence to support the claim. "Fannie" derives from "Frances," the name of W.C.'s favorite sister, and "Forrest" likely comes from Nathan Bedford Forrest, W.C.'s beloved Confederate leader. Her probable birth date (July 1864) accommodates the calendar of W.C.'s sporadic Civil War activities. There is no record of what W.C. was doing between his resignation from the Confederate army in the fall of 1863 and his purchase of a house in Pontotoc in 1865. Moreover, while Lizzie Vance Falkner did not live in that house during the 1860s, evidence suggests that Emeline did. Emeline's descendants always maintained that Fannie had been born in Pontotoc. Later census records indicate that by 1870, Emeline and Fanny had both left Pontotoc and were living in Ripley. The same records confirm that the two women were still in Ripley in 1880. By this time, as freed blacks, they were identified as "Servant" and "House Maid" in the home of none other than Richard J. Thurmond. This is the man, we remember, who bitterly quarreled with W. C. during the 1880s, and who would gun him down in 1889. As for W. C., the census for 1880 shows him owning only one servant, a thirteen-year-old mulatto named Lena. Williamson speculates that Lena was possibly Emeline's daughter as well, and that she might also have been sired by W. C. Whatever the case, we know that in 1886 Lizzie Vance Falkner took her two teenage daughters from W. C.'s home in Ripley, all three of them moving to Memphis. In August 1889—just three months before the Colonel's murder—an apparently outraged Lizzie announced to her husband that she was leaving his ornate Italian villa and Ripley forever.

Did Lizzie flee the Falkner villa in Ripley because of an intolerable scandal brewing there in the late 1880s? (The old man would not have been living alone during these years of her absence.) Was W. C. Falkner not only lover of Emeline and father of Fannie but, a few years later, father of Lena, too? Is it possible that, beyond those abusive relationships and deepening them exponentially, the old man took up in the late 1880s with his own illicit daughter, Lena, thereby scandalizing his wife Lizzie? Is the notorious murder of the Old Colonel by Richard Thurmond actually a dark-twinned love mystery? Both Emeline and Fannie had lived in Thurmond's household. W. C.'s abuse of Lena—if abuse there was—might have rankled Thurmond no less than the railroad and political imbroglios we know were at play. Certainty about these matters will not be forthcoming.[3] We are left, accordingly, with two sequels to this speculative narrative of miscegenation—each compelling in its own right.

First is the fact that in that Ripley cemetery where so few of W. C. Falkner's white family chose to be interred, Emeline lies buried, in the northeast corner reserved for blacks. Though there is no record of her ever having married, her tombstone speaks eloquently of her insistence on the marital state. "Mrs. Emeline Lacy Falkner," she had engraved on it. As Williamson notes, she could hardly have called herself the Colonel's wife, yet "she did establish firmly the fact—indeed had it written in stone—that she was 'Mrs. Falkner.' She is, in truth, the only Mrs. Falkner in the cemetery where *his* marble self rises above all" (WFSH 70, emphasis in the original). Second, did Faulkner know of this putative history? If he did, what difference might it have made to his understanding of race relations in the South? That last query trumps the earlier one. Faulkner's writerly grasp of racial abuse arrives at its greatest insights—in *Absalom, Absalom!* and *Go Down, Moses*—precisely as though the Old Colonel had risen from the grave and whispered into his great-grandson's ear. Whispered all of it, from miscegenation to miscegenation to miscegenation. Alone among white novelists of his time, Faulkner would grasp the genealogical dimension of racial abuse, the ways in which acts of miscegenation produced intractable reverberations, generations later. Put otherwise, Faulkner's profoundest understanding of cascading human trouble over time owes everything to what he was able to discern about racial abuse in the South—perhaps in his own family.

I have considered at some length the limitations of Faulkner's racial positions. Engaged black leaders were not impressed by his passionate exhortation to "go slow now." In the 1950s, Ralph Ellison and James Baldwin exchanged letters criticizing Faulkner's all-too-white anguish. Incarcerated in a Birmingham jail in 1963, an unillusioned Martin Luther King would say, "For years now I have heard the word 'Wait!' It rings in the ear of every Negro with a piercing familiarity. This 'Wait' has almost always meant never."[4] "Never" is what Faulkner meant, though it is not what he said. Nor is it all that he meant. He meant "never" only while he remained in the pole of disidentification, only so long as he could avoid seeing, in the mirror of race, his dark twin staring back at him. Riddling him with responsibility, that twin kept silently asking the same unanswerable question: when would Moses go down to Egypt and make Pharaoh let his people go? Recurrently in the life, and magnificently in the work, Faulkner would become penetrated by the all-troubling burden of that question. It is time to turn to the empathic pole of his imagination.

"BECAUSE THEIR SKINS WERE BLACK"

I have cast Faulkner's immersion in American race relations in the binary terms of blindness and insight, disidentification and identification. But this opposition is too stark. Rather, Faulkner's views and feelings oscillated stumblingly between the two poles. His twinship with blacks remained inalterably occluded, troubled. But it also became, at times, radiant. More, his troubled relation to racial turmoil is revealing in ways that simply "being right" could never be. There was for white Southerners no way of simply being right on this issue. Such men and women were incapable of seeing race with innocent eyes, but what they saw *was* race—inevitably affected by the ways their heritage conditioned them to experience race. One sees—at least in part—through the lenses that one's cultural training both proposes and imposes. But this is not all that one can see, and no act of seeing is predictable—condemned in advance to stereotype. Faulkner did not access racial turmoil as a nonwhite or non-Southerner might—how could he?— but he brought to his particular access all that his racial and regional experience, along with his global travels during the 1950s and his capacious imagination, permitted him to grasp. If his stance suffered from blindness, and was recurrently inconsistent, it did not reduce to those limitations.

It began with Mammy Callie. She wielded almost as formative an influence on Faulkner and his brothers as their mother did, and she was apparently more affectionate and more lovable than Maud. Like black maids throughout the early twentieth-century South, she would have cared for his bodily needs. She would have touched him, soothed him, protected him, scolded him: all acts of bodily acknowledgment—regular, assuring, enabling. One thinks of the possible screen memory behind his earlier reference to his great-aunt's daughters Vannye and Natalie: "Vannye was impersonal; quite aloof: she was holding the lamp. Natalie was quick and dark. She was touching me. She must have carried me." Are the remembered sisters stand-ins for memories—even further back—of Maud and Callie? The memoirs of both Johncy and Jack testify repeatedly to the strength of their bond with Callie. She regaled the boys with stories of the Civil War and her childhood in slavery prior to it. She introduced them lovingly to the nomenclature of natural phenomena: the variety of plants and animals, their specific names and habits and requirements, the folktales that go with them and provide bonding narratives between human and natural worlds. Callie entered Faulkner's parents' household in 1902, in Oxford. She was a crucial figure in the maturation of this five-year-old boy, and she would

Monument of the "Old Colonel" (William C. Falkner), cemetery in Ripley, Mississippi. *From the Jane Isbell Hanes Collection, Center for Faulkner Studies, Southeast Missouri State University.*

Maud Butler Falkner and her infant son William, c. 1898. *Cofield Collection, Southern Media Archive, Special Collections, University of Mississippi Libraries.*

The Falkner boys: Murry, William, John, and Dean, Oxford, Mississippi, c. 1910. *Cofield Collection, Southern Media Archive, Special Collections, University of Mississippi Libraries.*

Jaunty William Faulkner in flying officer's uniform, December 1918. *Cofield Collection, Southern Media Archive, Special Collections, University of Mississippi Libraries.*

Estelle Oldham Franklin
and her daughter Victoria,
Shanghai, c. 1924. *From the*
Brodsky Collection, Center for
Faulkner Studies, Southeast
Missouri State University.

William Faulkner: the artist as bohemian in Paris,
1925. William C. Odiorne.
From the Brodsky Collection,
Center for Faulkner Stud-
ies, Southeast Missouri State
University.

William Faulkner: notorious author (photo taken after publication of *Sanctuary*), 1931. *Cofield Collection, Southern Media Archive, Special Collections, University of Mississippi Libraries.*

Rowan Oak, Faulkner's antebellum home, purchased in 1930. *From the Brodsky Collection, Center for Faulkner Studies, Southeast Missouri State University.*

William Faulkner and
baby daughter Jill, Rowan
Oak, c. 1934. *From the
Brodsky Collection, Center for
Faulkner Studies, Southeast
Missouri State University.*

Radiant William Faulkner, beaming at Meta Carpenter, Hollywood, c. 1936.
Meta Carpenter Wilde. *From the Brodsky Collection, Center for Faulkner Studies,
Southeast Missouri State University.*

Meta Carpenter, William Faulkner's lover, Hollywood, c. 1936. William Faulkner (visible in the mirror taking this photo). *From the Brodsky Collection, Center for Faulkner Studies, Southeast Missouri State University.*

Worried William Faulkner, Oxford, Mississippi, 1942. *Cofield Collection, Southern Media Archive, Special Collections, University of Mississippi Libraries.*

William Faulkner, Nobel laureate, Stockholm, 1950. *Courtesy Robert Hamblin. From the Brodsky Collection, Center for Faulkner Studies, Southeast Missouri State University.*

William Faulkner, pipe-smoking, world-famous author, Oxford, Mississippi, 1962. *Cofield Collection, Southern Media Archive, Special Collections, University of Mississippi Libraries.*

William Faulkner, passport
photo, Oxford, Missis-
sippi, 1960. *Cofield Collection,
Southern Media Archive, Special Collections, University of
Mississippi Libraries.*

William Faulkner, gentle-
man rider, Charlottesville,
Virginia, 1961. *Cofield Collection, Southern Media Archive,
Special Collections, University
of Mississippi Libraries.*

remain an emotional fixture in his life until her death almost forty years later. "Mammy Callie was probably the most important person in his life," Faulkner's daughter Jill would later say to Judith Sensibar (OFA 19). Even if we discount the distortions that retrospective memory can impose, Callie figured centrally in the formation of Faulkner's emotions and beliefs.

Tellingly, Faulkner's brothers' memoirs dilate on Callie in ways that never fail to convey foreignness even as they proclaim intimacy. Both memoirs stress the delightful difference of her speech—its lack of book-taught grammar, syntax, and vocabulary. Jack lingers on the image of Mammy Callie sitting in her own rocking chair beside the family fireplace, placidly taking snuff. He recalls offering to take her for a flight in his new Aeronca (he flew commercially for a time). He was concerned that his proposal would frighten her: why would a black mammy want to set foot in an airplane? When he saw the anxiety on her face prior to takeoff, he suggested that she could still change her mind. Resolutely she refused to back away: "Whereat de fambly goes—Ah goes, too!" she declared (FOM 148). Pushing herself deeper into the passenger's seat, she enjoyed her experience in the air, so far as Jack could tell. Did Callie actually speak as Jack recorded her in this vignette, or did he unthinkingly exaggerate the otherness of her speech?

Faulkner has been much praised—and, by a smaller number, called into question—for pronouncing the eulogy at Callie's funeral in 1940. Since I am among that smaller number who have wondered in print what was at stake in his taking over that role, it seems appropriate to cite my reasons: "Presiding over her funeral," I wrote thirteen years ago,

> Faulkner emphasized Callie's "half century of fidelity and devotion," and he went on to identify her as one of his "earliest recollections, not only as a person, but as a fount of authority over my conduct and of security for my physical welfare, and of active and constant affection and love." On her tombstone he had these words written: "Her white children bless her." It detracts nothing from the sincerity of this engraving to note, at the same time, that the white Faulkner has taken over the roles of both wounded subject and grateful offspring, organizer of her funeral and spokesman of the grief her death caused others. In none of this do we register the reality of her own black culture, the friends and relatives who likewise (and surely with equal intensity) suffered her loss.[5]

So I wrote then, and I do not recant now. Yet I wonder if this is straining the ethics of racial behavior a touch excessively. Perhaps the question is unanswerable, or at any rate (as I proposed earlier in a different context) it has no right answer. Why must we refuse to credit Faulkner's love of Callie, just as why must we deny the sincerity of his brothers' love of her? Yet how can we ignore that they acknowledge her humanity only in its unceasing difference from their own—kindred, yes, but looking, smelling, talking, and acting differently from them. And to be treated differently from how they treat each other. Perhaps no love is innocent, and one that crosses the membrane of race is least so. But it is still love. Writing about Faulkner and Callie thirteen years later, I would close with two final considerations. First, according to Faulkner's authorized biographer, Callie had asked him to deliver the eulogy when the time came (F 413). He hadn't arrived at the idea on his own. Is it so strange to imagine that she would want this world-famous writer who loved her to cobble together some appropriate words after her departure? Not innocent, but not strange. Second, Jack's memoir mentions, as it draws toward its melancholy ending, that at the time of his mother's death (1960), Callie's rocking chair was to be found next to Maud's bed. It had remained there these twenty years between the maid's death and that of the mistress. The same object comes up different the second time. The snuff-smoking black woman's quaintly special rocking chair, on the one hand, and, on the other, the empty rocking chair where an intimate member of the family used to sit—and which her ageing and solitary friend liked to regard with the eye of memory and love.

Let us return to the Faulkner who stumbled throughout the 1950s in the mined fields of race. The blindness of his positions is clear enough. But stumbling is not only error—though it always *is* error—and there are dimensions of midcentury racial turmoil that you would have to have been there and stumbled through to grasp at all. In his "Letter to a Northern Editor," Faulkner identified one of those dimensions. Aligned with neither the Citizens' Council nor the NAACP, he described himself as "being in the middle" (ESPL 87), seeking to ward off disasters rising from either of the two extremes. Grace Hale and Robert Jackson have persuasively argued that the "middle" position Faulkner clung to—and which would not survive *Brown v. Board of Education*—was Southern white liberalism.[6] After *Brown*, the die was cast: either for integration or against it. Most Southern white liberals reluctantly retreated to a white moderate position. They wanted to avoid violence, but when the chips were down, they would not turn against the prerogatives of a society founded on segregation. Faulkner found himself even more isolated as he refused to endorse either side of the stark binary before him. He thus had no platform to stand on—no socially shared position to argue from—and that stance reveals both the strength and the limit of his racial understanding.

Although "in the middle" came increasingly to mean "on his own," Faulkner continued to speak out. The man who had refused as a boy to graduate from high school vigorously supported a single system of public education in Mississippi. It was absurd, he wrote the *Memphis Commercial Appeal* in 1955, "to raise taxes to establish another system at best only equal to that one which is already not good enough."[7] Attacked for this stance, he responded in another letter to the same paper as follows. "To Mr. Womack's last question: I have no degrees nor diplomas from any school. I am an old veteran sixth-grader. Maybe that's why I have so much respect for education that I seem unable to sit quiet and watch it held subordinate in importance to an emotional state concerning the color of human skin" (ESPL 219). More, he grasped the economic basis underlying Southern whites' hatred of blacks: "That's what the white man in the South is afraid of," he said in his most widely circulated essay about civil rights, "that the Negro, who has done so much with no chance, might do so much more with an equal one that he might take the white man's economy away from him" (96).

Faulkner's post–Nobel Prize travels for the State Department in the 1950s opened his eyes to how the rest of the world was watching America struggle with its race problem. A patriot before the Cold War, he was more emphatically one during it. He could not bear the possibility of the Soviet Union exploiting the United States' failure to grant equality to one-tenth of its people. "To live anywhere in the world of A.D. 1955," he announced to the Southern Historical Association, "and be against equality because of race or color, is like living in Alaska and being against snow" (ESPL 146). Perhaps it took his travels to make him realize that after the costly war to defeat Hitler, it was outrageous to oppose human equality. But his Oxford friends and family opposed it—his brother John pointedly wrote to the *Oxford Eagle* attacking one of Faulkner's arguments—and they would never understand his apparent apostasy. They knew he didn't want to live on an equal basis with blacks any more than they did, and they hated his pretending that he did. He was not pretending that he did. But he could not affirm any other position than equality in a mid-twentieth-century world.

His fellow white Southerners hated not only what they took to be his posturing: many of them hated him as well. When he publicly asserted that the evidence supporting the death penalty for Willie McGee (a black man convicted of raping a white woman) was insufficient to justify that decision, he was attacked as either a deluded writer or someone seditiously aligned "with the Communists" (F 539). A year earlier (1950), he had courageously criticized (in public) a Mississippi court's decision to spare white Leon

Turner the death penalty. No one doubted that Turner had murdered three black children, but the jury couldn't bring themselves to execute a white man for this crime. Faulkner knew how swiftly the jurors would have decided otherwise had the race of the killer and the victims been reversed. He wrote the *Commercial Appeal* that Turner, when eventually released, would at some point murder another child, "who it is to be hoped—and with grief and despair one says it—will this time at least be of his own color" (516).

Later, in September 1955, news of the savage murder and mutilation of young Emmett Till reached Faulkner in Italy. Having just completed an enlightening three weeks' visit (sponsored by the State Department) in Japan, Faulkner had come to Rome. Hearing this news from home was unbearable. For the next few days, he wrote and rewrote a statement he would release to the American press: "Perhaps we will find out now whether we are to survive or not," he said.

> Perhaps the purpose of this sorry and tragic error committed in my native Mississippi…is to prove to us whether or not we deserve to survive. Because if we in America have reached that point in our desperate culture when we must murder children, no matter for what reason or what color, we don't deserve to survive, and probably won't. (ESPL 223)

During this turbulent period, he seems at times to have feared for his own life. To his Danish friend Else Jonsson he wrote in June 1955: "I can see the possible time when I will have to leave my native state, something as the Jew had to flee from Germany during Hitler" (SL 382).

Man in the middle. Historians are probably correct to see that, politically, this was a disappearing position once *Brown* became American law. White liberal guilt would hardly light the way to a post–civil rights future. That would take wide-scale agitation, co-ordinated marches, tactical confrontations, multiple strategies. It would take mass media coverage, and above all courageous black leadership. Ultimately, in ways Faulkner was never positioned to understand, it would be blacks themselves—by the thousands and thousands—who masterminded the strenuous, nationwide campaign to emancipate blacks. Campaign: the work is still going on. Faulkner would never have been its architect, but that is only to say that he was not a significant political player in matters of race. Yet he sometimes managed to see—precisely from his unavailing stance in the middle—racial realities that went beyond, or beneath, political programs.

Despite his occasional avuncular claim that he understood blacks (as in the notorious Howe interview), his more abiding position was skeptical. In the same speech in which he urged the Negro "to cease forever more think-ing like a Negro and acting like a Negro," he also showed that he under-stood the concept of "Negro" itself to have no reliable meaning. Rather than the sign of a reality, it was a mask, a shield. "It is possible that the white race and the Negro race can never really like and trust each other," he wrote; "this for the reason that the white man can never really know the Negro, because the white man has forced the Negro to be always a Negro rather than another human being in their dealings, and therefore the Negro cannot afford, does not dare, to be open with the white man" (ESPL 157). Could a political program have based itself on this insight? It is doubtful, yet this insight went to the heart of his Southern experience, and it would recur powerfully in his finest novels. Whites did not know who blacks were, not because blacks were unknowable but because whites had for the longest time been fouling their own nest. They had abused blacks, broken faith with them, made them adopt the protective masks and strategies required to survive the whites.

Why did he so exercise himself in a cause he must have eventually recog-nized as unwinnable on his terms? Perhaps his most revealing answer came in a long and musing essay he wrote in 1954, "Mississippi." There, in barely concealed autobiographical terms (but using his fictional characters' names rather than those of his own family), he revisited his lifelong experience of "his native land: he was born of it and his bones will sleep in it; loving it even while hating some of it" (ESPL 36). Man in the middle: you love what you hate. You love it despite what you hate about it. What you hate is too deeply rooted to disappear simply because you wish it would. What you hate was not far to find: "But most of all he hated the intolerance and injustice: the lynching of Negroes not for the crimes they committed but because their skins were black" (37).

The middle is precisely where no effective racial politics could be con-structed in the mid-1950s. But it was where, stumbling and contradict-ing himself, seeing too many competing realities to get them into a single vision, Faulkner found himself. He didn't want to be there, but he felt he had no choice in the matter. The crisis was urgent; he had to engage it. Yet he knew, in his novelistic bones, that race trouble in America—however urgent—wasn't going away soon, no matter what the politics for addressing it. His much maligned phrase, "go slow now," meant all the reactionary or blindsided things it has been glossed to mean, but it also meant something more. The national malady of violent racism permitted of no specific rem-edy to cure it once and for all. No governmental antibiotics existed for ills in the body politic—ills so long established as to seem virtually constituent of American reality. Regions, let alone countries, do not remake themselves in a year or even a decade. Politicians often refuse to think in such long-range terms, for reasons both good and bad. But novelists do. "The human heart in conflict with itself," as he put it in his 1950 Nobel Prize speech, operates outside the instrumental terms of problem and resolution. Dramas of the heart are rarely about winners and losers. As Faulkner put away his speeches and his public letters in the later 1950s, entering his last five years of life (though he couldn't have known this), he might have felt an immense sense of frustration and fatigue. There was so much work on race still to be done, but he lacked the heart and energy to pursue it further. And he knew no one was looking to him for it. Could he have realized that his supreme contribution to the understanding of racial turmoil in his native land had already been done? It lay behind him, in his finest novels.

No reader of the early fiction would have guessed it though. His first writings were virtually free of black portraits or themes. *Soldiers' Pay* and *Mosquitoes* attended to white characters with white dilemmas. Some of the *New Orleans Sketches* did show signs of his power to enter racial territory—black vernacular rhythms caught and articulated, even the specific timbre of black distress. Blacks began to show up in number, and to open up to narrative development, though limited, only with *Flags in the Dust*. But they could not escape *Flag*'s plantation frame, its "whites only" emphases. Though skillfully drawn, the retinue of servants attending the Sartoris family—Simon and Leonora, Caspey and Isom—did not escape the repertory of stereotypes traditionally used to represent the black domestic. The rebelliousness of the returning Caspey might well have offered Faulkner a chance to explore the trouble-making restlessness of blacks coming home after the Great War. But Caspey's menace, given nowhere to go in *Flags*, loses its edge and portent, reducing to the familiar uppityness of a misbehaving servant. The book remained focused on its intricately suffering white protagonists.

"COMING BACK": *THE SOUND AND THE FURY*

Perhaps the most memorable black character Faulkner was ever to create appeared in his next novel, *The Sound and the Fury*. But he did not allow the Compsons' black maid, Dilsey Gibson, despite her resourcefulness, to break through the novel's undeviating focus on white postbellum dysfunction. Often reductively misread, Dilsey radiates dignity and a clear-eyed capacity to parse Compson misdoings well beyond the ken of any stereotypical mammy. The strongest character in the novel, she is nevertheless far from its most mesmer-izing. It is as though her achievement of mental health itself kept her from Faulkner's more penetrating scrutiny. Bounded by the demands of a failing white household, she was kept on the near side of emotional and mental free fall. Unpreparedness and vulnerability in the present moment—the signs of Faulkner's deeper investment in a character—are denied her.

Minor black characters in this novel share a good measure of Dilsey's composure. Versh, T.P., Frony, and Luster—three generations of Comp-son servants—caretake this unsavable family as efficiently as is humanly possible. With wry humor and unillusioned endurance, they deflect—or absorb—the racial slights coming their way. Deep down, they remain imperturbable, which is precisely the mark of their secondariness in this book: no onslaught of sound and fury *could* reach them. The most sugges-tive instance of such imperturbability is an unnamed black man sitting atop a mule. On a train heading home for Christmas vacation during his fresh-man year at Harvard, Quentin encounters him:

> I didn't know that I really had missed Roskus and Dilsey and them until that
> morning in Virginia. The train was stopped when I waked and I raised the
> shade and looked out. The car was blocking a road crossing…and there was a
> nigger on a mule in the middle of the stiff ruts, waiting for the train to move.
> How long he had been there I didn't know, but he sat straddle of the mule,
> his head wrapped in a piece of blanket, as if they had been built there with
> the fence and the road, or with the hill, carved out of the hill itself, like a sign
> put there saying You are home again….I raised the window.
>
> "Hey, Uncle," I said. "Is this the way?"
>
> "Suh?" He looked at me, then he loosened the blanket and lifted it away
> from his ear.
>
> "Christmas gift!" I said.
>
> "Sho comin, boss. You done caught me, aint you?"
>
> "I'll let you off this time." I dragged my pants out of the little hammock
> and got a quarter out. "But look out next time. I'll be coming back through
> here two days after New Year, and look out then." I threw the quarter out the
> window. "Buy yourself some Santy Claus."
>
> "Yes, suh," he said. He got down and picked up the quarter and rubbed it
> on his leg. "Thanky, young marster. Thanky." Then the train began to move.
> I leaned out the window, into the cold air, looking back. He stood there
> beside the gaunt rabbit of a mule, the two of them shabby and motionless
> and unimpatient. (SF 943)

"Coming back": the entire passage is suffused in the nostalgia of a return to the past. This black man—he has neither history nor name—radiates a bond with nature itself. Like the fence, the road, and the hill, it is as though he has been there forever. He seems planted like a signpost to reassure Quentin that whatever the Yankee surprises of his first semester at Harvard, "You are home again." The train moves with the technological velocity of a changing world, but not this black man, nor his motionless mule. The social ritual accompanying their encounter is likewise saturated in practices dating from antebellum times. "Christmas gift" was a game whites would play with friends and servants (or, further back, with slaves) during the last week in December. Whenever two people would cross paths, the first to say these words would be entitled to a small gift from the other. If the ritual involved a slave, the time-honored tradition insisted that the slave always said it first. Quentin gets to the ritual phrase sooner than the black man on the mule, but he does not fail to pass a quarter to him. They encounter each other as young marster and submissive darky. Fixed against the horizon by the train's hurtling motion away, the black man appears to Quentin as all but biologically bonded with his mule, "the two of them shabby and motionless and unimpatient." Faulkner seems to have invented the word "unimpatient" to convey the hard-won resilience of blacks in *The Sound and the Fury*. Eluding the onslaught of modernity (which is dispossessing and disorienting the white Compsons), this black man endures the indignities that come his way without succumbing to impatience. As though gifted with an instinctual component lacking in whites, he finds his way past the myriad reasons for frustration and recovers a contemporary "unimpatience" that replaces the traditional "patience" no longer available.

Faulkner accesses otherwise the damaged white Compson brothers—Benjy, Quentin, and Jason. He uses present-tense, first-person interior monologue to narrate their encounters. Their experience bursts upon them as assault, overwhelming their defenses. Remembering an earlier moment of distress when he had broken his leg and was trying to prepare himself for the ensuing pain, Quentin thinks: "*Wait I'll get used to it in a minute wait just a minute I'll get*" (SF 72, emphasis in the original). Go slow now, wait, stop: such language reappears in Faulkner's frantic later attempts to forestall a coming racial juggernaut (the violent move, in the 1950s, to integrate his beloved South). But Quentin—no more than Faulkner—cannot get ready in advance. His plea that the pain slow down is itself violently interrupted—"*wait just a minute I'll get*"—his distress overriding his linguistic effort to bind it. No hindsight or foresight possible: he is being crushed *now*. Caught in present-tense dilemmas, Faulkner's white protagonists lack "unimpatience."

In his early novels, Southern distress remained racially innocent. This fiction either ignored blacks or seemed to access them as inhabitants of another planet. More precisely, inhabitants of another time (antebellum-derived), embodiments of an earlier culture. More precisely yet, he imagined them as carriers of a separate blood. Even if they carried an admixture of white blood (like Elnora), Faulkner was not interested in probing the trouble that mixture might imply. But from *Light in August* (1932) through *Go Down, Moses* (1942), he would imagine blacks otherwise. And it was by seeing them as potentially scandalous carriers of white blood that he came upon a supreme insight. He grasped that racial turmoil in the South—at once yoking and dissevering white and black lives for over two centuries—centered on miscegenation. From 1932 forward, Southern trouble would no longer strike him as racially innocent. Innocence itself had lost its charm; Southern whites who basked in it had no title to it. *Light in August* would inaugurate Faulkner's attempt to probe the nightmare hiding in that simple phrase "dark twins."

"HE NEVER ACTED LIKE EITHER A NIGGER OR A WHITE MAN":
LIGHT IN AUGUST

I have already noted the unfamiliar sequencing of materials in this novel—the ways in which none of the opening chapters seems to prepare its reader for the one that comes next. Preparing one for what comes next is of course the role of tradition itself, and the very unfolding of *Light in August* sets off an alarm: tradition is useless here, you will not be ready for what is coming. Nor will you know whom to follow when it arrives. Seemingly minor, this deviation from standard novelistic practice is major. From Clarissa Harlowe through Emma Bovary, Anna Karenina, and Jake Barnes, the great novels of Western fiction tell us early on who matters more and who less—where to train our eye. They economize our passage through the *time* of reading, reassuring us that—though we still need to remain alert—we're on the right path. Faulkner takes five chapters and introduces a trio of possible protagonists—Lena, Byron, Hightower—before he settles in on Joe Christmas. He also insinuates, with increasing discomfort for his reader, that though we come to know Christmas intimately, we do not know a cardinal fact of his existence: his racial identity. Joe does not know this either. In any of Faulkner's previous novels, such not-knowing would be of no moment, since none of them engages racial identity as a question. This one does—its 375 pages do little else—and the consequences are astonishing.

How can racial identity be a serious question in a novel that has virtually no black characters? (A few young blacks wander the Jefferson streets late one night, a pair of older blacks figure in Hightower's memories of his nine-teenth-century childhood. None of them has much bearing on the book's events.) Yet racial hysteria—like a bomb threat—can flare up, uncontrollably, with neither blacks nor bombs anywhere to be found. In an essay entitled "Stranger in the Village," James Baldwin explains the logic of this hysteria: "At the root of the American Negro problem," he writes, "is the necessity of the American white man to find a way of living with the Negro in order to live with himself...'the Negro-in-America is a form of insanity which over-takes white men.'"[8] Dark twins: it is as though the American white man has been surreptitiously infected with Negro-ness. The insanity such infection foments is white alone. My figure of speech invokes the blood, which is *Light in August*'s obsessive concern. Joe Christmas is incapable of finding a way of living with the Negro in order to live with himself, and this is because he senses his dark twin living inejectably, blood-coiled, beneath his skin. How does Christmas come to believe this? How does Faulkner let us find it out?

The first scene where we realize that Christmas may be black occurs some seventy pages into the book. Far enough along for readers to feel tricked: which is to say, to resent the author not telling us in advance the racial infor-mation we require. Such resentment—deliberately fostered by Faulkner's pro-cedures—boomerangs on us once we ask what is at stake in our demanding to know, first off, a character's racial pedigree. Like the next two masterpieces focused on race, *Light in August* acts—mirror-like—as an uninvited dark twin bent on rousing into consciousness its reader's racial presuppositions. To read it is to reexperience one's own assumptions about race. Here is the scene in question. Joe Brown, Christmas's erstwhile partner and cabin-sharer, is being grilled as he tries to explain to an angry public what he has been doing with Christmas. The latter is suspected of having slit the throat of a white woman (Joanna Burden), set fire to her house, and fled. A thousand-dollar reward has been offered to anyone who can identify the killer, and Brown wants to collect it. The riled town, however, wants to know what Brown was doing at the scene of the fire. Byron Bunch narrates what comes next:

> "I reckon he was desperate by then. I reckon he could not only see that
> thousand dollars getting further away from him, but that he could begin
> to see somebody else getting it....Because they said it was just like he had

been saving what he told them next for just such a time as this. Like he had knowed that if it come to a pinch, this would save him.…'That's right,' he says. 'Go on. Accuse me. Accuse the white man that's trying to help you with what he knows. Accuse the white man and let the nigger go free. Accuse the white and let the nigger run.'

"'Nigger?' the sheriff said. 'Nigger?'

"It's like he knew he had them then. Like nothing they could believe he had done would be as bad as what he could tell that somebody else had done. 'You're so smart,' he says. 'The folks in this town is so smart. Fooled for three years. Calling him a foreigner for three years, when soon as I watched him three days I knew he wasn't no more a foreigner than I am. I knew before he even told me himself.' And them watching him now, and looking now and then at one another.

"'You better be careful what you are saying, if it is a white man you are talking about,' the marshall says. 'I don't care if he is a murderer or not.'…

"'A nigger,' the marshall said. 'I always thought there was something funny about that fellow.'" (LA 470–1)

Five times hurled into that space of contestation, the word "nigger" magically reconfigures the stakes involved. Brown exits from the scene of suspicion, as Christmas comes to fill (overfill) that space by himself. All eyes—previously blurred vision now corrected to twenty-twenty—are turned on this absent figure. "Nigger" is bad enough. What is intolerable, as the wordless vibration in the air suggests, is that none of them spotted him in advance. The marshall warningly trots out to Brown the South's hierarchy of crimes. To murder someone is less culpable than to call a white man a "nigger." Subsequent recognitions click into place: "I always thought there was something funny about that fellow," the marshall says. His access to this recognition is revealing. The lack of clarity he and his fellow white towns-people felt during their actual experience of Christmas has been satisfyingly dispelled. *Now* they know what that was all about. Retrospective judgment silently reconfigures earlier experience so that it fits later prejudice. Removing the gnats and tacks and broken glass from their confusing experience of Christmas, the town transforms the turmoil of *is* into the peace of *was*. Uncertainty gets "corrected" into fixed (and fatal) conviction. It doesn't stop there. Joanna Burden—while alive, a strange Yankee woman living alone in their vicinity—becomes, once dead, a martyr to Southern honor, the victim of black bestiality: "Among them [were those] who believed aloud that it was an anonymous negro crime committed not by a negro but by Negro and who knew, believed, and hoped that she had been ravished too: at least once before her throat was cut and at least once afterward" (LA 611). "Nigger," we now see, carries with it an entire subhuman narrative. As for Brown, wielder of this talismanic term, we can infer that he is lying about his own process of recognition. He was no less imperceptive than the others about Christmas's racial identity, until Christmas informed him otherwise. But he has forgotten that he *is* lying about it, so soothing is it to rewrite earlier blindness into later enlightenment. Except that it is not enlightenment. No one knows if Christmas is black: not others, not Joe, not the reader. None of this not-knowing will prevent the people of Jefferson from killing and castrating him. Only we and Joe are sure that we do not know, but there is nothing satisfying about such knowledge.

The novel wryly reveals that accurate knowledge doesn't affect irrational behavior anyway. The racial identity of Joe's father—the man who impregnated Milly Hines, "a fellow with the circus"—is forever uncertain. As Byron explains to Hightower, "She [Milly] told him [her father, Doc Hines] that the man was Mexican…Maybe that's what the fellow told the gal. But he…knew somehow that the fellow had nigger blood. Maybe the circus folks told him. I dont know. He aint never said how he found out, like that never made any difference. And I reckon it didn't, after the next night" (LA 678). Never made any difference because, after the next night, the man was dead anyway, gunned down by an insanely racist Doc Hines. Conviction explodes into lethal action. Reliable information is academic, beside the point. The racial makeup of this illegitimate child remains permanently under a cloud, however murderous its consequences.

Taken by his outraged grandfather to a Memphis orphanage, Joe grows up unmothered. The nearest he can approach a motherly figure is the orphanage's dietitian, whose hair reminds him of candy. Obscurely seeking nourishment from her, he makes his way secretly into her rooms where, in the privacy of her bathroom, he ritualistically takes and swallows her toothpaste. He seems to believe that ingesting this property of hers will secure her to him as well. One day, however, he comes to her room at the wrong time. Before he can slip away, she enters with a coworker, Charlie, who is intent on bullying her into intercourse. She resists feebly. Hearing their sounds, the little boy thinks "that it was a strange hour to be going to bed" (LA 488). Frightened, motionless, he keeps coiling toothpaste into his mouth, more than he has ever taken before. Soon all grows strange inside him—as the intercourse continues beyond the curtain—and the explosion occurs:

At once the paste which he had already swallowed lifted inside him, trying to get back out, into the air where it was cool. It was no longer sweet. In the rife, pinkwomansmelling obscurity behind the curtain he squatted, pinkfoamed, listening to his insides, waiting with astonished fatalism for what was about to happen to him. Then it happened. He said to himself with complete and passive surrender: "Well, here I am."

When the curtain fled back he did not look up. When hands dragged him violently out of his vomit he did not resist. He hung from the hands, limp, looking with slack-jawed and glassy idiocy into a face no longer smooth pink-and-white, surrounded now by wild and dishevelled hair whose smooth bands once make him think of candy. "You little rat!" The thin, furious voice hissed; "you little rat! Spying on me! You little nigger bastard!" (488–9)

The scene is passing strange. Joe's ingestion of the paste grotesquely imitates the passage of semen on the bed (Charlie's climax echoed by Joe's eruption), though in his case he is both receiver and releaser. His bids for a mother never get past this debacle in the dietitian's room. Nor will his later experience of sexuality—the passing and receiving of liquid—take place without violence. The would-be mother—transformed into a Medusa with disheveled hair—pronounces upon Joe a lifelong curse: "You little nigger bastard!" Identity in this novel involves not who you are but how you become penetrated by the names that others have called you. Under pressure, as Brown was earlier in the book, both characters "nigger" Joe to save themselves from scrutiny.

A few pages later, we learn that Joe has been called "nigger" before, on the playground. Though only five, he tried to figure out why he was singled out, treated as different. He knew it had everything to do with the janitor at the orphanage:

He knew that he was never on the playground for an instant that the man [the janitor] was not watching him from the chair in the furnace room door, and that the man was watching him with a profound and unflagging attention. If the child had been older he would perhaps have thought *He hates me and fears me. So much so that he cannot let me out of his sight* With more vocabulary but no more age he might have thought *That is why I am different from the others: because he is watching me all the time.* (500–501, emphasis in the original)

Over 150 pages later, a first-time reader learns that this janitor is Doc Hines, Joe's furious grandfather. Obsessed with the boy's satanic black

blood, Hines has taken him to a Memphis orphanage and become the janitor there, so as never to let the boy out of his sight. If the children code the
new boy's difference as "nigger"—which is not unlikely on an orphanage
playground in the early-twentieth-century South—the one focusing their
abuse is the ever-vigilant grandfather-janitor. It is as though in a bizarre
twist on the Calvinist God balefully scrutinizing his human subjects, Hines
unceasingly *looks* Joe's black difference into him—"niggers" him: a penetration from which the boy never recovers.

Years later, Joe grows up as the adoptive son of another brutalizing father
figure, Simon McEachern (the man who seeks with systematic violence to
force the catechism on the boy). Joe eludes McEachern's despotic control,
even falling in love with an older waitress in a seedy restaurant downtown.
That she is a part-time prostitute is something he will not recognize until—
like all genuine experience in Faulkner's world—he is knocked down and
forced to face it. Before this painful awakening, however, they become lovers—she is his first—and he invites her to figure out his single carefully
guarded secret. He hints that it has to do with his features, and she guesses
maybe he is a foreigner:

> "It's different from that, even. More than just a foreigner. You cant guess."
> "How more different?"
> "Guess."
> Their voices were quiet…"I cant. What are you?"…She asked him again.
> Then he told her. "I got some nigger blood in me."
> Then she lay perfectly still with a different stillness. But he did not seem
> to notice it. He lay peacefully too, his hand slow up and down her flank.
> "You're what?" she said.
> "I think I got some nigger blood in me." His eyes were closed, his hand
> slow and unceasing. "I don't know. I believe I have."
> She did not move. She said at once: "You're lying."
> "All right," he said, not moving, his hand not ceasing. (LA 543)

Only here does he offer his difference as something to be shared, an
intimacy that might bond them closer. She cannot believe him. It is incon-
ceivable to her that she could be having intercourse with a "nigger," though
she, too—like the others—will hurl his "nigger identity" at him when she is
under duress. For the moment she just denies it, in terms that spell out an
entire culture's racial phobia. He speaks of attribute—"some nigger blood
in me"—and she speaks of essence: "You're what?" Racial identity in the

South cannot be partial or mixed. To have a drop of black blood is to *be* black.

Deformed by Hines, brutalized by McEachern, betrayed by Bobbie the waitress, Joe finds himself, years later, in Joanna Burden's house and (eventually) in her bed. We have already glanced at the failure of that fraught relationship, and we know—it is one of the first things we learn in this book—that it ended with her throat being slit. We have known this since the early pages, and the town has obscenely dilated on it, embroidering the scenario according to their racist fantasies. Few things are more brilliant in *Light in August* than Faulkner's withholding this violent event itself, even as no one doubts that it occurred. Rather than give us the deed, Faulkner twice supplies—as already analyzed—the threshold scene: Joe outside her door, hearing the clock sound midnight, knowing that "something is going to happen to me," and making his way into her house one last time. Two hundred pages into the book, Faulkner finally unfolds the scene itself: what they say to each other, and what they do. There we learn—we alone, no one else in the novel is privy to this scene—that she is lying in wait for him, an ancient and loaded twin-barreled pistol in her hand. She has in mind a double suicide, since the affair is ruined and he will not become a good "Negro" worker in her behalf. He watches as she pulls the trigger point-blank, and the gun misfires. Rather than let her fire again, he reaches for his knife, slits her throat, and flees. Even in Mississippi in the 1930s, a killing that transpired thus would be legally a case of self-defense. Like our other unshared knowledge about events in this novel, knowing this does us no good. Joe must die the death, receive the castration, because—in all white eyes—he is, in essence, and therefore in behavior, a nigger-rapist-murderer.

Although Christmas outwits his pursuers, he chooses, finally, to turn himself in: "*I am tired of running of having to carry my life like it was a basket of eggs*" (LA 648, emphasis in the original). He makes sure that the day he starts trying to do so is a Friday. On Saturday, he succeeds in getting recognized and caught. I mentioned earlier *Light in August*'s brilliant moves, and this is perhaps the most stunning of all. Faulkner turns over the narrative of Christmas's capture to an anonymous townsman, who speaks to other anonymous townsmen as follows:

"He don't look any more like a nigger than I do. But it must have been the nigger blood in him. It looked like he had set out to get himself caught

like a man might set out to get married. He had got clean away for a whole
week....Then yesterday morning he come into Mottstown in broad daylight,
on a Saturday with the town full of folks. He went into a white barbershop
like a white man, and because he looked like a white man they never suspected him....They shaved him and cut his hair and he payed them and
walked out and right into a store and bought a new shirt and a tie and a
straw hat...And then he walked the streets in broad daylight, like he owned
the town, walking back and forth with people passing him a dozen times and
not knowing it, until Halliday saw him and ran up and grabbed him and said,
'Aint your name Christmas?' and the nigger said that it was. He never denied
it. He never did anything. He never acted like either a nigger or a white man.
That was it. That was what made the folks so mad. For him to be a murderer
and all dressed up and walking the town like he dared them to touch him,
when he ought to have been skulking and hiding in the woods, muddy and
dirty and running. It was like he never even knew he was a murderer, let
along a nigger too." (657–8)

A culture's racial vernacular speaks here, with energetic conviction. In this
vernacular, "niggers" are all too likely—it is their "default" position—to be
rapist-murderers who skulk and hide in the woods. They are typically dirty
as well—and recognizable as such. One recalls the speeches Faulkner made
twenty-five years later in which he reminded black people that, to deserve
equality, they should act, dress, and smell like white people. In *Light in
August* there is no place for such condescension. The novelist imaginatively
knew, in 1932, what the letter-writer of the 1950s seems to have forgotten.
Joe Christmas does not need to be reminded how to dress. With exquisite
irony, he bestrides the town as though he owned it. A white barbershop,
a new shirt and tie and hat, an unhurried parading through Mottstown
as he waits to be recognized: his moves eloquently counter white racist
expectations, point for point. He does not say a word. His performance says
it for him: "I look like you, perhaps better than you. I am clean, tall, and
self-possessed. I enter and exit your segregated spaces—your barbershop
and stores—and you do not see my difference. You do not see it because it
does not exist. It takes you forever to catch up to me." I have invented this
silent speech, yet something like it roils inside this mob of enraged whites.
Confusedly, they register his insult and grasp that he is mocking the racial
conventions that underwrite their sanity. "The Negro-in-America is a form
of insanity which overtakes white men," Baldwin wrote. *Light in August* is
the first of Faulkner's masterpieces to express the fallout of that insanity.

"LOOK[ING] AT ALL THE OBJECTS FROM THE OTHER SIDE":
ABSALOM, ABSALOM!

Absalom, Absalom! was not easy for Faulkner to write, and it is not easy
to read. An all but intolerable amount of implication is wrought into its
charged three hundred pages. It is not a matter of erudite meanings like
those inserted by T. S. Eliot and Ezra Pound into their allusive modernist
poems *The Waste Land* and the *Cantos*. In those overladen poems—countless
scholars have made careers tracing the allusions—the concrete text serves
as a locus for the most rarified musing. Not so for *Absalom*. Its allusions
are helpful but supply no key. Rather, in an onslaught of emotionally laden
prose that is remarkable even for Faulkner, the book twists and turns as it
strains to give shape to an overarching racial vision of the South. Coleridge
spoke of poetry as language expressing a "more than usual state of emo-
tion" brought under "more than usual order." On that model, *Absalom* is
Faulkner's most poetic novel.

The events of the novel are crucial, but *Absalom*'s identity lodges in its
way of delaying and repositioning those events. Events happen in time:
Absalom conveys how we actually go about grasping their meaning. Our
tactic for doing so—as Faulkner's earlier masterpieces suggest as well—is
retrospection. We live forward, even as we understand by later looking back.
A comparison between the linear events of the story and Faulkner's way
of circuitously plotting the same events—letting them come clear, or look
different, later—makes this plain. Here is *Absalom* synopsized into linear
sequence:

A boy named Thomas Sutpen is born around 1808, in the mountains
of (what would become) West Virginia. After his mother dies, his father
takes him and his sisters eastward. He joins his father in working on a
large Tidewater plantation, and he encounters there the plantation's black
slaves. At age fourteen or so, he is told by his father to take a message to
the planter in the big house. A black butler stops him at the front door,
forbids his entrance, and tells him (in effect) that trash like him may enter
only through the back door. He is never to forget this humiliation. Trying
to avenge the wound to his psyche, he determines to become as rich as the
planter whose butler had humiliated him. To do this, he heads to the West
Indies, never seeing his family again. End of part 1.

Thomas Sutpen succeeds on a Haiti plantation. After putting down a
slave revolt, he is offered as reward the planter's daughter. They marry, and
a son is born. Later, Sutpen learns that the planter's wife is part black. In

the American South (if not in Haiti), this fact would doom his design to establish a plantation dynasty. So Sutpen abandons his family (paying for this handsomely) and heads to Mississippi. He arrives in Jefferson in 1833 with slaves (one of whom is a child named Clytie), money, and a "design" in place: to become a wealthy planter. He buys his land (Sutpen's Hundred), builds his mansion, and takes as (second) wife the daughter, Ellen, of a local tradesman, Goodhue Coldfield. By 1841, they have produced two children, Henry and Judith, and in the next two decades he becomes the region's most powerful planter. End of part 2.

In the late 1850s, Henry attends the University of Mississippi, where he falls under the spell of a sophisticated young man, Charles Bon, of New Orleans. Henry brings Bon to Sutpen's Hundred, where Bon meets and falls in love with Judith. Ellen is overjoyed at the prospective marriage. In November 1860, Lincoln is elected president. That Christmas, Henry inexplicably breaks with his family, traveling to New Orleans with Bon. Henry and Bon enter the war the following spring, seeing action during the next four years. Ellen dies in 1863, heartbroken; a year later, Ellen's father dies. The much younger Coldfield daughter, Rosa, moves to Sutpen's Hundred. Bon returns to Sutpen's Hundred in 1865 to claim Judith as his bride. Henry comes with him and, for unknown reasons, shoots Bon dead. Henry then flees. Sutpen returns home after the war, proposes to Rosa, and is rejected. He takes up with Milly, the granddaughter of his poor white worker Wash Jones. Milly gives birth to a girl whom Sutpen repudiates (he wants a son for his dynasty). Wash overhears Sutpen's insult to Milly—"too bad you're not a mare too. Then I could give you a decent stall in the stable" (AA 236)—and, incensed, kills Sutpen, along with Milly and the newborn baby. The sheriff's party comes, and when Wash does not surrender, they kill him. End of part 3.

In 1870, an octoroon with her eleven-year-old, white-skinned son appears at Sutpen's Hundred. Judith learns that she is Bon's New Orleans widow, and the boy, Charles Etienne, is Bon's son. Mother and son return to New Orleans, the octoroon dies soon after, and Judith sends Clytie to bring the boy back to Sutpen's Hundred. Forced to be negro in Mississippi, when he had been comfortably creole in New Orleans, Charles Etienne does not adapt. As a young man, he seeks out violent racial encounters. He then leaves home, returning with a mentally deficient black woman as his bride. They produce (in 1882) a brain-damaged child, Jim Bond. Charles Etienne and Judith Sutpen both die of yellow fever in 1884. Clytie remains with Jim Bond in the dilapidated Sutpen mansion during the next twenty-five years. Rosa lives alone in her father's Jefferson home. In September 1909 Rosa summons Quentin Compson to come see her. She tells him someone is living at Sutpen's Hundred, and she passes on to him her understanding of the tormented family history. That night Quentin goes with her to Sutpen's Hundred. They find a dying Henry Sutpen, home after forty years of flight, being cared for by Clytie. Quentin discusses with his father the events he has heard and witnessed, shortly before departing for Harvard that fall. End of part 4.

With his Canadian roommate, Shreve, Quentin probes the Southern tragedy that has been foisted on him. In January 1910, Quentin receives a letter from his father telling him that Rosa has returned to Sutpen's Hundred, trying to save Henry. Seeing her coming—and thinking the purpose is to arrest Henry for the murder of Bon forty-five years earlier—Clytie sets fire to the mansion, killing herself, Henry, and (eventually) Rosa. Of Sutpen's tormented family, only Jim Bond remains alive, howling in the distance. Quentin and Shreve discuss these distressing events, laboring to produce a story that might make sense of it all. They want most to know why Henry would have killed Bon in 1865. They decide that this act of violence did not spring from Bon's being already married to an octoroon. Instead, they see Bon as the son of Sutpen and his first wife, Eulalia. Bon would have been returning (in 1865) to Sutpen's Hundred not just to claim a wife but to compel acknowledgment from his father. Finally, they believe that Sutpen could not acknowledge Bon because this son suffered from black blood. Referring to Jim Bond howling in the night, Shreve poses a last question to Quentin—"Why do you hate the South?" Quentin responds in agony, "*I don't hate it. . . . I dont. I dont!*" (AA 311, emphasis in the original). End of part 5 and of the tragedy of the South.

Why didn't Faulkner narrate the materials of *Absalom* in something like this sequence? The answer is that my linear summary does not tell how, in ongoing time, its actors and tellers (and readers) actually encountered all this experience. Converting earlier (mis)understanding into retrospective clarity, my paragraphs assume an all-knowing perspective, omitting the confusion that precedes enlightenment. From the beginning, I provide the comprehensive mapping that only retrospective mastery can provide—later. Of course my grasp of the events *is* retrospective. Drawing on repeated readings, I have straightened out and made sequential *Absalom*'s tangled time-weave, providing the orderly peace of *was* rather than the chaotic turmoil of *is*. By contrast, Faulkner's creative effort centers on rendering the stumbling and confusion as it might have felt when it was happening. Only by attending to the events as Faulkner narrates them can we home in on the novel's racial freight.

Absalom opens in September 1909. The Sutpen it first features is no infant in West Virginia (in the early 1800s) but a tyrannical adult who has ruined Rosa Coldfield's life and who—dead these past forty-three years—cannot be forgiven. As with Joe Christmas, Faulkner has us first encounter Sutpen as an adult who has damaged others, long before showing him as a child damaged *by* others. Rosa's conversation with Quentin—suffused with anger toward this "demon"—fills the first chapter. On Sunday mornings (so Rosa learned from her deceased sister Ellen) Sutpen would have his carriage—Ellen and the children inside it—roar up to the church at breakneck speed. Rosa closes the chapter by telling Quentin of Sutpen's more offensive, indeed bestial, wrestling match with one of his own slaves. It seems that he used to permit his own children to watch this monstrous event in a ring—white and black onlookers surrounding it—where the two men would fight "not like white men fight with rules and weapons, but like negroes fight to hurt one another quick and bad" (AA 20). Monstrous: in the antebellum South, whose priorities Rosa passionately defends, no white master would treat his slaves thus. The master could have them beaten, even maimed. But he would not touch them intimately, as an equal, in a public setting. Henry responded to this scandalous racial intimacy by vomiting, while Judith, we're told, gazed on imperturbably. The scene ends in Rosa's voice: "But I was not there. I was not there to see the two Sutpen faces this time—once on Judith and once on the negro girl beside her—looking down through the square entrance to the loft" (24).

Rosa reads the fight between Sutpen and his slave as scandal, but it comes to look different when we are allowed (many chapters later) to put into play the realities of Sutpen's upbringing. In the mountain territory where he grew up, one proved one's mettle by physical strength. In that space uncontaminated by racial difference or private property or invidious wealth, personal identity and value got established by dint of one's fists. A couple of decades later, Sutpen might have stepped into the ring with one of his slaves with no aim of wounding the sensibilities of his wife or children. In nostalgic fashion ("his only relaxation fighting his wild niggers in the stable" [AA 214]), he might have been confirming an earlier model for understanding his self-worth. He might have been demonstrating that he deserved to be master because he was still physically in charge. Likewise, when we learn later about his past, we realize that the furiously speeding carriage—read by Rosa as demonic—echoes an earlier humiliation involving a carriage. As a boy, he had helplessly watched as his older sister, walking on the road, refused to give ground before the planter's approaching carriage. The horses had reared, the slave driver had cursed, the elegant occupants had glared: "then he was throwing vain clods of dirt after the dust as it [the carriage] spun on" (191). A defiant gesture some twenty-five years later, we now see, echoes and poignantly attempts to reverse an earlier class-inflicted humiliation. For the reader, it is not a matter of later correcting a wrong reading of these scenes with a right one. Rather, both are true to the place and time where they occur. Rosa could see only as she saw, while a racially innocent Sutpen might have seen according to his earlier mountain schema. Faulkner ensures, by his structure of delayed information, that we read the scene both ways, and both times, as real.

The second chapter has Quentin and his father (the same September night in 1909) narrate again the creation of Sutpen's Hundred and its furnishing. The chapter then dilates on the details of Sutpen's marriage to Ellen Coldfield. Later we will learn—but only later—that this was his second marriage; we then realize why he was in such a hurry. Humiliated by the insult at the door, deceived later by the racially mistaken first wife, he had no time to lose if he was to build his plantation, launch his dynasty, and get his revenge. Likewise, the children born of this second marriage could not know—yet—that they were shadowed by an earlier sibling, their dark twin. Here again both views are true, incompatibly so. Faulkner forces the two views—rising from different times and places—eventually, and violently, to encounter each other. Charles Bon is relentlessly on his way to Sutpen's Hundred, driven by his mother's thirty-year-old, race-wounded history. Retrospectively, we grasp that the long-simmering anger caused by Sutpen's abandonment of her was not to be gainsaid. Up close, however— to everyone but Sutpen—the unfurling courtship of Judith and Bon reads as sweetness and light.

When Quentin presses his father for more information about Rosa in the third chapter, Mr. Compson furnishes the town's understanding of her warped childhood. He tells of her father's death during the war, and he closes on Wash Jones riding a mule to her house in 1865, saying: "Air you Rosie Coldfield?" (AA 72). Talking further to Quentin during the same night in September, Mr. Compson launches the fourth chapter by envisaging Henry and Bon traveling together to New Orleans, after Henry's mysterious break from his family. Mr. Compson enters their drama empathically, and both young men come powerfully to life: Henry choosing love for Bon over fidelity to his own family, Bon riskily revealing to Henry the details of his exotic New Orleans experience. That revelation culminates in Bon introducing Henry to the octoroon mistress whom he has morganatically married and by whom he has a child. (*Morganatic* designates a marital arrangement in which neither wife nor offspring may legally inherit. It was a procedure often used by French royalty and their nonaristocratic mistresses, centuries earlier, and it still flourished in nineteenth-century New Orleans. This arrangement would have ensured that when Bon later married a white woman, the line of descent and inheritance would be protected.) Unable to supply other motives for their quarrel, Mr. Compson tries to believe that Henry killed Bon because of the octoroon. This chapter concludes virtually where the preceding one left off, citing again Wash Jones's words to Rosa Coldfield: "Air you Rosie Coldfield? Then you better come on out yon. Henry has done shot that durn French feller. Kilt him dead as a beef" (AA 110).

Thirty-eight pages later, we are only three brief sentences further along! What could justify such circular movement? The answer is that the murdered Charles Bon we earlier knew of had no narrative density—his was merely the name of a man who had inexplicably been killed—whereas the fourth chapter has created him, generously and generatively. He has begun to matter. We learn of his love for both Henry and Judith, and we are invited by Faulkner's narrative procedure to identify with his plight. In the next chapter, he will speak movingly in his own voice, by way of an 1865 letter to Judith (in Mr. Compson's possession). There he wryly recounts to his fiancée the disasters of the war and his decision to return to Sutpen's Hundred so that they may marry. We know—but still not why—that Henry will end by killing him rather than permit the union to take place. The climactic eighth chapter accesses Bon in yet a different fashion—this time by way of Quentin and Shreve, as they imagine him traveling earlier to Sutpen's Hundred, filled with expectation and anguish. This last version of Charles Bon is a young man who—informed by his mother who his father is, but not why his father repudiated mother and son—desperately seeks paternal recognition. He has waited patiently, all his life and now these four years of the war, for Sutpen to recognize him.

By providing present experience before revealing that experience's long-concealed antecedents, Faulkner allows us to grasp both the innocence of the Sutpen children's love for Bon and the tangled noninnocence behind Bon's appearance at the university. Their love for him—which in Henry's case will not survive the scandalous (later) revelation of black blood—takes *Absalom* into racial territory Faulkner had never entered before. Whites loving blacks, always on condition of not knowing that they are black: this narrative arrangement bristles with implication. Half French in his sophistication, half American in his vulnerability; half female in his charm, half male in his strength; half white by his father, part black by his mother: Bon blends elegance and power, unillusioned shrewdness and generosity of spirit. These come together to produce a suppleness of being that no pure line of descent could make available. He is the text's utopian image of what miscegenation might *really* enable, though no one in the story is prepared to consider this possibility once he is "outed" as black. Identified thus—his history exposed and communicated—Bon cannot be loved, nor admired, nor admitted into the precincts of his white family. Once racially fixed, he must either submit to be "nigger" or die the death. Given Bon's unflinching courage, his choice is not surprising.

But more than courage is now involved in this novel of black and white relations in the South. Bon emerges as the most strenuously reinvented character in the novel—reinvented because, as in *Light in August,* the facts are not all in, never will be. Bon cannot be objectively known, he can only be interpreted—by the other characters in their present experience of him, by the narrators later seeking to make sense of what happened. The narrators perforce encounter the Sutpen saga as a mix of the known (never enough) and the plausible (never fixed once and for all). Though each of them grasps that Bon's motives were the key to this "bloody mischancing of human affairs" (AA 84), they read him in different ways. We have seen how Mr. Compson enters Bon's life, imagining his unillusioned wisdom as that of a "youthful Roman consul" come to visit northern Mississippi's "barbarian hordes" (77). His Bon is above all *curious:* a curiosity for Mr. Compson to figure out, a man curious to understand these quaintly uncivilized Mississippians.

When Quentin and Shreve, in the last chapters of *Absalom,* turn toward Bon, they see him no less as the key to the novel's murderous enigma. For them, though, the "bloody mischancing" must circulate around something more than fate or curiosity, must have risen from the tormented human heart. They decide on an "overpass to love"—a history that, at its racial core, must have centered on heartbreak—and their Bon (the novel's final version) is no merely sophisticated traveler. "*I am a good deal younger than I thought,*" this Bon muses, "*My God, I am young, young, and I didn't even know it*" (AA 265, emphasis in the original). Young, confused, stumbling in his present 1859 crisis (however long ago it happened for his twentieth-century interpreters), this Bon—like Joe Christmas—doesn't know what he's going to do next. He seeks only the merest sign of recognition from Sutpen—with that he'd leave for good—and he'd accept even less: "*a sheet a scrap of paper with the one word 'Charles' in his hand, and I would know what he meant and he would not even have to ask me to burn it. Or a lock of his hair or a paring from his finger nail and I would know them because I believe now that I have known what his hair and his fingernails would look like all my life*" (269, emphasis in the original). A lock of hair: it has become a love story.

Henry pleads with Bon—"You are my brother"—to forego his quest, not force the issue. Bon replies: "No I'm not. I'm the nigger that's going to sleep with your sister" (AA 294). Bon is unpacifiably both. No other novelist approaches Faulkner when it comes to loving what you hate, hating what you love. This unmanageable heart-truth underwrites *Absalom* and makes it live and breathe. "The human heart in conflict with itself": so Faulkner characterized his core concern when receiving the Nobel Prize in 1950. What is this but to center his great work on the plight of human beings who find themselves intolerably self-entrapped? Doomed by what their culture has taught them they must be—yet can no longer bear to be? Faulkner's most compelling protagonists seethe with convictions at odds with their feelings. Over time, agonizingly, they lose their inner coherence. The territory Faulkner opens to anguished reilluming is not—as in his own life—the confusions of love, or the war that was missed at first and mendaciously claimed later. In *Absalom* it is the reality—at once his own and his region's—of interracial intimacy cohabiting with repudiation. They are us and not-us, cherished and abandoned—dark twins inseparably bonded by blood, beyond joining because of that shared blood.

By the end, *Absalom* has revealed in Charles Bon all that he is and cannot be. Bon a nigger? Given what we have seen of the suave and sophisticated white-skinned Bon, the inappropriateness of "nigger" virtually explodes on the page. In mid-nineteenth-century Mississippi, if Bon "were" black, he would have been a slave, and none of *Absalom's* love-investments would have been possible. Since he "is" black—as we learn after many hours of reading him as white—we recognize with renewed power the absurd brutality of racial stereotype. Absurd because Bon so transcends the stereotype, brutal because its daily imposition prevented Mississippi slaves from remotely becoming Bon. Faulkner has created, in the guise of this socially impossible figure, so much that the South had experienced but could not allow itself to conceptualize.

Nor does it stop here. Bon has a child, though not by Judith, and this child's story comes to figure as the mixed-blood nightmare that replaces

Sutpen's lily-white dream of dynastic descent. Unlike his father's, Charles Etienne's racial awakening is brutally swift. He was born in a New Orleans in which he "could neither have heard nor yet recognised the term 'nigger,' who even had no word for it in the tongue he knew who had been born and grown up in a padded silken vacuum...where pigmentation had no more moral value than the silk walls and the scent and the rose-colored candle shades" (AA 165). Suddenly, this child is seized by Clytie and transported—without explanation or shared language—to a northern Mississippi where the space he inhabits has altered beyond recognition:

> the few garments (the rags of the silk and broadcloth in which he had arrived, the harsh jeans and homespun which the two women bought and made for him, he accepting them with no thanks, no comment, accepting his garret room with no thanks, no comment, asking for and making no alteration in its spartan arrangements that they knew of until that second year when he was fourteen and one of them, Clytie or Judith, found hidden beneath his mattress the shard of broken mirror: and who to know what hours of amazed and tearless grief he might have spent before it, examining himself in the delicate and outgrown tatters in which he perhaps could not even remember himself, with quiet and incredulous incomprehension) hanging behind a curtain contrived of a piece of old carpet nailed across a corner. (165)

The courtly twinned image at which ragged Charles Etienne stares in this shard of broken mirror reveals the chasm between what he was and what he is. Each present item of clothing reads as the despoliation of a former item of clothing. His New Orleans–furnished body has been displaced by his Mississippi-furnished body, none of this his own choosing. Like his father, Charles Etienne materializes as culturally impossible, torn between here and there, now and then. Puritan northern Mississippi and Catholic New Orleans, the jagged racist present and the harmonious race-neutral past share him incoherently. His solution to these incompatible cultural markings is to combine them as crucifixion. One needs (as one needed with his father) an infrared light to read the black man in this white man. But Charles Etienne makes it easier by guaranteeing, through premeditated acts of violence, that he be recognized as both at once. He chooses for wife exactly the kind of black woman that white and black alike will read as scandalous. Abreast of the nuances of every stereotype that entraps him, he projects nothing except trouble upon black and white alike.

And it is not over yet. The book ends on the note of his brain-damaged, dark-skinned son, Jim Bond. The last of the Sutpen line, this orphaned figure remains howling somewhere in the woods. No one is left who could claim him—unless it be Quentin Compson. Paralyzed by his own race-tormented inheritance, how could Quentin either recognize or fail to recognize—in the mirror of this unassuageably howling idiot—his own dark twin?

Cognition can take forever to become more than cognition. Quentin pores over this story, seeking the detail, the clue, that will unravel its mystery. I have already quoted the innocent detail that later ignites into illumination: "I [Rosa] was not there to see the two Sutpen faces this time—once on Judith and once on the negro girl beside her—looking down through the square entrance to the loft." So casually said by Rosa: Sutpen's face on the negro girl Clytie as well as his own daughter. Quentin's climactic trip to Sutpen's Hundred (occurring in narrative time at the beginning of the novel, but opened up and passed on to the reader only at the novel's end) lets him figure out the portent of that white-engendered dark face. "And she didn't tell you in the actual words," Shreve says about Quentin's seeing Clytie there, "nevertheless she told you, or at least you knew" (AA 289). At least you knew: if Sutpen could beget one black child, he could beget others. He could and did beget Charles Bon.

The murder finally takes on its meaning. The morganatic marriage only goes so far, not very far at all. The incest motive goes further, tormenting Henry for the four years of the war. Finally, though, there is miscegenation, and this barrier is nonnegotiable—Henry "thinking not what he would do but what he would have to do. Because he knew what he would do" (AA 292). Perhaps the book's brilliance is most at work here. *Absalom* must manage to *think through* something that its actors—once they know that the obstacle to marriage is miscegenation—are incapable of thinking about at all. *Absalom*'s strenuous withholding of information—the reasons for its circuitous movement through time—reveals its purpose. We are all but finished with the book when we learn that Bon is not just brother but black brother. Faulkner has suspended that discovery over the entire narrative, releasing it only in the penultimate pages. All previous interpretations of Bon's murder remain intact. But the racial motive is both the most decisive (the one that can command life-altering behavior) and the last Faulkner can supply. He must withhold it from Bon himself, from most of the other characters, and from the reader as well.

It must come last because he, we, and the others in the novel must experience Bon otherwise until the end. We internalize (as Henry does) the developing emotional value of his becoming a brother. We live inside his subjectivity as a man who does not know he is black. He figures it out, finally, because the refusal of acknowledgment he receives at the hands of his father tells him eventually, by process of elimination, who he has to be. He must be suffering from the one condition no white Southern patriarch *can* acknowledge: black blood. Finally it clicks into coherence. Sutpen himself long ago suffered the same searing illumination that Faulkner's tortured narrative technique springs upon Bon. Brutally refused entrance into the plantation's front door, the young Sutpen

> seemed to kind of dissolve and a part of him turn and rush back through two years they had lived there like when you pass through a room fast and look at all the objects in it and you turn and go back through the room again and look at all the objects from the other side and you find out you had never seen them before, rushing back through those two years and seeing a dozen things that had happened and he hadn't even seen them before. (AA 190)

Still the same, yet wholly different now. Likewise, the reader of *Absalom* stumblingly reads on, believing that the objects and others encountered are themselves—until later revealed as dark inversions when seen from "the other side." To read *Absalom* is to undergo a racial education that moves—over time—from cognition into tragic recognition.

"BUT THERE MUST HAVE BEEN LOVE": *GO DOWN, MOSES*

Blacks had hardly been the catapult for tragic recognition when he began writing fiction. Either absent from his earlier fiction or "unimpatient" decor within them, they had commanded no special attention. In *Light in August*, however, Faulkner had found his way into a realm where race mattered imperiously. It is as though he suddenly sat up in bed after a nightmare and asked himself: what would it feel like—to me—if I suddenly found myself to be one of them? To me: there was no question of what *they* might feel like. The novel didn't ask who (as a community living in segregated "freedman's" districts of every town in the South) they might be. No empathic entry into Southern blackness, virtually no blacks in the novel at all. This absence is ultimately telling, for it reveals what conditions Faulkner required to turn—for the first time seriously—to race relations in the South. Those conditions mandated that the one suffering from such relations be white—a man trapped in a weave of racial rumor about his identity at its core genetic level. The man had to be unable to know what blood ran in his veins. If this narrow optic radically limited Faulkner's vision of race, it simultaneously brought to focus an extraordinary insight. Beneath the surface confidence of Southern whites ran a racial insecurity bordering on hysteria. If a drop of black blood was thought to make a white person black, who might not unknowingly carry this toxic drop? No one could see the internal wreckage that drop would have wrought. Invisibly infected carriers might be anywhere, and they might not even know the illness they were bringing into the white community. Such anxiety might be enough to make many a white man in the segregated South have trouble going back to sleep, once he had sat bolt upright at three o'clock in the morning and wondered: what if I were black and didn't know it?

Racial hysteria, the insanity that overtakes white men in the South confronting their dark twin, served as Faulkner's entry point in *Light in August*. In *Absalom*, he would go further. Less violent than *Light in August*, *Absalom* extensively explored the prehistory of that putative drop. Suppose our nineteenth-century "white" brothers and sisters were already, ever since the genesis of the plantation design itself, infected carrriers of that drop of black blood? Suppose the foundation of the South's abiding dream—its plantation paradigm of wealth, civility, and achievement—were invisibly steeped in impure blood? Such blood would not only be pressing from outside to get inside that plantation's front door but also simmering inside and threatening to get outside. In a culture founded for over two centuries on racial relations at once intimate and barbaric, how could that drop of black blood *not* be already at work, subverting the meaning of the planterly dream? *Absalom* took Faulkner more time to write than *Light in August* not least because its reverberations went further: a racial malaise that had been gathering for over two hundred years, endemic to the slaveholding South. And not just a malaise. Because that drop was invisible—and, as Faulkner sometimes recognized as well, genetically meaningless—whites might embrace blacks (unidentified as such) as beloved siblings and offspring. They would be loved inside the family so long as they were thought to be white, though passionately repudiated from it once marked as black. The malaise manifested at the same time as a foredoomed love story.[9]

In 1938, flush (briefly) with money from MGM's purchase of film rights to *The Unvanquished* ($25,000), Faulkner purchased a 320-acre lot in the countryside named Greenfield Farm. He would later, in the post-Nobel years, insistently self-identify as a farmer. This was not just an identity he recurrently drew on to beg out of pressing engagements (as he would try in 1950 to beg out of the Stockholm trip to receive his Nobel Prize). It was also an abiding component of the person he had long imagined himself to be, perhaps ever since his childhood exposure to woods and wilderness.

Greenfield Farm demanded more agricultural expertise and managerial energy than he possessed or could afford to provide, so he put his brother Johncy in charge of running it. Against professional advice, he insisted on raising mules—and lost money doing so. Though Johncy ran the farm, Faulkner footed the bills and spent a good deal of time there as well. He came to know his black workers—including the familiar Uncle Ned—in more sustained and intractable ways. His role toward them was approaching that of the master of the plantation, and they were looking more like tenant farmers. Such would become, in *Go Down Moses* (1942), the fundamental roles played by the forty-three-year-old Roth Edmonds, frustrated landowner, and his wily black tenant farmer Lucas Beauchamp.

A vignette recounted by Faulkner's authorized biographer conveys something of the tenor of race relations on the farm and in the novel as well. It seems that Faulkner had unwisely bought a scrawny little bull called Black Buster. This bull soon became Uncle Ned's favorite, but was not much good at impregnating cows. So at considerable further expense, Faulkner bought a large pedigreed bull that answered better to these needs. As the Fourth of July (1938) approached, Faulkner told Ned to slaughter Black Buster so that they could at least (and for once) get something profitable out of him, in the form of tasty ribs. The master had proposed a noon barbecue to his friends and family; Black Buster would be the plat de résistance. Ned agreed to take care of the details. By noon the guests had arrived, the ribs and other dishes had been set out on the table, and the lunch was under way. In the midst of the delectable meal, Faulkner happened to glance toward the field where he saw—Black Buster. Startled, he looked at Ned and asked, "Who's that?" Ned responded, "that's Black Buster." "Then," looking at the meat roasting on the spit, Faulkner asked, "who's this? I thought I told you to kill Black Buster and I thought you told me you did." As Faulkner began to realize that he hadn't seen his pedigree bull for the past couple of days, Ned rose swiftly, answering in retreat, "Master, I calls them all Black Buster" (F 398). Such a story would have no place in either the brutal *Light in August* or the tragic *Absalom, Absalom!* but would fit perfectly into the wryly comic white master–black tenant shenanigans of *Go Down, Moses*.

A comic undertone runs through much of this novel, and its prehistory explains to some extent why. As often, Faulkner was out of money in 1940. He wrote Bob Haas at Random House that he desperately needed $10,000—$1,000 immediately and the rest in monthly installments. Haas helped as he could, but Faulkner's financial urgency seemed to outpace Haas's (or anyone else's) ability to pacify it for long. In this context,

Faulkner started to conceptualize *Go Down, Moses*. The new book must first of all be profitable. His working model for making it profitable was *The Unvanquished*, also composed (four years earlier) by his revising a cluster of previously published stories. Here he would do the same, trying to place the stories in the same high-paying popular magazine market. Thus he began, so to speak, with defective materials—stories written as potboilers and published (eight of them) in magazines as varied as *Harper's*, *Collier's*, the *Atlantic Monthly*, and the *Saturday Evening Post*. The problem before him—as he was the first to realize—was to make the novel itself greater than the sum of its parts ("stories about niggers," as he had characterized them to Haas [SL 124]). Almost miraculously, he succeeded in this, though an ineradicable residue of the stories' prehistory still lives in their racially insouciant tone. That tone—sometimes flawless but recurrently facile when not condescending—penetrates "Was" and "The Fire and the Hearth" (which together account for over a third of the book). Blacks on a working twentieth-century white-owned farm are portrayed as wily, lazy, and cleverer than their white master ever anticipates. Whenever they are not kept under strict supervision, they start to make trouble. As Roth (the frustrated, landowner) puts it to Lucas, "As soon as you niggers are laid by trouble starts" (67). The premise is clear. Black workers get away with murder, and all the burden is on the white landowners trying to keep them in line. Since there was no way Faulkner could remove this premise, he thought of something better. He would make it pay. And he would begin by using the perspective of an uncomprehending nine-year-old boy, Cass, to tell a story that took place years before his younger cousin, Ike, was even born.

Go Down, Moses opens in 1859 (a racially portentous year) with a merry chase. "Was" begins with two white bachelors—Cass's uncles Buck and Buddy McCaslin—rushing to recapture their runaway slave, Tomey's Turl. Turl is hotfooting it toward another plantation where his mate, Tennie, who is owned by Hubert Beauchamp, is forced to live apart from him. Casually operative already are two of slavery's disturbing features: runaway slaves and slaveholders' right to divide their slaves' families as they see fit. The most disturbing feature soon enters the narrative with equal casualness. Hubert, not about to make matters easier for the separated couple, refuses to have "that damn white half-McCaslin on his place even as a free gift" (GDM 7). This slave hunt is about two white McCaslins chasing their white "half-McCaslin" brother. But Buck and Buddy hardly think of either whiteness or fraternity when they regard Turl. When Buck hunts Turl incorrectly (there are rules for this sort of thing) and gets run over by him, he realizes his error: "Afterwards, Uncle Buck admitted that it was his own mistake, that he had forgotten when even a little child should have known: not to ever stand right in front of or right behind a nigger when you scare him; but always to stand to one side of him" (16). The story ends with the runaway slave recaptured and Tennie now set to join him by way of a tortuously complicated set of gambling wagers. Everyone in the story knows what a "nigger" is and how to hunt him. No reflections, no concession that anything strange is going on.

The next chapter, "The Fire and the Hearth," focuses on Lucas Beauchamp—of all the black men in Faulkner' work, the most intricately represented. Almost obsessively, Faulkner returns to Lucas's independent bearing: his "face which…was a composite of a whole generation of fierce and undefeated young Confederate soldiers" (GDM 91). Usually that face is haughtily inexpressive, and at all times its owner proudly dates himself back to his white grandfather, Lucius Quintus Carothers McCaslin. Moreover, Lucas's most riveting memories—focused on an encounter with Carothers's white descendant Zack—circulate around the enabling resources bequeathed by his grandfather. When Zack's wife was dying in childbirth, Lucas's wife, Molly, went to her bedside, to nurse the newborn baby (Roth). Molly remained at the big house for six months; Lucas would never know what roles she played there. Finally he could take it no longer. In a ballet-like ritual of challenge and counter-challenge—suffused with enmity and intimacy—Lucas confronts Zack in the bedroom, coming within an inch of taking Zack's life. At the ultimate moment, his gun misfires, the crisis ends, and Lucas returns home: "*Old Carothers,* he thought. *I needed him and he come and spoke for me*" (45, emphasis in the original). In calling Zack to account, Lucas drew precisely on what he had inherited from the imperious and unyielding progenitor. Does one hear a precursor of Faulkner's later claim that the black man "is competent for equality only in the ratio of his white blood"?

In dramatizing Lucas's remembered struggle—his standing up like a man, let the consequence be what it will—Faulkner compellingly represented a black man in distress. No longer picturesque racial décor, Lucas was granted a significant past. In that recalled scene, his chest heaved, his mind lurched, as he sought to confront the assault on his manhood. It comes as no surprise to learn that Faulkner added this scene when he revised the magazine version of these materials (*Collier's* would have had little interest in this flashback). More broadly, Faulkner wrote a black capacity for memory itself into *Go Down, Moses*—by way of revisions and with considerable consequences. The novel exits the brittle cleverness of current-day games, rising into a brooding sense of what has been cumulatively endured over time.

Ike McCaslin—Old Carothers's white grandson—functions as the central bearer of memories. But Lucas (the other grandson, Ike's "dark twin") is likewise bathed in the flow of time past—territory that had heretofore been reserved for Faulkner's privileged white figures. Like their author, these figures (and these alone) are granted the searing consciousness of their missteps and blunderings over time. Lucas's appeal for Faulkner lodges essentially in the temporal shadow he casts. Seen over decades of past time, he luminously harbors dignity, endurance, survival. Seen in the present alone, he appears at best as a wily black tenant farmer. At worst, he appears—so the chancellor's clerk angrily addresses him—as an "uppity nigger."

The next story, "Pantaloon in Black" speaks black distress more starkly—more starkly than Faulkner ever managed again. This story attends to the agony of one of Roth Edmonds's black tenants, Rider, whose wife has suddenly died. All but inarticulate, he says little; Faulkner writes his distress in bodily fashion. A powerful man, bristling with life-energies, Rider's very strength keeps him from bridging the distance between his pulsating anguish and his wife's unbreathing state. Dead and buried, she nevertheless suffuses the space of the cabin she tended during their two years of married life. Entering the cabin, he sees her there and tries to approach:

> "Mannie," he said. "Hit's awright. Ah aint afraid." Then he took another step. But this time as soon as he moved she began to fade. He stopped at once, not breathing again, motionless, willing his eyes to see that she had stopped too. But…she was fading, going. "Wait," he said, talking as sweet as he had ever heard his voice speak to a woman: "Den lemme go wid you, honey." But she was going. (GDM 106)

Faulkner focuses hypnotically on Rider's foredoomed moves: his attempt to drink himself into not-feeling, his running all night through the woods (as though he could bodily exorcise his grief), and finally his suicidal provocation of a white night watchman in a late-night poker game. Rider has long known of this man's cheating, but now he calls him on it. When the watchman goes for his gun, Rider swoops from behind his back the razor he always carries there. With the rhythmic power that has characterized all his bodily moves during the past twenty-four hours of distress, he slits the man's throat a second before the gun goes off. We next see him lynched on a black schoolhouse bell rope, murdered by the watchman's family and strung up for view.

The story then shifts focus to a bewildered white deputy talking to his wife, trying to explain what his work has been like for the last two days. Responsible for keeping Rider in jail, he has misread every sign of his prisoner's grief—perceiving only the unfeeling animal barbarity of niggers. The reader knows otherwise. "Lemme go wid you, honey," Rider had pleaded with the spirit of his dead wife. Finally he has succeeded in provoking whites to "help" him find his way there. "Hit look lack Ah just cant quit thinking," the deputy quotes Rider saying at the end—unable to get his breath in prison, unable to bear his widowed life. The deputy's inattentive wife hardly hears these words, and the deputy doesn't understand them as he recites them. But few words ever uttered in a Faulkner novel carry deeper resonance. In heavy black vernacular, they voice the distress the writer himself endured throughout his life, and was no more able than Rider to put to sleep with booze or other strategies. That distress—the anguish caused by *is*'s incapacity to restore, or forget, *was*—gave Faulkner his most compelling material; out of it he made his greatest art. The same distress he bestows on Rider.

Perhaps no single work of Faulkner is more widely reprinted than "The Bear," the centerpiece of *Go Down, Moses*. It is the finest hunting story Faulkner ever wrote—perhaps the finest in American literature. Centered on Ike McCaslin's quest for the legendary bear Old Ben, this story shows why—thanks to his experience of the wilderness—Ike chooses to relinquish his race-tarnished inheritance. Part 4 of "The Bear" goes inside Ike's memories so as to show what is at stake in his choice. It rehearses a debate in the plantation commissary between Ike and his older cousin Cass. Ike has turned twenty-one and is trying to explain to Cass why he must refuse his inheritance. Even more resonant, part 4 rehearses—through Ike and Cass—Faulkner's largest meditation on slavery and the Civil War that followed it. Finally, part 4 narrates Ike's attempt to repair some of the earlier wrong committed by his grandfather. As grandson, Ike comes to recognize himself in the mirror of race posed by the spectral history of his own family, and he cannot live with what he sees there.

"That damn white half-McCaslin," the strange but insouciant phrase in "Was," takes on in "The Bear" its delayed resonance. Hubert saying it so casually indicated that everyone knew that the runaway slave (Tomey's Turl) carried the blood of the white master, Carothers McCaslin. Faulkner does not provide specifics, but one assumes the following: Carothers McCaslin took as mistress the mulatto slave Eunice whom he had bought in 1807 in New Orleans. In 1810, Eunice bore a daughter, Tomasina—fathered

162 BECOMING FAULKNER

by Carothers, though married off to another slave, Thucydus (a common enough practice in antebellum times). Thus Tomasina's offspring Turl was widely recognized as the grandson of Carothers McCaslin—however "slave-like" the treatment that came his way. So Ike assumes as well, as he presses further (at age sixteen) upon ledgers kept for decades in the plantation commissary. Eventually, those yellowed pages begin to reveal their secret.

Ike's Uncle Buddy had noted there, some fifty years earlier, that Eunice "*Drownd in Crick Cristmas Day 1832.*" A little later appeared Uncle Buddy's ledger entry: "*Drownd herself.*" Incredulous, Buck responded two days later with another entry, "*Who in hell ever heard of a niger drownding him self.*" Undaunted, Buddy repeated his claim in a later entry: "*Drowned herself.*" Reading and rereading the ledger, Ike keeps thinking, "*But why? But why?*" Then a page later he comes upon this: "*Tomasina called Tomy Daughter of Thucydus @ Eunice Born 1810 dide in Child bed June 1833 and Burd.*" And following that ledger entry, this one: "*Turl Son of Thucydus @ Eunice Tomy born June 1833...Fathers will*" (GDM 198, emphasis in the original).

Illiterate, cryptic, unexplaining, yet—on reflection—these ledger fragments intimate a devastating story. Eunice did indeed drown herself in the creek, six months before her daughter Tomasina died while birthing her baby Terrel (Turl). Piecing the shards together and taking into account the portent of "fathers will," Ike imagines his way into their unspoken meaning. In 1810 Old Carothers impregnated Eunice, begetting a daughter named Tomasina; twenty-two years later, he impregnated Tomasina, begetting a son named Terrel. When Eunice grasped that her daughter was three months pregnant, and this by the man who was both her own lover and her daughter's father, she found her life no longer worth living: "he [Ike] seemed to see her actually walking into the icy creek on that Christmas day six months before her daughter's and her lover's (*Her first lover's* he thought. *Her first*) child was born, solitary, inflexible, griefless, ceremonial, in formal and succinct repudiation of grief and despair who had already had to repudiate belief and hope" (GDM 200, emphasis in the original).

Ancestral echoes, dark twins: Carothers McCaslin eerily echoes Colonel W. C. Falkner. Both men—imperious masters in the time of slavery— seemed likely to have taken mulatto mistresses, produced offspring, and then impregnated their own offspring. Tomey's Turl suddenly rises for Ike into uncontainable significance, becoming the marker of generations of white sexual abuse. "*Fathers will*": the phrase reverberates—a legal document, but more darkly a despotic power. Rather than acknowledge Turl openly, Carothers bequeathed him money in his will, leaving his sons Buck and Buddy to regulate the bequest. *"So I reckon that was cheaper than saying My son to a nigger he* [Ike] *thought. Even if My son wasn't but just two words. But there must have been love* he thought" (GDM 199, emphasis in the original). There must have been love, Ike has to believe, in the face of ledgers bleakly suggesting otherwise.

Turl never collected during his lifetime the $1,000 bequeathed to him in his father/grandfather's will. Apparently feeling implicated by Old Carothers's behavior, Buck and Buddy increased the legacy to $3,000 so that they could assign $1,000 apiece to the three children of Tomey's Turl and Tennie. One of those children, James, disappeared from view in 1885. Another, Fonsiba, left her white planterly family when a black man from the North came to claim her as his bride. Ike has by then recognized his own blood-complicity in his grandfather's acts of miscegenation and incest, and he is desperate to bestow the guilt money. But he can neither locate James nor accept Fonsiba's leaving her white family. A sense of white Southern entitlement—an urge to protect one's own blacks (one's "own" as intimacy and possession both)—fuels Ike's frustration. He remembers with bitterness the black Northerner casually walking into the commissary and demanding Fonsiba as his bride. "You dont say Sir, do you," an affronted Cass had replied. "To my elders, yes," the man had responded. He had come to notify Cass as the head of the family, not to beg for favors. Furious, Cass ordered him to "Be off this place by dark" (GDM 264)—the standard white Southern male's warning to uppity blacks. Thus Fonsiba departed with husband-to-be. Ike soon afterward sets out to find her, determined to bestow the $1,000: *"I will have to find her. I will have to. We have already lost one of them. I will have to find her this time"* (205, emphasis in the original).

He does find her. She and her husband are living on a bedraggled farm in Arkansas, in squalid conditions that epitomize the novel's criticism of Reconstruction practices. Fonsiba's Northern black husband knows nothing about farming—despite the government pension he clutched in his hand when he claimed her—and the glasses he wears lack lenses. Faulkner ungenerously allows those missing lenses to signal the hollowness of the man's pretense to culture. Ike lectures him sternly. The entire scene of desolation weighs on Ike as something "permeant, clinging to the man's very clothing and exuding from his skin itself, that rank stink of baseless and imbecile delusion" (GDM 206). "Rank stink"—this revealingly familiar phrase connotes centuries of racial prejudice about black uncleanliness. Just when we think that Faulkner is engaging in the most knee-jerk of Southern stereotypes, he turns the scene upside down. Ike pleads, "Fonsiba, Fonsiba. Are you all right?" In words that conclude the scene by making further argument irrelevant, she answers, "I'm free" (207).

An aftermath to "The Bear" remains: "Delta Autumn," a brooding narrative that somberly reconfigures the comic tone on which the novel opened. Faulkner revised an earlier version of "Delta Autumn" so that it would center on the old and fragile Ike McCaslin, attending perhaps his last hunt. The time is now the 1940s, the wilderness has receded another two hundred miles from Jefferson, a way of life is coming to an end. Yet Ike tries to remain ensconced in his innocent memories, lying on his cot unsleeping, thinking "there was just exactly enough of it [the wilderness]" (GDM 261) to last him out. And then the surprise: a woman the younger men have pointedly alluded to as the "doe" enters their campsite, approaching Ike's tent. A sullen Roth Edmonds has the night before given Ike an envelope for her, no explanations offered. He had no intention of being present himself. Uncle Ike was to hand her the envelope if she made an appearance. The woman enters his tent, carrying an infant in her arms. She has been Roth's mistress, and she is to be repudiated and paid off rather than acknowledged. As she talks to Ike, she reveals that she knows the entire history of his family. Speaking of her own family, she tells Ike that, to support themselves, they used to take in washing:

> "Took in what?" he said. "Took in washing?" He sprang, still seated even, flinging himself backward onto one arm, awry-haired, glaring. Now he understood what it was she had brought into the tent with her….the pale lips, the skin pallid and dead-looking yet not ill, the dark and tragic and foreknowing eyes. *Maybe in a thousand or two thousand years in America,* he thought. *But not now! Not now!* He cried, not loud, in a voice of amazement, pity, and outrage: "You're a nigger!" "Yes," she said. "James Beauchamp— you called him Tennie's Jim though he had a name—was my grandfather." (GDM 266, emphasis in the original)

Maybe in a thousand or two thousand years, but not now! Go slow now! The act of miscegenation—initiated by Old Carothers 130 years earlier and once again enacted within the same family, embodied seven generations later in the form of that sleeping infant—stares out at him. Ike cannot at first acknowledge the dark twin he sees in the mirror she provides. He urges her to go North and find a black man, anyone other than his great-nephew Roth. Her difference from his white line is too great. "Took in washing": from antebellum days through the Memphis garbage strike that cost Martin Luther King his life in 1968, black people have been cleaning up white people's dirt, and they have been treated like dirt while doing it. Except that at the same time that she cannot be him, she is undeniably his. Tennie's Jim—the offspring of the long-ago mating of Tomey's Turl and Tennie Beauchamp that was set up in "Was"—did not disappear into oblivion in 1885. Over the subsequent decades, beyond narration, he sustained a name of his own, James Beauchamp, and a life of his own, too. In 1940, he reemerged in *Go Down, Moses*—at once the grandfather of the "doe" and Ike's long-lost kin. Even as Ike backs away in recoil, his hand reaches out to touch hers: "the gnarled, bloodless, bonelight bone-dry old man's fingers touching for a second the smooth young flesh where the strong old blood ran after its long lost journey back to home. 'Tennie's Jim,' he said. 'Tennie's Jim'" (GDM 267). The story of repudiation is also—inextricably—a story of family and love.

In all of Faulkner's portrayals of relations between blacks and whites, there are few moments more moving than this one. Centering on a frail old white man reconnecting—in his mind and through his fingers—with his long-absent black kin, the scene is unashamedly paternal, but it is not condescending. This startling connection transforms the woman before him and her infant into beings at once beyond acknowledgment yet his own. He ends by giving her not just the envelope of money Roth has left but also General Compson's ancient hunting horn. Henceforth the wilderness hunt—so hierarchical in its arrangements of race and gender—will take on in Ike's memories blackness as well. The recognitions he has been forced to undergo in this scene are—like most genuine recognitions—unwanted and beyond accommodation. He has lived too long, his innocence painfully ending before his life does.

Something similar is true for his creator as well. In his most compelling fictions of race, Faulkner recognized himself—uncomfortably, guiltily, responsibly—in the mirror of black distress at which he gazed. Paternal, not paternalistic. He knew he was complicit—that his entire life in the South entailed ineffaceable complicities. The solution to the race dilemma in America, should one ever be put into practice, would not be proposed by him. Rather than solutions, his work—at its best—would act as an unnerving dark twin intimating to its white reader: "yes, you, too, are in this mirror, you will need to find a way to live with yourself insofar as you see yourself here." *Light in August* and *Absalom, Absalom!* and *Go Down, Moses* constitute the most capacious mirror Faulkner was able to construct. It is not a magic mirror, and nothing we see reflected in it is likely to give much cause for satisfaction. But none of his white peers in the twentieth century even attempted to see—and say—what he saw when he gazed into it.

He would write once again about race relations. And he would seek to play his part—confusedly and at some risk to himself—in the civil rights turmoil that was already brewing. His last race-focused novel, *Intruder in the Dust*, appeared in 1948. Its keen (and easily decipherable) attention to contemporary racial agitation doubtless played a part in his being awarded the Nobel Prize two years later. But that novel's stance moved from paternal to paternalistic. Its plot was simple. Lucas Beauchamp, now an old man charged with a murder he did not commit, had to be saved from lynching. Faulkner ensured that it would take white people cooperating together to save him. Lucas's efforts in his own behalf were to be quietly stymied (he remained locked up in jail). Thus the motion and emotion in this novel belonged to the Southern whites who labored to clear him. Not that this number was large. Lucas's rescue turned on a pair of boys and an old lady who refused to sit by and see injustice done. Because Faulkner was too honest to propose that the larger adult white South wanted anything other than to lynch this "uppity nigger," the novel's strategy for liberating Lucas emerged as more than a little sentimental. On one matter, Faulkner was crystal clear. Lucas's dilemma was not one in which well-meaning Northern outsiders had any business interfering. Lucas's defense lawyer, Gavin Stevens, referred to his silent client throughout as Sambo. One wonders how much is gained by freeing a black man only on condition that he continue to answer to Sambo. Once again, looking forward and looking backward merge as incoherently fused dimensions of Faulkner's racial imagination.

Intruder, at any rate, was commercially successful (its first several weeks of sale outpaced even *Sanctuary*'s record). MGM not only paid $50,000 for screen rights but went on to produce the movie. Much of it was shot in Oxford during the spring of 1949—Faulkner helped the director, Clarence Brown, cast local acquaintances in several bit parts—and the world premiere would take place in Oxford that fall. The town appreciated the business generated by the several weeks' work required to shoot the film, whatever their private thoughts about their most celebrated citizen. As the filming hullabaloo approached its end, Estelle decided that a fitting conclusion would be a party at Rowan Oak itself. There was only one hitch. A Puerto Rican named Juano Hernandez had been signed on to play the principal role in the film—that of Lucas Beauchamp. Faulkner had even helped Hernandez work on a black accent that would sound more like Mississippi than the islands. Such professional cooperation was one thing, but attendance at a Rowan Oak party was another. Hernandez was himself presentable, but if the Faulkners invited him, they would have to invite his Negro hosts in Oxford. After some soul-searching, they determined they could not do that. "So the whole crew, with the exception of the portrayer of Lucas Beauchamp, came out to Rowan Oak" (F 503). We recall an earlier arc of nonrecognition launched by the closing of a door in young Thomas Sutpen's face. Trash like him were to use the back door of a white plantation. A kindred arc repeats itself in 1949 at Rowan Oak. *"Maybe happen is never once,"* Faulkner had written in *Absalom*. Whatever images he saw in that mirror posed by Juano Hernandez's black hosts, they did not figure for him as dark twins deserving acknowledgment.

CHAPTER 4

IN SEARCH OF SANCTUARY

ROUGH SPAS: FAULKNER AND ALCOHOL

He was not unconscious the whole time. Specific details would flare into focus, then flee as swiftly as they had come. All he knew for sure was that he could not move, though he could not remember why. Where was he anyway? Sprawled out—half sitting, half lying—he pressed tentatively on his pounding head, trying to frame this moment of pure distress. An image arose in his mind: he was in New York, at his favorite hotel, the Algonquin. He had come here to complete the contracts with Random House for *The Unvanquished*: which meant that it was November 1937. He had come here to forget something as well—he suddenly knew what that was—but he had less luck there. Meta Carpenter was who he wanted to forget, who now appeared in his mind's eye with aching clarity. He concentrated again, his screen of consciousness widened. Depressed—he had his reasons for it—he had been drinking steadily the night before. He had drifted from bar to bar, then seen no need to stop once he returned to his room. He vaguely remembered the sensation of booze sliding down his throat, the sought-after numbness it radiated. But how had that moment led to this one? Straining once more, he got hold of another image. The last thing he had done was to make his way into the bathroom and settle onto the toilet seat, bottle in hand. Time for one more swig before bed.

Bright sunlight bore down on him, and the room was unaccountably full of cold, moving air. A glance downward showed him he was wearing only his undershorts. Looking up, he saw an open bathroom window. Had he imagined last night that he was still in Mississippi, where on going to bed he would often open the window a crack, even in winter? Then he recognized the noise he had been hearing for some time now: the hiss-ing sound of a steam pipe, just behind him, his back resting on it. He had passed out in this bathroom. His mind, still whirling, permitted larger oases of lucidity. He realized suddenly that he was in the wrong place: he had no business lying against that pipe. He could tell from its sound how hot it had to be, but his back—which ought to know—had reported no signals of pain. It didn't even hurt now. How long had he been in this position? When would he find the energy and focus needed to get up again? Like Joe Christmas caught in the dietitian's room in *Light in August*—lying flat out in his own vomit and realizing that, for better and surely for worse, he was completely in others' hands—Faulkner waited for someone to come. Eventually someone always did. This was a hell of a way to begin the day.

The moment is emblematic in its self-destructiveness, though its gravity is new. He had been drinking heavily—and occasionally passing out—for over twenty years. But up to now he had been lucky enough to avoid New York hotel steam pipes, as well as other complications linked to a lifetime of boozing. Some time later that morning—minutes? hours?—he heard knocking, at first cautious and then louder. He could not move, and he had nothing to say, so he waited. Within a few minutes Jim Devine—Random House fellow writer and boon drinking companion—had managed to get the door opened. Devine found him there, moved him gingerly, then gasped. The wound inflicted on his lower back by the steam pipe must have looked pretty alarming. Though it didn't hurt yet, Faulkner had done him-self real damage this time. The sought-after numbness that the booze pro-vided was at the same time a dangerous abdication, an invitation to further troubles. These third-degree burns (the size of a man's palm) would even-tually require several skin grafts—grafts that in turn became infected and never entirely took. His sleeping, not good in the best of times, was all but impossible for the next few months, and his lower back would never forgive how cavalierly he had treated it. The doctor that Devine took Faulkner to stared at his patient's back, then at the patient himself, and asked, "Why do you do this?" Grimacing with incipient pain but showing no other emo-tion, eyes hooded by emphatic curved brows, Faulkner responded, "Because I like to" (F 387).

Abdication: such excessive drinking—revealing his incapacity to man-age himself—led to his need to be managed by others. In this instance, Jim Devine not only nursed him through the worst of his convalescence, but (urged by Bob Haas) accompanied him by train to Oxford, once Faulkner was well enough to leave New York. Hal Smith had played a similar chaperone role at the Virginia Writers' Conference in 1931. Later, both Bob Haas and Saxe Commins of Random House would more than once find themselves drafted into the service of managing their self-destructive genius. Malcolm Cowley occasionally stepped in as well, to play the role of nurse-manager in the late 1940s and early 1950s. Joan Williams and then Jean Stein inherited something of the same responsibilities later. In Hollywood during the 1940s, his friend and fellow scriptwriter "Buzz" Bezzerides recurrently took on this job.

In addition to these caretakers, there were the various black servants Faulkner would employ to drive for him and tend to domestic needs. Nor is this to take into account the policy adopted by larger institutions that occasionally sponsored him (like the State Department): to make sure that potential crisis managers would be on hand whenever Faulkner served as an unofficial cultural ambassador during the 1950s. He had become widely identified as a man who required handlers, and he recognized himself in that mirror. For some time now he had been casting himself in that role. To an annoyed Hal Smith he had written (in January 1932)—after one of his hurriedly summoned managers had persuaded him to part with some unpublished poems—"I'm sorry....goddam me for getting mixed up with it and goddam you for sending me off...in the shape I was in. I don't think it will happen again. But if I should do so, for God's sake find Ben [Wasson] and turn me on to him next time" (SL 55). If I mess up again, "turn me on to" a more trustworthy manager. The stance is that of a self-accepting *ingénu*—a man who sees himself as a receptive "me" rather than an active "I." Such a man cannot be expected to take care of himself in intricate situations: his calling as writer of genius preempts the responsibilities that normally go with adulthood.

Convalescence after the 1937 Algonquin disaster was slow. He was unable to keep to his commitments in the next week or so—including an emotionally fraught lunch with Meta Carpenter and her new husband, the gifted German pianist Wolfgang Rebner. She had recently introduced the two men; she was intent on them liking each other. Faulkner knew only too well that Rebner had become her husband because he himself had refused to go through the distress—divorce from Estelle and separation from his daughter, Jill—required to step into that role. His back by now was torturing him; he was not up to seeing the Rebners together at this moment. Meta would have to understand. But she didn't understand, and his failure to show up at the restaurant sent her into panic. She rushed (with Rebner in tow) to the Algonquin and then up to his room. Like Devine earlier, she knocked softly, then loudly, then managed to get the door open. She found him lying naked on the bed, barely able to move, his body reeking with burn medication. Rebner looked on at a distance, nonjudgmentally. Meta and Faulkner stared at each other, then he mumbled, "I started drinking....You know why" (ALG 224).

Drinking had become a sort of rough spa meant to provide sanctuary—a place where no one else could follow, an attempt to distance himself from the unmanageable stresses of his life. The foregoing vignette reveals a number of the elements motivating Faulkner's dependence on alcohol. Three places are here involved—Hollywood (Meta's setting), New York (his publishing center), and Oxford (home: the opposite, in different ways, of both other places). Three people are involved as well: Meta (his mistress, his single chance at successful love) silhouetted against Estelle and Jill (his now-rejected wife, whom he would divorce if he could, and his precious daughter, whom he would lose if he left Estelle). The elements that come together to launch a bout of uncontrolled drinking can be reshuffled. Sometimes such drinking is called forth by the near-hysterical rush of feeling set loose in him by the completing of a novel. Sometimes it erupts as a means for negotiating (i.e., avoiding) encounters that raise his anxiety level beyond tolerance: a group of professors and writers discussing "southern letters," a major New York interview for discussing race relations in America. Sometimes it occurs for reasons no one—including Faulkner himself—can fathom. But it does not occur as mere bodily event, as the predictable reenactment of an illness—alcoholism—with no psychological profile. That "diagnosis" would make Faulkner's chemical dependence essentially the same as anyone else's: alcohol calls the shots, not the profile of the alcoholic. It omits the intricate algebra of this troubled man's encounters with the world.[1] In what follows, I argue that alcohol provides a revealing window into Faulkner's psychological and social makeup.

Alcohol penetrates to Faulkner's private core as a human being. But several aspects of its appeal locate more broadly outside him—as dimensions of a larger (and typically masculine) history of family, region, and country. Male Falkners had been drinking excessively, and being dragged to clinics to dry out, long before William was born. Colonel W. C. Falkner was an inveterate drinker; legends of his alcoholic exploits were passed on to his great-grandson. As for the Young Colonel's extravagance, Faulkner could draw on both recounted stories and personal experience. He remembered the Buick/brick/bank vignette as though it had happened to him, and long-ago afternoon séances with the charming but irascible and often sodden old man remained in his mind. Faulkner had seen a good deal of his grandfather in those early years; Murry's quarrel with J. W. T. was never his. Finally, his father himself was widely known in Oxford as a "mean drunk"—one all too likely to move from intoxication to violence. As well, Faulkner was unlikely to forget those vivid instances of Murry being hustled off by Maud to take the "Keeley Cure." The boys were brought along, so they could recognize the evils of alcohol (and—this part unspoken—witness at pedagogic length the degradation of their father). The logic was inescapable and, for Faulkner, perfectly normal. Men in his family drank to excess—all of his brothers had trouble with alcohol as well. Wrought into the fiber of their identity, alcohol was their tacitly affirmed way of (not) coping.

That notion of manhood-and-alcohol went beyond Falkners. It partook more broadly of a Southern male mystique—one not limited to the South but prevalent there. Southern boys (long before Faulkner, all during his youth, and during mine as well some forty-five years later) often learned to drink excessively, early on. Faulkner not only stole from his grandfather's cache of whiskey while working in his Oxford bank, during his late teens, but was already engaging in sustained bouts of drinking two or three years earlier. He did not, as a young man, gain the sobriquet of town drunk without having put in some effort. More speculatively, one can say that many Southern men sought, and found, a haven of male camaraderie by way of drink. The shared bottle of booze was a talisman allowing them to secede from the world of womenfolk and adult responsibilities—to declare once more their untamed independence. "We don't want him tame," Sam Fathers says of the wild dog, Lion, that eventually takes down the great bear, Old Ben, and forfeits his life in doing so (*Go Down, Moses*). There are few values more abidingly lodged in Faulkner than the desire to remain untamed. Throughout his life, he would refuse to compromise, come to terms—as though doing so would amount to caving in.

Alcohol-soaked behavior stands out as a salient dimension of Faulkner's rebellious teens and twenties. The forays with Phil Stone to Clarksdale, Memphis, and the Gulf Coast; the gambling ventures and speakeasies with Reno De Vaux; the heavy drinking with Sherwood Anderson's New Orleans coterie: these experiences unfolded as rituals of male bonding as much as they embodied a deliberate intent to flout the law. It is as though early on in Faulkner's psyche, the law began to take the shadowy form of a humorless judgmental female who said No. It's not hard to see Maud Falkner lurking behind this figure, as well as admirable Jenny DuPre in *Flags in the Dust* and odious Mrs. Compson in *The Sound and the Fury*. Such older women seem to have accepted the social decree to abide by the rules and be grown up, but boys—and then men—in the South liked to escape by getting drunk. It was a sanctioned form of playing hooky. Faulkner did not refuse to go past the eleventh grade for nothing.

In addition, there was the influence of Prohibition. Getting hold of liquor was already an enchanting notion for underage boys together on a night out. It became doubly alluring when federal law mandated that the mere possession of liquor could land you in jail. To the risk of purchasing it was added the risk of drinking it. One could end up unknowingly with "Old Jake," a villainous rum-based concoction that often paralyzed its drinkers.[2] And a range of entertaining narratives attached to illicit booze: what it was composed of, where it originated, the travails undergone in transporting it to the places of purchase and consumption. To engage in such activities was to enter the romance of law-breaking, to show oneself a risk-taker among others fraternally bonded by the same daring. Thanks to Prohibition, drinking excessively—under dangerous conditions—became for many men a normal expression of independence.

Finally, there was for Faulkner the decades-long ritual of hunting in the Delta. As early as his midteens, he had joined Phil Stone to participate in General Stone's annual November bear and deer hunting expedition. Each year he looked forward to renewing this ceremony. It confirmed his sense of himself as a woodsman in the female-free company of other woodsmen, as well as in relation to the wilderness and its creatures, rather than an impecunious youth yet to accept a place in the labor force. Those two weeks in the big woods were amply lubricated by sustained nighttime drinking, during which the pleasures of the day, memories of the past, and expectations of the future would find their way into men-speech. As Faulkner put it in *Go Down, Moses*,

> the best game of all, the best of all breathing and forever the best of all listening, the voices quiet and weighty and deliberate for retrospection and recollection and exactitude....There was always a bottle present, so that it would seem to him [Ike McCaslin] that those fine fierce instants of heart and brain and courage and wiliness and speed were concentrated and distilled into that brown liquor which not women, not boys and children, but only hunters drank. (GDM 140–1)

But this sanctuary of retreat from women and domestic responsibilities could not last forever. A heavy bout of drinking during a hunting trip in late 1940 ended for him in unconsciousness and something alarmingly like kidney seizure or a perforated ulcer. Frightened, the other hunters rushed Faulkner home, where he soon recovered. He would continue for the next decade and longer to participate in the November Delta hunts, but his heart seemed less in it, and his drinking got increasingly out of control.

The first hospitalization for alcohol abuse had occurred in June 1936, at Wright's Sanatorium in Byhalia, Mississippi. Wright's would also, twenty-six years later, be the locus of his last hospitalization for drinking—and his sudden death by coronary one day after he was admitted (July 6, 1962). Between these two hospitalizations were too many others to recount. One of his critics reckons that by the 1950s, Faulkner was undergoing hospitalization as often as every three months.[3] The cluster of underlying reasons for his alcoholism probably never altered much, but no form of therapy made any lasting difference. Such therapies ranged from injection into the body of chemicals designed to make alcohol repugnant to the system (the Keeley Cure) to electroshock treatment and psychoanalytic sessions. None of it succeeded in separating Faulkner from the bottle. Rough spas: he seems to have believed, at the deepest level of his being, that he *needed* periodically to drink himself into oblivion. It was his chosen way of shaking off anxiety, as a wet dog shakes off water. When younger, he would emerge from these binges refreshed, even energized, and ready to return to his commitments—as though he had drained the battery all the way, and it was now being effectively recharged. For the last twenty years of his life, he tolerated the booze less and less well, though he indulged in it with the same frequency.

His wrestling with friends and family who sought to keep him from alcohol could seem comic if it weren't laden with pathos. Here is Buzz Bezzerides' account of trying, in Hollywood in late 1944, to get Faulkner to stop. The two of them were in Faulkner's rented rooms, and he was already well on his way to oblivion. Bezzerides' first ploy was to threaten to cut off the supply. He left the room, and on returning found copies of all of Faulkner's novels lined up on the coffee table and autographed for Buzz. "Now will you give me a drink?" Faulkner pleaded. Remembering that a doctor had once mentioned that excessive drinking could bring on heart trouble, Bezzerides changed tack and appealed to Faulkner not to "go that way" (F 461). When he returned to the room a few minutes later, Faulkner was nowhere to be seen, and two bookshelves were bare. Bewildered, Bezzerides rushed to the porch, where he glimpsed Faulkner some distance away, struggling to heave two large sacks full of books up a steep hill. "Bill, what are you doing?" he cried. Through gritted teeth Faulkner answered,

"I want to see if I've got a bad heart or not." Desperate now, the athletic Bezzerides sprinted toward Faulkner, gathered him in his arms, and headed toward his car. He was taking his friend to the hospital. Apparently understanding Bezzerides' intentions, Faulkner twisted wildly in his arms. "Bill, what are you trying to do?" the overwrought Bezzerides screamed. "I'm trying to get down," Faulkner answered. They both stopped, looked at each other, and broke into hysterical laughter.

His stance toward alcohol was sometimes more casual. When Dave Hemphill, a Hollywood acquaintance in early 1936, grasped the gravity of Faulkner's boozing, he asked incredulously, "Bill, how can you keep this up?" Faulkner's reply, recycled in various situations for decades, varied but little: "Dave, there's a lot of nourishment in an acre of corn" (F 364). As he entered his fifties, he was saying this mantra less, and ending up in hospitals more. His plight had become desperate by August 1952. He had suffered a number of serious riding falls that spring and summer, producing two compression fractures. A few months later he injured his back again—while sailing—and X-rays showed five compression fractures (some of them probably dating much further back). He was suffering convulsive seizures as well. At a doctor's suggestion of a spinal tap he fled as usual—he had a lifelong distrust of the medical establishment—and holed up in Rowan Oak. By then he looked so ravaged that even Estelle—inured to seeing him in states of alcoholic disrepair—panicked. She summoned Random House's Saxe Cummins to come down from New York for emergency help. Cummins came and managed to get Faulkner readmitted into the Gartley-Ramsay psychiatric hospital in Memphis. Writing home about his incapacitated author, Cummins said: "He mumbles incoherently and is totally incapable of controlling his bodily functions. This is more than a case of acute alcoholism. It is a complete disintegration of a man" (WFSH 285).

There remains a final vignette perhaps sadder than all the others. Jill Faulkner told this one, culled from a reservoir of painful childhood memories. ("Given his independent personality," she once said with considerable restraint, "he shouldn't have burdened himself with a family" [WFSH 294].) As one of her childhood birthdays approached, she saw her father moving toward a binge. Such binges, she knew better than most, typically lasted from a few days to a couple of weeks. Faulkner would consume bottle after bottle in his bedroom—dressed only in underwear and uninterested in eating—and would not stop until ready to stop. Alarmed, Jill begged him to hold off until after her party. Hearing this plea once too often, Faulkner told her, "No one remembers Shakespeare's children." Perhaps, but Faulkner's child remembered that zinger—whether her father did or not—and I heard her cite it in a TV interview some two decades later. Faulkner's tenderness toward his daughter was demonstrable and deep, but she grew up a troubled child, in the shadow of an unpredictable and (often) unapproachable father. (As she told one biographer, she "ached for mediocrity" [294].) When in 1954 Jill met her husband-to-be, Paul Summers, she was enraptured to learn how Summers had responded on hearing of her famous father. "Who's he?" Summers had said—a remark that elicited from Jill an instant conviction: "he's for me" (294).

No single cause emerges as the key to Faulkner's abuse of alcohol. A chorus of contributing motives—all of them dimensions of his encounter with the world—cooperate, increasing his susceptibility to this disease.[4] Hypersensitive from childhood on, Faulkner toughened himself as he could. At an early age he knew himself destined to write, but he knew as well that Southern culture viewed writing as a sissified vocation appropriate for women. Malcolm Cowley—who came to know Faulkner well during the later 1940s—was alert to this cultural dynamic. He saw that to withstand his fellow white Southerners' dismissive incomprehension, Faulkner had had to overcultivate the resources of "pride, will power, and tough-hided indifference" (FCF 167). Faulkner remained a loner who never confided easily in others—including those he loved: his wife, his mother, his daughter, his siblings, his mistresses. Confession of any sort seems to have been torture to him: an exposure of his being. His extensive letter to the world was indirect and indirectly signed, via a lifetime of stories and novels. This virtually visceral reticence was one reason why later sessions of psychoanalysis (in New York in the 1950s) not only failed but were offensive. No one was entitled to know what was going on inside him—not that he always knew either. But this he did know: it was himself against the "sinister gods," and they held the better cards.

Faulkner was unprepared for experience as it actually arrived. At the crucial juncture with Estelle—to elope or not to elope—he didn't so much decide against it as found himself unable to decide for it. She seems to have been ready to take the leap. What emerges with increasing emphasis are the lineaments of the "untimely" man explored earlier—the man on whom "they stopped the war," the man who married (too late) the woman he had failed to marry at the right time, the man who couldn't fly a plane but pretended he could, who hadn't seen action in the Great War but limped and lied to persuade others otherwise. He would be "a figure in the world"—the "figure" he saw when he envisaged his own identity—but "the Ones who set up the loom" seem to have determined otherwise. Conflicting impulses, a penchant for Keatsean dream scenarios, an incapacity to accommodate emergent realities, the intransigent difficulty of writing *A Fable* (he spent a decade trying to get control over it): all these contributed, during the 1940s and early 1950s, to an acutely troubling gap between what he was and what he wanted to be.

Faulkner's stumbling descended more broadly from a shared cultural malaise. A Southerner whose regional ideals had been decapitated ever since 1865, Faulkner dreamed backward, not forward. His dreams took the form of negative sanctuaries, holding patterns, attempted stays against the pell-mell forward movement of his life. A primary model for the domestic dignity he sought to maintain—as a bulwark against rampant, profit-driven American "progress"—was antebellum largesse. He wanted to display the valor and courage of his military progenitor—Colonel W. C. Falkner—and he wanted to inhabit the big house (Rowan Oak) built in antebellum times. Eventually, he would purchase the Bailey woods (neighboring his property) as well as Greenfield Farm. As he saw it, a Southerner was meant to be a rural (Jeffersonian) figure—one requiring an expansive mirror of land and animals to reflect his proper identity. A life of Southern graciousness should follow, enabled by a retinue of black maids and butlers, punctuated by ceremonial hunting in the big woods. As head of the household, Faulkner took on the expenses of his extended family. Such responsibilities defined the master as one who paid incumbent bills without evasion or negotiation downward.

Even as he played this role honorably, he bitterly recognized its incompatibility with his artistic calling. To Bob Haas he wrote in 1940: "Beginning at the age of 30, I, an artist, a sincere one and of the 1st class, who should be free even of his own economic responsibilities and with no moral conscience at all, began to become the sole, principal and partial support—food, shelter, heat, clothes, medicine, kotex, school fees, toilet paper and picture shows—of my mother...brother and his wife and two sons, another brother's widow and child, a wife of my own and two step children, my own child; I inherited my father's debts and his dependents, white and black without inheriting yet from anyone one inch of land or one stick of furniture or one cent of money" (SL 122). A footloose and unshaven maverick artist (beholden to no one) on the one hand, an antebellum paterfamilias (responsible for everyone) on the other: Faulkner awkwardly straddled these opposed stances. He had learned the rebellious bohemianism in Oxford during his teens, and then perfected it later in New Orleans, New

York, and abroad. He had been absorbing the requirements of noblesse oblige ever since his mother's milk and the childhood vignettes of Old South civility and rectitude. A maverick artist without income—who is at the same time a married gentleman with costly notions of propriety—is a man under considerable stress.

He drank to forget his defections as husband, son, father, uncle, and citizen of the South—roles he both accepted and submitted to ruthless critique. Like Jason Compson and Gail Hightower laboring furiously to escape something inescapable—themselves—so Faulkner grasped (even as he refused to know) that his forays into sanctuary were doomed. "Truth is the constant thing," he would say in a 1955 interview in Japan, "it's what man knows is right and that when he violates it, it troubles him…and he'll try to escape from the knowledge of that truth in all sorts of ways, in drink, drugs, various forms of anaesthesia, because he simply cannot face himself" (LG 145). "The human heart in conflict with itself," so Faulkner declared in his Nobel Prize speech (1950), is the core concern of great literature. It was no less the conflict gnawing at his own core.

He may also have been drinking because of professional anxiety. His big book—*A Fable*—was stalled. Its snail-paced composition would menace for over a decade his sense of artistic identity. Critics have marveled at how Faulkner had conceived, by 1930, most of the materials that would flower into novels during the next three decades: *Go Down, Moses* (1942) leading to *Intruder in the Dust* (1948); *Sanctuary* (1931) followed by *Requiem for a Nun* (1951); *The Hamlet* (1940) inaugurating the Snopes trilogy—*The Town* (1957) and *The Mansion* (1959). Less often noted is that, in the 1940s and 1950s, Faulkner generated little that was genuinely *new*—except for *A Fable* (1954). It would be hard to overestimate the dreams and anxieties that accumulated for over a decade during the stop-and-start composing of this novel. Deep down, as he conceded more than once, he knew that the book—his major new departure—was in trouble. What did the difficulty getting it written mean, if not that it went obscurely against the bent of his own genius? I shall return to the strange intensity—the rhetorical insistence mounting at times to a deafening roar—of Faulkner's work between 1948 and 1954 (*Intruder, Requiem, A Fable*). For now the point is clear. The longer this belated novel took him to write, the more it had to become his *Moby Dick* or *War and Peace*.[5] However wistfully he spoke of its promise, it comes as no surprise that, faced with its unending unfinishedness, he took to drink.

Finally, though, the distress sending him with rising frequency to the bottle may have arisen most from emotional needs. These had been thwarted ever since his disastrous marriage in 1929 to Estelle. "I started drinking…You know why," he had muttered to Meta Carpenter Rebner in his Algonquin room in November 1937. Those cryptic words suggest that burn-sick and booze-sick and heart-sick were fused together in him, and that Meta serves as a key for exploring all three.

META

He met her in Hollywood in December 1935, one of the most fraught periods of his life. Dean's crash had occurred just a month earlier. He was trying to complete *Absalom,* to survive guilt for his brother's death, and to make enough Hollywood money to gain control over his debt. Meta was eleven years younger, slender, attractive, demure, and Southern. She was Howard Hawks's script girl—as he would later, in a different sense, become Hawks's screenplay guy—and her Mississippi provenance meant much to him. Thousands of miles from home, he missed his region—and especially his infant daughter. He felt that he had no respectable reason for being in California. It was only and always about the money. Meta's shared background and mannerisms charmed him: a Southern oasis in the great Babylonian desert. But in a deeper sense, she offered no oasis of difference. His affair with her—though it might have happened elsewhere—took on its precise contours in Hollywood. Hollywood *existed* as the timeless, place-less stage set for launching the heart's longings and liabilities. No less, the relationship with Meta was doomed because it happened in Hollywood.

"A loving gentleman," she called him in the title of her 1976 memoir, written fourteen years after his death, almost twenty-five after they had last seen each other. The title is both sentimental and accurate. "Miss Meta," "m' honey," "dear one," "ma'am": these were the courtly, distancing terms he used for addressing her. Though mannered, they exude his delight in her presence, his Southern appreciation of this charming woman. His respect for her never failed—she responded to it from the beginning—and it was in keeping with his need to idealize her as a woman on a pedestal, his young maiden. "The idealization of me as a girl far too young for him was to last for a number of years," she wrote. "I never protested, and my acceptance of his vision of me as a maiden nourished his fantasy" (ALG 78). As though she were Estelle as Estelle had been meant to be, Meta opened up, for him, a hermetic space of fulfillment at once erotic and sublime.

Her bared body aroused him; at the same time he wanted to know only certain things about that body. At their first dinner together (after his assiduous courtship that December in 1935) she noted how repelled he was by nearby diners consuming their meal. "There's something about human mastication that's downright unattractive" (ALG 35), he explained to her. As the courtship developed into an affair during the early months of 1936, and their physical intimacy deepened, his squeamishness about the body's basic functions struck her more forcefully. He would run water in the bathroom to muffle the sound whenever he urinated or defecated and she was nearby—a delicacy that touched and amused her. It also strengthened her awareness that he was sequestering the two of them into a rarefied love-space that had room for little else. Others were not to enter. "Bill had placed me in a bubble," she wrote, "and we were using up the air in it; one day we would not be able to breathe" (67). But in his mind, where would ideal lovers live, if not in a Keatsean world of bliss beyond the mundane needs of eating and breathing and socializing? He was a troubadour courting his lady; she was to be his alone.

Six years earlier, his world had come crashing down when a married and possessed Estelle had been superposed on an earlier and unpossessed Estelle. The two images were radically incompatible, and the later one did not so much annihilate the earlier one as exile it to a space in his mind where it would remain compelling and unrealizable. Their 1929 honeymoon was in many respects a disaster; by 1933 they might not have been sleeping together any longer. At least he told Meta that after Estelle's difficult delivery of Jill that year—followed by months of unstable health—Estelle had shown no interest in intercourse. With Meta, for the only time in his life, he would enjoy a coalescence of the ideal and the actual. If his language of courtship suggested the need to maintain distance, it no less expressed his amazement that this lovely woman could be his.

Soon he was drawing (doodling would be closer to it) erotic, cartoon-like figures of their intercourse, and he was writing her tenderly obscene phrases and poems of sexual gratitude. "Meta/Bill/Meta/ who soft keeps for him her love's long girl's body sweet to fuck Bill" (ALG 75). Showing her his unexpurgated copy of Lawrence's *Lady Chatterley's Lover,* he developed for the two of them a kindred erotic lexicon: not *Chatterley's* "John Thomas" and "Lady Jane" for their intimate parts, but "Mr. Bowen" and "Mrs. Bowen." His correspondence with her delighted in these terms; the phrase-maker was Faulkner, not Meta. In another letter he wrote in the same vein, "For Meta, my heart, my jasmine garden, my April and May cunt; my white one, my blonde morning, winged, my sweetly dividing, my honey-cloyed, my sweet-assed gal. Bill" (76). "Keeps for him," as well as that string of "my"'s: such terms intimate less a couple's shared richness than his astonishment at possessing her: all this is *his*. With Meta, during the passionate early months of 1936, he enjoyed the honeymoon ("honey-cloyed") that had failed with Estelle six years earlier. A photo she took reveals a grinning Faulkner seated in the courtyard of her Hollywood apartment complex—grinning in appreciation of his fabulous luck. This photo joins that other one of him grinning, his hand pointing proudly to his Waco, taken a few years earlier. I know of no others of Faulkner that approach these two as unguarded expressions of delight. In each, he expresses his joy in possessing something he had assumed to be beyond his reach. The "sinister gods" must have been napping: this was too good to be true.

If he treated her as a maiden whom life had miraculously made available to him, she saw him as a lover at once strong, fatherly, and reliable. For their first few months together, she had no idea he drank heavily. When her friends told her of his reputation, she was shocked—though she would soon enough see him inebriated. At any rate, these first months of passion were the crucible in which they forged their bond together. "I was the girl he would surely have married," she wrote, "if our paths had only crossed before 1929" (ALG 24). In her mind this was never an affair. She was not a promiscuous woman, nor—she thought—was he a promiscuous man. ("Sensualist, yes....Womanizer not at all" [127].) A Southern girl brought up to be docile in the presence of men—and to charm them with her pliancy—Meta did not threaten Faulkner. When she sought to learn more about his inner life, she soon learned it would not be forthcoming. Even his intimately obscene phrases and poems emerged as written documents, arising in absence and communicating safely across it. She came to recognize that she learned more about him from his letters than ever in their conversations. He was, and would remain, a "moated man," "a great carapace," one who drew his "insularity...over himself like a second, tougher skin" (50). She was not to know until after his death that he had not fought and been wounded in the Great War. From first to last she responded to him as the famous William Faulkner. His stature acted as a screen that both brought them together and separated her from the precincts of his intimate thoughts. Which is probably how he wanted it to be.

That summer of 1936 he returned home, and when he came back to Hollywood he had bad news. Divorce—he had done some research—would be difficult, if not impossible. He could not lose Jill, and he had been counseled that divorcing Estelle would mean losing his daughter. There was more bad news. Estelle and Jill were coming out to Hollywood. That Faulkner wanted

Meta to meet his infant daughter is understandable; that he insisted as well on her meeting Estelle is less so. His affair brought out a new streak in him—at once detached and sadistic—as he schemed how to bring his two women together. He arrived at the bizarre scenario of drafting his friend Ben Wasson (working in Hollywood as well) into the performance. Wasson and Meta—Ben's supposed date—would join the Faulkners for dinner together in the Faulkners' rooms. Meta immediately recoiled, but he was adamant. It was an awful evening; apparently only Faulkner enjoyed the charade. Estelle drank heavily, chattered intensely, then called Wasson the next morning in fury. She had not been fooled. Wasson remembered Faulkner's saying shortly thereafter, "Aint there something you can do to get her off my back? Get her a lover, anything, so she'll leave me alone" (CNC 148). The phrasing is cruel, conveying both the besottedness of a lover who has glimpsed his escape and the vindictiveness of a husband who has paid too dearly. As for Meta, she came away from this dinner, as well as from later masquerade-encounters with Estelle, convinced of the wife's shrillness and inadequacy. "Let him go, Estelle," she thought. "I can grow with him. You can't. I'm younger. Prettier. I can hold him, grace his life, keep him from alcohol, slake his passion, calm his volcanic rages" (ALG 180). Could she possibly have managed all of this? Did she glimpse, even then, that she'd never have the chance to try?

By the summer of 1936, they both seem to have realized that he would not divorce. He urged her (against his own desire) to get free of him, and—perhaps surprising to him—she took him at his word. Another dimension of Meta Carpenter revealed itself in such behavior: pliant and docile though she was, this woman knew how to secure her own interest. At twenty-eight, she was aware that she would not remain forever well-positioned in the marriage market. If Faulkner would not rise to the mark, it was time to locate the right person who would. Some months earlier, close friends had introduced her to Rebner—a brilliant German pianist, a few years younger than she—and he had swiftly fallen for her. She had resisted his advances, without exactly rejecting them. By September 1936, she was emitting signals of receptivity sufficient for Rebner to propose to her. In December, she accepted his proposal; with it came her decision to refuse Faulkner entry into her bed. By early 1937, she and Rebner were married—a move Faulkner could neither criticize nor tolerate. His drinking spiked sharply during the following months. His anger toward Estelle, whom he must have seen as his jailor-wife, escalated, often brimming over during this first year of his involvement with Meta. In June 1936, unable to contain his annoyance at Estelle's spending habits, he wrote a letter to the *Oxford Eagle* (picked up by the *Memphis Commercial Appeal*) saying that "I will not be responsible for any debt incurred or bills made, or notes or checks signed by Mrs. William Faulkner or Mrs. Estelle Oldham Faulkner" (F 372). Enraged and embarrassed by such antics, Estelle's father lectured Faulkner sternly. The letter was not reprinted.

The Rebners' marriage did not prosper. Twice they tried to make it work; twice they divorced. Faulkner's role in those collapses is as undeniable as it is unknowable, but the available evidence suggests that he never sought to intervene as Rebner's rival. Nor did Rebner seem to resent Faulkner's prior place—sometimes prior in both senses—in his wife's affections. The decency with which all three seem to have treated each other over the next decade is remarkable. But Meta's off-and-on marriage allowed, at the same time, an intermittent relationship with Faulkner that was going nowhere. In 1939, weakened by an operation to remove a tumor and depressed by the failure of her marriage, she wrote Faulkner of her misery. She was heading home to her parents in Arizona, to recuperate and to see if she could straighten out her life. He responded at once, urging her to route her train trip by way of Louisiana, where he would meet her. In a blinding rainstorm, he drove to the train junction and saw her emerge, feverish. They drove for hours through the storm to New Orleans, then checked into a hotel in the Vieux Carré. After a night of drinking and lovemaking, she awoke at noon, free of fever. Looking up in amazement, she saw him grinning at her as he answered her unstated question, "Good whiskey, and Mr. Bowen" (ALG 242).

Reinvigorated after her stay in Arizona, Meta returned to New York and tried to put her marriage together again. But by 1942 she was divorced, and when she returned to Hollywood alone, it was inevitable that she would return to Faulkner. They seemed now to have become more tempered lovers, realizing that they could never live together on a longtime basis. "You'd rail at me," Meta remembered him saying, as he playfully put words into her mouth: "'Bill, don't put your pipe on the table. Hang up your coat. Don't feed Chloe [their dog] at the table. Wipe your shoes on the doormat, for heaven's sake.'" To these bantering (but not only bantering) words she had responded, "'And you'd see me in all my imperfections.'" This he had answered, with a grin, "'Let us be faultless one to another'" (ALG 297). "Faultless": something like the Keatsean opposition between ideal and reality seems to have reinserted itself—either a sustained real-life-in-time love relationship (faulty of course) or a sublimely rootless (but faultless) one. They both knew, perhaps ruefully, that they could have the second, maybe, if they no longer sought the first. The second was in its way quite wonderful. She recognized him, retrospectively, as "my lover, my rock; it was not enough, but I made it enough" (283). As one of Faulkner's biographers has written, "There were no institutions that insisted that she had to love this man, and continue to love him regardless of circumstances. The love she gave was given—and apparently freely given—from within herself" (WFSH 249). Thanks to the erotic and emotional generosity of Meta Carpenter, the same critic claimed, "the marble faun unfroze" (253). One hopes he did.

In 1945, Meta remarried Rebner, but their union could not come right. As she and Faulkner continued to write to each other, their mood became increasingly autumnal, past-focused. He wrote in 1949: "I know grief is the inevictable part of it, the thing that makes it cohere; that grief is the only thing you are capable of sustaining, keeping; that what is valuable is what you have lost, since then you never had the chance to wear out and so lose it shabbily" (ALG 317). A few years later, subsequent to their last love-making, another of his letters rehearses the same sentiments: "Change in people, saddest of all, division, separation, all left is the remembering, the dream, until you almost believe that anything beautiful is nothing else but dream" (326). These are dark and touching claims. They cast this love relationship—his only one that could be called happy—as destined for grief and destruction. As though genuine love and its actualization over time (and within institutional constraints) were simply incompatible notions. If it is real, if one has not trucked with it—exploited it or cheated on it—it cannot endure. What endures gets worn down, lost shabbily, held hostage to division and separation. Chronos is our mortal enemy, indeed the carrier of our mortality. It is only in refusing the negotiations and compromises that occur over time that love can flourish: as flame, but also as doom.

At some point in the mid-1950s, divorced again and her life in tatters, she found herself reduced to borrowing $150 from Faulkner. By then—a celebrated Nobel laureate—he was free of money troubles. Tortured by exploiting her relationship thus, she sent him a check for $75 as soon as she could, promising to repay the remaining $75 swiftly thereafter. Within days she received his letter enclosing her torn-up check: "You can't possibly owe me anything like money," he wrote. "I remember too much" (ALG 327). It was at about this time that she realized, all at once, that he was never coming back. "[H]e was past the time of the blood's violent flood," she thought. "It was not Bowen so much as memory…that tormented him in the still hours of the night" (329).

Memory: this is perhaps the appropriate note to sound in closing a discussion of Faulkner and Meta Carpenter. He had sought her as a sanctuary in which he could escape the miseries of his actual life—his marriage's failure, his California-enforced separation from his adored daughter, his guilt for the violent death of Dean, his discomfort at being caged in the money-trap that was Hollywood. She figured for him the illusion of transcendence. Together, they would create an erotic utopia, made up of their two bodies and their two souls. Themselves alone, sealed off from society and change. Wonderful as it was—for a time—it could not be sustained. Nothing good, he came to believe, could be sustained. Alcohol soon found its way into their love nest; so did Estelle and Jill and Rebner and the conflicting needs and desires of each of them. Conceived as the other of normal life, this affair became, gradually, a part of normal life. It became inextricably enmeshed with the other commitments that made up their quotidian lives.

It was helplessly open, he finally saw, to the pain that memory is uniquely capable of inflicting. Memory as the unwanted resource that keeps reminding us, like a bell tolling, that we live our lives in ever-changing time, that what comes later mocks (and is mocked by) what came earlier. "Hit look lack Ah just cant quit thinking," Rider realized at last (in *Go Down, Moses*). To be conscious is to remember, and to remember is to grieve for what is gone. "Between grief and nothing, I will take grief," Faulkner wrote Meta in 1937. He had already decided that the novel he was then writing—*If I Forget Thee, Jerusalem,* the most autobiographical he was ever to write—would pivot on that choice. He would never have sought sanctuaries as aggressively as he did if he had not known that—lurking within them all, alcoholic binges as well as passionate affairs—was the day of reckoning. The bell would sound, he would be in time again, and he would remember. There would be grief, and he would take it.

TINSEL TOWN

In December 1931, the first "summons" to Hollywood was set in motion. Though no great reader himself, Sam Marx of MGM gathered that the author of *Sanctuary* was a property worth acquiring. To Leland Hayward in New York (Ben Wasson's boss), he sent the telegram quoted earlier: DID YOU MENTION WILLIAM FAULKNER TO ME ON YOUR LAST TRIP HERE. IF SO IS HE AVAILABLE AND HOW MUCH (F 296). William Faulkner was available, and "how much" did not pose great difficulties. Hayward ended by negotiating an MGM contract at $500 per week.

Given that Cape and Smith—publishers of *The Sound and the Fury, As I Lay Dying,* and *Sanctuary*—was going into receivership, Faulkner realized that the hefty royalties he anticipated from *Sanctuary's* notoriety might never materialize. (He was right. Smith was never able to pay him the $4,000 that was his due.) So, expecting from Hollywood nothing but the cash that had compelled him to sign on, Faulkner set out on his journey west. The scene of his arrival there intimates his larger relation to Tinsel Town.

On May 7, 1932, a man bleeding profusely from a head wound walked into Sam Marx's office. He said that he was William Faulkner, and that—en route to Los Angeles—he had been hit by a taxi while in New Orleans. He was now ready to begin work. Marx, perhaps stunned and certainly suspicious, responded that Faulkner would be working on a Wallace Beery picture. "Who's he?" Faulkner asked, then added, "I've got an idea for Mickey Mouse." Marx explained that the famous mouse was a Disney property, then instructed an office boy to take Faulkner to the projection room where some footage of the Beery film was being shown. Faulkner entered the room but refused to look at the screen. Instead he turned to the office boy. "Do you own a dog?" he demanded. When the boy responded negatively, Faulkner retorted, "Every boy should have a dog." He then informed the group of speechless adults around them that they should all be ashamed if they did not own a dog. At that point—although the Beery footage had barely gotten under way—Faulkner turned to the projectionist, "How do you stop this thing?" He said he already knew how the story would come out, and he abruptly left the room. When Marx later asked where he had gone, no one had the faintest idea. Nine days later he reappeared at MGM—as mysteriously as the first time, and again unsteady on his feet. By way of explaining his absence, he allowed that he had been wandering about in Death Valley. His MGM contract was not renewed a month later, and without the intervention that summer of Howard Hawks, his Hollywood stint might have ended then and there.

This vignette suggests in summary fashion the absurdity of Faulkner's tenure in Hollywood. He cared more for dogs than for film (he'd rather have been that hound scuttling back under the wagon than have to deal with these strange folks and their stranger business). He didn't know the difference between Disney and MGM. A Wallace Beery film bored him to death after the first fifteen minutes, since any fool could see how the story would turn out. Heavy drinking predated his arrival in Hollywood, lubricated his off-and-on twenty-year stay there, and would continue once he left for good. His entries and exits were unpredictable. He would never—one sees this right away—be a company man. The moguls who ran this multimillion dollar industry did not appreciate such erratic behavior.

Howard Hawks made possible Faulkner's Hollywood career, at least money-wise. A graduate from Exeter and then Cornell, Hawks had the strenuous masculine profile—accomplished, risk-taking, self-contained if not taciturn—to which Faulkner responded. Hawks had flown army planes in the Great War and later done a stint of car racing. Moreover, he already admired Faulkner's fiction to the extent of purchasing screen rights for the story "Turn About." That summer (1932), he approached Faulkner to see if he would do the script for it, entitled *Today We Live*. Hawks offered Faulkner a drink, then settled into more detail about how he envisaged the film. Faulkner was silent while Hawks spoke, seemed positive about the idea, and then rose to leave. "See you in five days," he told Hawks. When Hawks demurred that it shouldn't take that long to decide, Faulkner answered, "I mean, to write it" (F 307). He was as good as his word, and both Hawks and his boss, Irving Thalberg, liked the script. The studio gave the green light. In almost no time, *Today We Live* became one of the few projects Faulkner would work on that made it to the screen. Not that it did so without considerable revision. Joan Crawford, it turned out, was an expensive MGM property waiting for a film. Higher-ups decided that a starring role would be created for her in *Today We Live*. When Faulkner demurred—"I don't seem to remember a girl in the story" (307)—Hawks explained that this was Hollywood. Highly paid top stars had to be placed in films. Faulkner accepted the rules without further rejoinder and adroitly wrote her role into the script.

Hawks was Faulkner's principal Hollywood mainstay. *Today We Live* premiered in 1933, and in 1934 Hawks rehired Faulkner—at $1,000 per week—to work on the script for *Sutter's Gold*. Better yet, understanding Faulkner's intense dislike of Hollywood, Hawks arranged more than once for Faulkner to remain on payroll while working at home in Oxford. A year later, Hawks hired Faulkner again for *The Road to Glory*, this time with Twentieth Century Fox. For more than fifteen years, Hawks was to procure work for Faulkner that would not otherwise have come his way: screenplays for *Battle Cry* in 1942,[6] *To Have and Have Not* in 1944 (one of Faulkner's finest scripts, and one of the least revised by others), *The Left Hand of God* in 1951, and *The Land of the Pharaohs* in 1953. Through Hawks, Faulkner met not only Meta Carpenter in 1935, but Clark Gable and other of Hawks's Hollywood friends with whom he would later hunt, fish, and carouse. If Hollywood could have been turned into a home-like space, one would have to credit Hawks for it.

But Hollywood could never, for Faulkner, be other than a perversely willed invention, a huge stage set, a scene of bloated egos and untrustworthy performances: all of this resting on a meretricious art form. It was a place of exploitative machinations disguised by tinselly mirages—alluring surfaces with nothing reliable underneath. It battened on sentimental illusion. The unceasing hum of high profit—greed—bespoke its subterranean motor if one listened hard enough. When Jack Falkner, aware of his brother's intensified drinking and fearful for his health, joined Faulkner in 1937, he asked if Faulkner could recognize his rented house from the air. Faulkner answered no, saying that it "was practically impossible to distinguish even when driving along the street right in front of it" (F 382). Later he would say of the entire region, "Nobody here does anything. There's nobody here with any roots. Even the houses are built out of mud and chicken wire" (467). Los Angeles was a city invented by the car, rather than a set of communities where people had long lived together, prior to Henry Ford's abstract organizing of their shared space. No house had its unique insertion, its own history. No abiding stories attached to dwellings, giving them an irreplaceable personality, a patina of time. Seemingly built yesterday, the whole place could disappear tomorrow.

As I have noted, though Meta was Southern, his affair with her was pure Hollywood. There they could be unknown in a sense that would have been impossible back home. Acquaintances in Oxford were encumbered with parents and grandparents, uncles and aunts and cousins and offspring, friends and enemies. Extensive family stories predated them, intermingling with other families' stories. Three generations earlier, Hindmans and Falkners had intimately and publicly done damage to each other. His grandfather was abidingly interwoven into the texture of Oxford banking, business, and politics—a friend or enemy of important and unavoidable men and women. His father Murry had grown up under the shadow of an extensive family history that he could have wished less oppressive—but that he could not wish away. Faulkner's own identity presupposed a sustained Falkner/Oldham/Stone history whose duration was inescapable—for better and for worse. Toward the end of his life, when he was preparing to shift his primary residence from Oxford to Charlottesville, Virginia, the idea of slipping that lifetime noose of "known-ness" must have appealed to him. In Charlottesville, he could fantasize being only who he now was: a universally acclaimed writer, an occasional professor, a doting grandfather, a sartorial fox hunter. He would be just William Faulkner, not also the former but unforgotten Billy Falkner whom his Uncle John had openly ridiculed in Oxford's public square some thirty years ago.

Faulkner's fictional genius required, as one of his critics has noted, several generations of intertwined family histories as their enabling premise.[7] There are no Sartorises at all if you strip away their nineteenth-century avatars; likewise no Compsons or Sutpens or McCaslins. Even Snopeses presuppose extensive passing time. At the end of *The Mansion,* an outraged Mink Snopes makes his way from Parchman prison back to Jefferson, revenge on his mind. He has returned to kill his cousin Flem for not protecting him thirty-seven years earlier and allowing him instead to rot in prison all that time. Remove the complications of "all that time" and there is no plot in *The Mansion.* The entire sequence from *The Hamlet* to *The Town* to *The Mansion* sits squarely atop the frame of extensive, ongoing time. Faulkner is a *time* writer (as Hemingway is not). It takes cumulative changes—with their unpremeditated consequences—for him to come to life as a novelist.

Hollywood understood time and space differently. It had no interest in the cumulative, in the unfolding of trouble-making causes and consequences— traps that would unavoidably involve others in unforeseeable ways. Hollywood promised time as nirvana and space as utopia, and it promised them now—or if not now, within the scope of a two-hour film. Its model for an enrooted place was a stage set, its model for an entangled time was a love story simplified enough to be compassed on two hours of celluloid. Faulkner never tired of cursing Hollywood as a betrayal of his calling. Although he rarely identified the specifics of that betrayal, Hollywood's cheapening of the actual texture of experience must have been crucial. He knew perfectly well how the popular magazines required shortcuts—in language and in sequence— that his own more intricate sense of unfolding would have forbidden. He had accepted those short cuts then, and he accepted them now. Off and on for some twenty years, he labored in Hollywood to produce the scripts the moguls wanted—some ten thousand pages of writing, it has been estimated. But he could neither accept nor escape the Hollywood stamp irremovably placed on his affair with Meta Carpenter.

At first they had dreamed of his divorce and their marriage. But the more she envisaged Oxford's endlessly repercussive response to her replacing Estelle, the more Meta realized that it was doomed. Too many people, long since part of his established world, would refuse to endorse this new marriage. She would never be accepted, and she was not cut out for confrontation or ostracism. For his part, he seems to have understood even earlier—by the summer of 1936—that only as a pair of lovers did they have a chance at all. Take into account three people or four (Estelle and Jill), and it could never work. The puppet strings controlling their movements were inextricably entangled with those of others—as he had put it in *Absalom*. Too many incompatible human wills were engaged for their union to thrive. It had one chance and one only: in Hollywood. There, in rented rooms and during stolen weekends—in that setting dedicated to the heart's release, licit or not—they experienced their love for each other. It was not enough, as she later said—a beleaguered sanctuary—but they both made it enough. It could not save their lives, and it arguably damaged hers beyond repair. But gentle Meta Carpenter was the dark flame that both consumed him and made him—during the troubled years of their affair—a novelist of irresistible, hopeless love.

"WHERE DO WOMEN BLEED?": *IF I FORGET THEE, JERUSALEM*

By September 1937, he had begun a novel that both poured out of him and dried up on him, unpredictably. *If I Forget Thee, Jerusalem*—published as *The Wild Palms* and given its proper name only in 1990—draws intimately on his ongoing experience with Meta Carpenter. Or more accurately, it draws less on Meta herself than on his experience of the bodily phenomenon she brought to a crescendo: orgasm. Charlotte Rittenmeyer, one of the two protagonists, hardly resembles Meta Carpenter. Marked by "a faint inch-long scar on one cheek" (IIF 520), Charlotte burns with an unsmiling ferocity foreign to Meta's well-bred docility. Perhaps because of the scar, critics have proposed Helen Baird as the model for Charlotte: Helen was similarly scarred, forthright, demanding. But Helen was an unpossessed flame some fifteen years earlier, on Faulkner's voyage out. The crucial event here is erotic consummation. The entire novel pivots on the unmanageable force of sexuality.

It is true that one half of the novel ("Old Man")—oddly interwoven with the love-story half ("Wild Palms")—features no acts of sexual intercourse. But no great leap of imagination is required to grasp that the intercourse enacted literally in the love story of "Wild Palms" is enacted figuratively in the landscape of "Old Man." Faulkner was never to describe a more hallucinatory landscape than that of the ferocious Mississippi (Old Man) flooding its borders and wreaking havoc on all the puny schemas of order meant to contain its force. The protagonist of this narrative—an unnamed convict sent out on the water to rescue a stranded and terminally pregnant woman, equally unnamed—has only a frail boat between him and the exploding waters:

> [Suddenly the place] where the phosphorescent water met the darkness was now about ten feet higher than it had been an instant before and...it was curled forward upon itself like a sheet of dough being rolled out for a pudding. It reared, stooping; the crest of it swirled like the mane of a galloping horse....He continued to paddle though the skiff had ceased to move forward at all but seemed to be hanging in space while the paddle still reached thrust recovered and reached again; now instead of space the skiff became abruptly surrounded by a welter of fleeing debris—planks, small buildings, the bodies of drowned yet antic animals, entire trees leaping and diving like porpoises above which the skiff seemed to hover in weightless and airy indecision like a bird above a fleeing countryside...while the convict squatted in it still going through the motions of paddling, waiting for an opportunity to scream. He never found it. For an instant the skiff seemed to stand erect on its stern and then... (IIF 601)

Immersed in water like this, one does not steer; there is not even time to scream. Time disappears. Spatial demarcation vanishes as well. What was earlier dry land with fixed orientational markers (trees, farms, roads) is now a roiling universe of water. Horizontal becomes vertical, down becomes up, forward becomes backward, fixed things swirl by as moving and dangerous debris. The sexual dynamic interior to "Wild Palms" has here transformed into outer apocalypse. The setting of this story has slipped its mapped and masculine fixity, becoming bottomless, unmanageable, female waters. Fall into these and you drown. At their symbolic core—the targeted but unlocated object of the convict's quest—is a nameless nine-months-pregnant woman, swollen, and with her own waters ready to rupture. The landscape of "Old Man" keeps screaming the same message to the hapless convict trapped upon it: *you can't live here*. In this, it squarely intersects the kindred message at the heart of the love story—one Charlotte passes on to Harry: "You live *in* sin; you cant live on it" (IIF 551, emphasis in the original).

Both stories circulate around something more primordial than fixed forms: liquid that has escaped its normal boundaries and is flowing uncontrollably. In the love story, that liquid is Charlotte's blood. The narrative opens in the perspective of a puritanical older doctor suddenly summoned to treat a badly—but invisibly—injured woman. Charlotte and Harry have rented the doctor's bungalow on the Gulf Coast. She is bleeding—fatally, it turns out—from Harry's botched abortion. Although the doctor senses immediately "the secret irreparable seeping of blood" (IIF 496), his defenses keep him from knowing more. He has to ask, "Where is she bleeding?" and Harry responds, "Where do women bleed?" (504).

Female bleeding marked Faulkner's imagination long before this novel. In *The Sound and the Fury*, Quentin was mesmerized by women's menses—"periodical filth between two moons balanced" (SF 975). *As I Lay Dying* and *Sanctuary* both attended hypnotically to an illicit rupture of the hymen—Dewey Dell's pregnancy, Temple's rape. *Light in August* went on to consider more broadly this male obsession. "Womanfilth!" the incensed Doc Hines thunders at both of Joe's "mothers" (the dietitian who substituted as mother, his real mother, Milly, who died in childbirth virtually at Hines's hands). Christmas is likewise fascinated and terrified by where women bleed. When other boys first told him about female periods, he rushed into the woods—horrified—where he found a stray sheep, slaughtered it, and immersed his hands in its blood. He was seeking inoculation from an intolerable leakage at the core of the woman one desires. Joe thought he had got such inoculation until—years later—he tries to bed the waitress Bobbie and learns that she is having her period. Shocked speechless by the invisible liquid moving beneath her apparent stillness, he erupts into violence, jabbing her hard twice in the head, then fleeing. When he stops within a grove of trees to get his breath, he sees all the trees, hallucinatorily, as deformed and bleeding urns, issuing drop by drop a deathly, foul-smelling liquid. Menstruation figures in Faulkner's masculine imaginary (and not just his) as an unbearable confession of instability and bodily rot—of "liquid putrefaction"—lurking within what ought to manifest as an intact female form.

But none of these earlier novels—no matter how intense their interest in female menses—centered on orgasm. And none of them drew so openly on recent personal experience. If *Pylon* and *If I Forget Thee* both deal with autobiographical experience (flying and intercourse), only the latter imagines it as something like a perpetual drowning. Here is Faulkner trying to say it to Bob Haas in 1938: "To me, it [*If I Forget Thee*] was written just as if I had sat on the one side of a wall and the paper was on the other and my hand with the pen thrust through the wall and writing not only on invisible paper but in pitch darkness too" (SL 106). Here is Harry trying to say it in the novel proper: "Yes out of the terror in which you surrender volition, hope, all—the darkness, the falling…you yet feel all your life rush out of you into the pervading immemorial blind receptive matrix, the hot fluid blind foundation—grave-wound or womb-grave, it's all one" (IIF 589). And here is the diagnosis offered by a doctor in "Old Man." To the convict—who has been bleeding through the nose for much of the narrative, as well as battling with raging waters and trying to deliver the liquid-swollen, stranded mother—the doctor says, "Anyone ever suggest to you that you were hemophilic?" (658).

Common to these three passages is the uncontrollable release of liquid—through the pen, out the body, from the nose. The release seems to occur "in pitch darkness," and its recklessness is steeped in fatality: "grave-wound or womb-grave, it's all one." The bursting is at once ecstatic and transgressive of every boundary that makes selfhood recognizable. "Hemophilic": let us take the term figuratively as suggesting an unstanchably porous and "leaking" imagination. Things surge in and out too easily. It has long been noted that vomiting plays a large role in Faulkner's fiction. Vomiting first shows up as the result of binges in the aviator stories, as well as in Bayard in *Flags*, Gowan in *Sanctuary*, Jiggs in *Pylon*. But in the greater work—*The Sound and the Fury* and *Light in August*—vomiting begins to signify more broadly the drama of the ego's exposure, its incapacity to ward off coming assault. Honeysuckle threatens to choke Quentin (drenching him in Caddy's sexuality); Benjy's vomiting after drinking sarsaparilla at Caddy's wedding expresses a violation of his entire psychic economy; and Joe Christmas's throwing up in *Light in August* enacts the breaching of his meager resources for self-sustaining. In the presence of a black girl in a shed—this is to be his sexual initiation—the young supposedly-white Christmas explodes into violence. Her "black" scent has penetrated him, undone his sense of racial distinctiveness. He goes briefly berserk.

"Hemophilic": Faulkner suffered from—and tapped unforgettably in his work—the overwhelming of his defenses. Eventually he would realize that bodily distress was at the same time cultural distress. His hypersensitivity to the dynamics of "taking in" and "leaking out" made him a virtual seismographer of unnegotiable cultural encounters. Outrage—the signature event in his tragic work—is precisely the overwhelming of culturally inculcated boundaries. Outraged, invaded, one is no longer oneself. Like Freud, Faulkner seems to have known that only what hurts—what cuts *"across the devious, intricate channels of decorous ordering"* (*Absalom*, emphasis in the original)—is instructive. The lacerating wound carries the bad news that one's defenses have been breached, one's map of selfhood now in shambles. In a Southern culture fixated on mapping and maintaining differences between male and female, white and black, aristocrat and white trash, Faulkner reveals with extraordinary power the phenomenon of cultural hemorrhage: the collapse of identity-sustaining boundaries. What is the invisible spectacle of such a collapse if not light-skinned Joe Christmas parading in Mottstown's central square, waiting to be recognized as "black"? What is the miscegenation at the heart of both *Absalom* and *Go Down, Moses*—not to speak of Faulkner's own ancestral shadow family—if not the transgression of sanctuaries meant to keep out the secretly desired but socially intolerable other?

Invisible to the eye but not to the nose: the idiot Benjy in *The Sound and the Fury* "sees" Caddy's ruptured virginity with his nose—"he smell hit." More broadly, the larger social armature of segregation itself was installed to quarantine a black difference impacting whites at the level of smell itself. In a white South obsessed with maintaining racial distinctions, smell becomes hypercharged. More primitive and disturbing than sight—which satisfyingly keeps others at a distance by identifying them as "out there"—smell does its work retroactively. Once you smell it, it is too late: the damage is done. The other has invaded you, is in your nostrils, your entire body—without warning. Your only recourse is a violent, virtually orgasmic expulsion of the intolerable. "Hemophilic": Faulkner *matters* because he did not manage to keep his borders (at once personal and cultural) intact and stanch the bleeding, and because he somehow grasped what was at stake in such overwhelming. The troubled life and the troubling work are inseparable.

If I Forget Thee, Jerusalem is certainly centered on trouble. "You live *in* sin; you cant live on it." You cannot make a life out of it; sin cannot be tamed—willed into familiar spatial or temporal order. The novel takes this core conviction all the way. At the level of plot, one could call both stories scorched-earth narratives, if they weren't so saturated in liquid. Place as we know it—familiar, stabilizing—disappears in "Old Man." The story deals in frantic motion on the water, with minor intervals alongside larger boats or interludes among incommunicable Cajun hunters. The expelled convict longs to return to the dry enclosure of Parchman prison: anything that will keep him away from the watery and unfathomable female world. In "Wild Palms," place doesn't so much disappear as take on kaleidoscopic motion. The narrative lurches from New Orleans to Chicago to Utah, then back to New Orleans and finally to a Mississippi prison. At the story's end, Harry is set to spend the rest of his days in the same prison as the convict, sent there for having killed Charlotte with his botched abortion. Though offered escape, Harry has no interest in taking it. None of these settings is sustaining, provided with a stabilizing history, populated by others one might come to know. None is available for normal activities (getting a job, buying a house, marrying a spouse, raising a family). Fleetingly, other people and places flash by in "Wild Palms," like two-dimensional landscapes glimpsed on a speeding train. The train is the lovers' sexual bond(age): it has room for only two figures—Charlotte and Harry—and it is at home nowhere.

Harry first meets Charlotte at a party she and her husband are giving (and to which he has not been invited). A page later, she has grabbed him by the arm, "ruthless and firm, drawing him after her" (IIF 520). Within the next two pages they have spoken, casually but portentously. Then, a page later—he has gone home and a couple of days later returned to the Rittenmeyers' for dinner—she says it all: "What to—Do they call you Harry? What to do about it, Harry?" (523). A few hours together at most, but the die is cast, their *Liebestod* is launched. From this point on, unsmiling and lecturing him as needed, Charlotte directs the lovers' moves. This involves systematically destroying all moorings, refusing all compromise, cutting all cords. Grasping his hair, striking his body, "rous[ing] him to listen with a hard wrestling movement" (557), hammering his belly, jabbing him with her "hard and painful elbow," Charlotte conducts her lover undeviatingly into the fatal conflagration ("grave-wound, womb-grave, it's all one") that is their erotic union. Apparently, he needs to be directed. For her part, she knows from the beginning that it must be tragic: "love and suffering are the same thing and…the value of love is the sum of what you have to pay for it and any time you get it cheap you have cheated yourself" (526).

"Do they call you Harry?" His name does not matter, just as no character in "Old Man" is granted a name. We are dealing with nameless liquids, not stable solids; only fixed entities have names that they fondly believe bestow reliable identity. The element in him to which she has all but chemically bonded is anonymous. *If I Forget Thee* reaches for the indescribable motions of "pitch darkness"—where the perquisites of identity lose their purchase, on the roiling water, in the heaving bed—and the awful release or inundation of liquid begins. "As though the clotting which is you had dissolved in the original, myriad motion"—so Faulkner described (in *As I Lay Dying*) this exposure to currents stronger than selfhood. But characters retained their names and identities in that novel—Darl and Jewel and Cash and Addie. With their names came both the richly textured turmoil of a family's distress and the dark and abiding humor of siblings who have long lived in each other's presence. Family drama and humor are absent from "Wild Palms" (there is dark humor aplenty in "Old Man," albeit mainly at the convict's expense).

Charlotte's children are whisked out of the narrative after two brief mentions. When Harry reminds her of what she is about to abandon— her children—she replies, smoking, "I wasn't thinking of them" (IIF 526).

More brutal yet, Harry has earlier identified them (at the party) as "two not particularly remarkable children" (522): as though they might be more text-worthy—and to be parented rather than orphaned—if they had been more "remarkable." It is a quietly callous narrative moment, and one wonders if Faulkner has not—in wish-fulfillment fashion—imaginatively reversed his own heartbreaking dilemma: either Jill or Meta. Here it is different: forget the children, head pell-mell toward the "womb-grave," indict everything else as defection. "I told you once," Charlotte lectures Harry late in the narrative, "it isn't love that dies, it's the man and the woman, something in the man and the woman that dies, doesn't deserve the chance any more to love" (643).

Love is figured as an appalling invasion. Not just that it is bound for destruction: Harry's abortion knife will end Charlotte's life as inevitably as the convict's sharp tin can will cut the pregnant woman's umbilical cord and let her baby live. More deranging than the fatal destination is the night-marish journey. There is no foreplay here, no intimacy, no pleasure—no evidence that they even *like* being in each other's company. The story insists on this searing condition as love, but it has equal title to be called torture. As in *Requiem for a Nun* later (1951), Faulkner is at his grimmest when he envisages erotic love. Scorched earth: there is no place they can stand, no place they can go, no activity other than intercourse they can engage in together. They have deliberately burned up possibility itself. Was this the underside of Faulkner's doomed affair with Meta Carpenter? As though beneath her docility and charm, he found the iron of impossibility: they could not live in society, and they could not sustain a sanctuary outside it. Reduced thus, they had no choice but to consume each other—and then to swear solemnly not to forget the pain that went with consummation. "I know grief is the inevictable part of it, the thing that makes it cohere," he had written her. In kindred fashion, ensconced in his prison cell and dedicated to the lifelong memory of what has been lost, Harry ends "Wild Palms" by claiming loyally, "Between grief and nothing I will take grief" (IIF 715). How powerfully this story testifies—more powerfully perhaps than Faulkner knows—to the destructiveness of illicit love, even as it insists that only illicit love is authentic.

It is well known that Faulkner had trouble writing this novel. His inge-nious solution was to pursue each of the narratives until it petered out, and then to switch to the other until it, too, dried up, and then back again. Each story, divided into five subparts, is interwoven with the other; Faulkner's novel remained faithful to its rhythm of conception. Critics ever since have wondered about the aesthetic logic of *If I Forget Thee*'s narrative structure. I argued earlier that, fundamentally, the two narratives rehearse the same explosive materials. They intersect as point and counterpoint in a common dance of carnivalesque disaster.

Yet Faulkner's difficulty in completing this book may be as telling as any unifying pattern implicit in its structure. As with *A Fable* later, something stubbornly lodged in the writer's imagination was reluctant to keep plunging into these materials. Does the fact that, by contrast, he was able to write *As I Lay Dying* in two months testify not only to the earlier Faulkner's creative fecundity but also to his grasp on the familial and regional interrelationships that propel that novel to its conclusion? He sometimes described *As I Lay Dying* as a "tour de force"—a narrative in which he exposed his characters to fire and flood—but the phrase is even more apt for "Old Man." Family and region have dropped away: the narrative pits a single man existentially against the elements. "Old Man" lives mainly in the convict's beleaguered (but not otherwise interesting) head, as it attends to his endlessly violent encounters. Fabulous though "Old Man" be, it is—by comparison with *As I Lay Dying*—perhaps overwritten. It cannot vary its slew of operatic scenes of vertiginous assault. "Not again!" the reader thinks, when yet another catastrophe careens upon the convict (and starts the blood flowing again from his nose). "Not again!"—as in "not another disastrous encounter!"—hardly characterizes the reader's response to the emotional trials of the Bundren family. Put otherwise, Faulkner's entry into the Bundren family's astonishing projections and identifications ("My mother is a fish") has little counterpart in this nonrelational narrative of disasters grimly engaged and survived.

As for the difficulty in completing "Wild Palms," the reasons may not be far to seek. Faulkner's chaotic emotional life is perhaps too implicated in these erotic materials. It is not for nothing that he pictures a pen thrust through a wall, an invisible piece of paper, and pitch darkness. Something in the writer wants to withdraw that pen even as it wants to extend it further. Finally, adult intercourse is—without exception—traumatic territory in Faulkner's imaginary. It is one thing for Benjy and Quentin to anguish over their beloved Caddy. Their distress is bathed in the softened light of balked desire, not the scorched-earth glare of orgasmic consummation. (Caddy's sexual release is narratively off-stage; so is her daughter Quentin's, at novel's end.) "The man called Harry" and the woman named Charlotte enact their love affair on-stage. Not that this novel is Lawrentian in its narrative of intercourse—Faulkner has no interest in body parts or the moment-by-moment experience of coitus—but it remains dedicated to articulating his thinking about intercourse. Sexual release emerges as both devastating and sublime. It is as though Faulkner had to make fictionally coherent a realm of experience that remained for him beyond cohering.

A year later, at any rate, his fiction would return to Jefferson and Yoknapatawpha County—replete with that setting's familiar space, linear time, and interrelated family histories. Rural humor, penetrating social analysis, and the texture of class relations would feature prominently in *The Hamlet*, making it one of his most admired—indeed, Balzacian—novels. (Readers who do not otherwise care for Faulkner often esteem *The Hamlet*.) But that novel would continue to explore, more briefly but no less forcefully than *If I Forget Thee, Jerusalem*, the madness of love. It was 1940, after all, and Meta Carpenter was still raging in his blood.

"BREATHING IS A SIGHT-DRAFT DATED YESTERDAY": *THE HAMLET*

Faulkner was in his early forties when he put this book together, largely out of stories already published. He had been meditating Snopes materials ever since 1925, and *The Hamlet* expertly taps a Yoknapatawpha County mastered into its narrative possibilities. Unlike a world composed of two lovers in "Wild Palms," Frenchman's Bend (a village near Jefferson) in *The Hamlet* sports a generous cast of characters and a capacious setting and history. Uncle Will Varner seems to have been running the place forever. The novel opens on a challenge to his hegemony: the arrival of the first Snopes at the community's social and financial hub, Varner's country store. The skeletal plot for the entire trilogy involves the Snopeses' economic takeover of the region, beginning in the opening scene. Flem Snopes—the major Snopes, though flanked by his truculent father Ab and an unending slew of bizarrely named cousins and nephews—competes silently, systematically, and successfully with the Varners for power. By the time of *The Mansion* (1959), Flem will have made his way into Jefferson and attained wealth, power, and respectability.

Critics sometimes portray this as a struggle between the Old South of Compsons and Sartorises and the New South of Snopeses. Will Varner, the boss of Frenchman's Bend, is no aristocratic master, however, but one of the boys—the most powerful, to be sure, but not a man descended from the plantation model. More, Faulkner does not heavily moralize the Varner/Snopes conflict. Varners are as likely as Snopeses to exploit their neighbors, but in more traditional ways. The moment when Flem, now the chief clerk of Varner's store, makes Uncle Will pay for his plug of tobacco identifies the key change taking place. A traditional scene of exchange—where the players know each other, even realize, while being financially accommodated, that they are being exploited—is ceding to an abstract, contractual model. Even the boss must pay; the transaction goes down on the books. Flem fleeces his clientele on a scale hardly attempted by the Varners, but he does so legally.

Legal outmaneuvering functions as the lifeblood of *The Hamlet*. Its vignettes circulate around one-upmanship transactions—horse-trading, goat-purchasing, the buying and selling of land. Totally lacking in personality, Flem would seem an unlikely protagonist, yet he remains (with Ratliff) the central figure of this trilogy it took Faulkner almost two decades to complete. Although the narrative refuses to access his consciousness— either Flem is unknowable or there is nothing inside to know—it shrewdly delineates his outer features:

> He did not speak. If he ever looked at them individually, that one did not discern it—a thick squat soft man of no establishable age between twenty and thirty, with a broad still face containing a tight seam of mouth stained slightly at the corners with tobacco, and eyes the color of stagnant water, and projecting from among the other features in startling and sudden paradox, a tiny predatory nose like the beak of a small hawk. (HAM 777)

"Predatory," but otherwise blankly impenetrable (his age undisclosed, his mouth a closed seam), Flem is in a community but not of it, as he is in a family but not of it. His cousin Mink will ultimately put him to death for his lack of family piety. If we ask what in the characterologically impoverished Flem Snopes commands Faulkner's attention, one trait emerges already. He is his own man, independent, unreachable, impregnable. He is a hard-wired virgin—or better, a eunuch. Surely this is why, with extravagant irony, Faulkner chooses to marry off the luscious Eula Varner to emotionally barren Flem. Faulkner emphasizes the sheer waste of Eula's Dionysian fecundity, the incapacity of contemporary rural society to rise to her erotic challenge.

Flem's predatory impenetrability requires a balancing counterpart. Another impenetrable figure—as communal as Flem is a loner, as loquacious as Flem is silent, as playful as Flem is driven, but equally private at the core—shares center stage with him. The "pleasant, affable, courteous, anecdotal and impenetrable" (HAM 741) Ratliff functions as Faulkner's Hermes:

> He sold perhaps three [sewing] machines a year, the rest of the time trading in land and livestock and second-hand farming tools ... retailing from house

to house the news of his four counties with the ubiquity of a newspaper and carrying personal messages from mouth to mouth about weddings and funerals....He never forgot a name and he knew everyone, man mule and dog, within fifty miles. (741)

Such catholic interests point to Ratliff's role as village custodian. He knows the region's players, joins in their identity-defining rituals and activities. His commitment to "sewing" helps knit a group of individuals together into a community. Finally, he possesses a cardinal virtue necessary for taking on Snopesism: sexual immunity, a sutured heart. Faulkner emphasizes Ratliff's "air of perpetual bachelorhood," his "hearty celibacy as of a lay brother in a twelfth-century monastery—a gardener, a pruner of vines, say" (769).

Ratliff and Snopes serve as structural antipodes grounding the concerns of the trilogy. Their primacy tells us that these novels will return repeatedly to exploitative transactions and to the larger struggle between traditional and contemporary ways of doing business. Irrational excess is foreign to both men: Ratliff is there to spot and rein it in before it becomes dangerous, Snopes is there to fan it into action and exploit its consequences. These two figures preside over an ongoing drama that is economic at its center, moral and erotic at its margins. Moving forward in linear time, this drama accommodates traditional narrative techniques. The Balzacian cultural historian in Faulkner flourishes here.

But it is the irrational erotic energy lurking in the margins that fuels *The Hamlet*'s most memorable vignettes. A number of interrelated love stories establish this novel's kinship with *If I Forget Thee, Jerusalem*. Through Eula Varner and the schoolteacher Labove, as well as a pair of harassed men—Jack Houston and Mink Snopes—transformed into mortal enemies, and finally the idiot Ike Snopes and his beloved cow, Faulkner narrates tormented private histories that give this otherwise sunny novel much of its somber power.

We have already glanced at Eula and noted the irony of her father's bestowing her (as a tactical move) on the sexless Flem. An early description of Eula reveals the dimensions of such waste:

[H]er entire appearance suggested some symbology out of the old Dionysic times—honey in sunlight and bursting grapes, the writhen bleeding of the crushed fecundated vine beneath the hard rapacious trampling goat-hoof. She seemed...to exist in a teeming vacuum in which her days followed one

another as though behind sound-proof glass, where she seemed to listen in
sullen bemusement, with a weary wisdom heired of all mammalian maturity,
to the enlarging of her own organs. (HAM 817)

Eula is often paired with Caddy Compson and Dewey Dell Bundren—
those other sexually intense young women—but this passage accesses her
in a unique fashion. The woman delineated in this over-the-top description will never escape her narrator's categorizing impetus, never be granted
her own language for expressing her thought and feeling. The texture
of Eula's subjectivity is closed to articulation. She means only what the
(male) narrative perspective emphatically sees her as meaning. Caught up
thus, Eula remains imprisoned—throughout the trilogy—in mythological
language that expresses male response to her fabulous body. Put otherwise,
she tends to reduce to her organs. Her later love affair with Manfred de
Spain (in *The Town*), like her subsequent suicide (in *The Mansion*), gets
clear of such organ-emphasis, but this trajectory is likewise never narrated from her point of view. Rather, the idealistic and garrulous Gavin
Stevens—of whom we have decidedly too much in the last two novels of
the trilogy, and who remains both infatuated with her and incapable of
acting on it—most often speaks Eula's thoughts and feelings, from his
own exalted perspective.

By contrast, *The Hamlet* effortlessly grants subjectivity to the schoolteacher Labove—some fifteen years older than Eula and obsessed with her:

> a man…with straight black hair…and high Indian cheekbones…and the
> long nose of thought….It was a forensic face, the face of invincible con-
> viction in the power of words as a principle worth dying for if necessary.
> A thousand years ago it would have been a monk's, a militant fanatic who
> would have…passed the rest of his days and nights calmly and without an
> instant's self-doubt battling…his own fierce and unappeasable natural appe-
> tites. (HAM 827)

Labove's inner orientation is before us—as a set of thoughts and convictions and appetites—as clearly as Eula's outer body is before us, as a
set of male-arousing organs. It is through Labove that *The Hamlet* reen-
gages the erotic intensity of *If I Forget Thee*. He is the monkish man
who lives for principle, the gaunt self-willed hermit intent on his ideal.
In his name, we see prefigured his coming ordeal—both "bovine" and
"above"—a man who would transcend the demands of his animal body.
It is not to be.

Then one morning he turned from the crude blackboard and saw a face eight
years old and a body of fourteen with the female shape of twenty, which
on the instant of crossing the threshold brought into the bleak, ill-lighted,
poorly heated room dedicated to the harsh functioning of Protestant primary
education a moist blast of spring's liquorish corruption. (HAM 835)

He is instantly felled. Try as he might, he cannot expunge her erotic scent
from his skin and glands. Soon he begins to hunger for the encounter—
any encounter—that will end this sexual torture: "And he did not want her
as a wife, he just wanted her one time as a man with a gangrened hand or
foot thirsts after the axe-stroke which will leave him comparatively whole
again" (839).

As with Harry and Charlotte, there is neither intimacy here nor desire for
it. Labove wants to penetrate Eula so powerfully—once will be enough—
that he might manage to expel her from his bodily system. The passage
glosses only his lust. It would be irresponsible to claim that Faulkner's
sexual feelings for Meta were the same, though the following letter to her
vibrates with a kindred erotic force: "I weigh 129 pounds and I want to
put it all on you and as much in you as I can can can must must will
will shall" (ALG 264). Both passages bespeak male sexual besottedness: he
must have her. But where *If I Forget Thee* traveled uncertainly into the territory of erotic consummation, *The Hamlet* remains safely (in this instance)
on the near side of coition. It thus finds its way into the comic dimensions
of Labove's frustration.

As luck would have it—but there is no luck in Faulkner's novels, only
fate—she re-enters the schoolroom just as he has his nose buried in the seat
those Olympian buttocks have recently vacated. Seeing him there, she says
(sublimely), "What are you doing down there?" (HAM 841). This launches
him. As during the football games he had earlier played with sufficient
brutality to garner a college scholarship, he now closes in on his prey: "He
caught her, hard, the two bodies hurling together violently because she had
not even moved to avoid him, let alone to begin resisting yet" (842). Slowly
she gathers herself together, then they wrestle: "'That's it,' he said. 'Fight
it. Fight it. That's what it is: a man and a woman fighting each other. The
hating. To kill, only to do it in such a way that the other will have to know
forever afterward he or she is dead'" (842). How much biographical conviction speaks in this quietly terrifying passage? How much male puritanical
disgust caused by eruption of carnal desire—desire that it is the everlasting fault of the female to have awakened? An entire culture's unthinking

misogyny can here be glimpsed: the abiding anger men feel toward women for arousing them, stripping them of their self-control and undermining their idealized image of themselves.

Labove is ecstatic in this career-destroying moment of encounter: "He held her loosely, still smiling, whispering his jumble of fragmentary Greek and Latin verse and American-Mississippi obscenity" (HAM 842). She manages to free an arm, elbows him under the chin, strikes him hard in the face. Stunned, he goes down. Standing over him, neither panting nor disheveled, she speaks the novel's most hilarious line: "Stop pawing me, you old headless horseman Ichabod Crane" (842–3). With those words—the epitaph awaiting every aging male teacher of English who has dreamed of bedding one of his nubile female students—Labove sinks into defeat and oblivion. Material that—thanks to its erotic unmanageability—had no choice in *If I Forgot Thee* but to head toward disaster and the abortion knife here ends in comic resolution.

Jack Houston—like Labove, memorable for his private anguish—serves to focus the next narrative of fatal passion. Biographical echoes abound. Like Faulkner and Estelle, Houston and his wife Lucy Pate "had known one another all of their lives" (HAM 922), and like Faulkner, Houston had tried to flee "the immemorial trap" (922). Suggestively recalling his creator, Houston realizes he must escape this woman. "He was...possessed of that strong lust, not for life...but for that fetterless immobility called freedom" (922). He first sought to escape her by failing his grade, then (though the brightest student in the class) she did likewise. At this sign of her determination, he panics: "It was a feud, a gage, wordless, uncapitulating, between that unflagging will [hers]...for the married state, and that furious and as unbending one [his] for solitariness and freedom" (924).

He flees, "not from his past, but to escape his future. It took him twelve years to learn you cannot escape either of them" (HAM 927). He lives for a time in El Paso, hundreds of miles away, bedding down for ten years with another woman, but cannot escape Lucy's long-range spell. Finally, putting his head in the noose, he returns home, self-compelled. They marry. (She has been waiting the entire time.) However—in an untypically overt piece of symbolism—he buys her a stallion as wedding present, as if "that blood and bone and muscles represented that...bitless masculinity which he had relinquished" (931). The stallion soon kicks her to death—an event whose reverberation forever after stalks Houston. Dead, she remains—like Mannie for Rider—inejectably inside him. He lies at nights on his narrow cot, "rigid, indomitable, and panting. 'I don't understand it,' he thinks to himself.

'I dont know why. I wont ever know why. But You cant beat me. I am strong as You are. You cant beat me'" (933).

At this precise moment in the text—when the biographical echoes seem strongest—Houston meets his death: "He was still alive when he left the saddle" (HAM 933). In a magnificent further paragraph, Faulkner writes Houston's last moments of consciousness. It is Mink Snopes who has shot him, and Houston silently struggles to handle the unbearable pain:

> It [the pain] roared down and raised him, tossed and spun. But it would not wait for him. It would not wait to hurl him into the void, so he cried, "Quick! Hurry!" looking up out of the red roar, into the face which with his own was wedded and twinned forever now by the explosion of that ten-gauge shell— the dead who would carry the living into the ground with him; the living who must bear about the repudiating earth with him forever, the deathless slain—then, as the slanted barrels did not move: "God damn it, couldn't you even borrow two shells, you fumbling ragged—" and put the world away. His eyes, still open to the lost sun, glazed over with a sudden well and run of moisture which flowed down the alien and unremembering cheeks too, already drying, with a newness as of actual tears. (HAM 934)

A minor figure in *The Hamlet,* Houston takes on depth and pathos through his haunting memories and mesmerizing death. It is in more ways than one a posthumous portrait. Faulkner enters Houston by having him retrospectively grasp the compulsions that have dominated his life—looking back and seeing how he could live neither with nor without Lucy Pate. Because Houston's death occurs at just this moment, it resonates as a dying man's recognitions. It is as though Faulkner could narrate the ordeal of an indestructible and all-destroying sexual bond only through the lens of a double murder: first the wife's, then the husband's. Next to the cadaver of Charlotte and the incarcerated Harry who "accidentally" killed her, we might place the murdered Houstons. There are no accidents in Faulkner. What happens is what must, according to the logic of his characters' being. Labove played out in a comic mode what unfolds here as disaster: men and women obsessed with each other are doomed to suffer for it, to die for it. The relationships are unforgivable. Or, looking back at his own fatal marriage—or at his doomed affair with Meta?—Faulkner seems unable to narrate such obsessions in a forgiving mood. It is as though he can enter them narratively only by way of envisaging both partners' punishment and extinction. Finally, the relationship that follows the suffocating heterosexual one is strangely homosocial. Mink and Houston have become forever bonded by their violent embrace. Without skipping a beat—these are the most compelling sequences in *The Hamlet*—Faulkner moves to the ordeal of Mink Snopes.

Mink's marital experience darkly intersects with Faulkner's. "Almost a half a head shorter" (HAM 937) and meaner than his wife (both of these details arguably biographical), Mink often threatens her, even hits her full in the face. He believes he has his reasons, inasmuch as he had first met her—been taken by her—at a timber camp deep in the woods, where she was the experienced one and he the virgin: "He had been bred by generations to believe invincibly that to every man, whatever his past actions, whatever depths he might have reached, there was reserved one virgin, at least for him to marry; one maidenhead, if only for him to deflower and destroy" (953). It was not to happen. Imperious—she has her take of all the men in the camp—she summons him: "He entered not the hot and quenchless bed of a barren and lecherous woman, but the fierce simple cave of a lioness—a tumescence which surrendered nothing and asked no quarter, and which made a monogamist of him forever, as opium and homicide do of those they once accept" (954).

Sexual congress figures here as a madness, like opium or homicide. Like Eula's penetration of Labove's being with the scent of her sexuality, this woman has gotten inside Mink: a "tumescence" has arisen between them that he can despise but cannot escape. Despise it he does: raised (like all Southern males of his time, including Faulkner perhaps) to believe that a virgin has been reserved even for him, he daily experiences humiliation. He cannot approach her without being "surrounded by the loud soundless invisible shades of the nameless and numberless men" there before him— "the cuckolding shades which had become a part of his past too" (HAM 938). Quentin Compson in *Absalom* has long moved readers by his awareness of himself as no longer an individual but a crystallization of his region, "a barracks, a commonwealth." Mink's plight is oddly similar. The body of his woman is multiply occupied. In every act of intercourse, her previous men—still in her—mock him for his belated "scratching" of what they had earlier "scratched" to their hearts' content.

It is not so much that Faulkner constantly replays the sordid dimensions of his marriage to a divorced woman, but rather that its sordidness does not go down, go away. Faulkner gets done with nothing. Time—in the sense of gradual, healthy oblivion—seems not to exist for him. "The past is never dead. It's not even past" (RN 535) he has Gavin Stevens magisterially declare in *Requiem for a Nun*. This conviction about time is easier to pronounce than to live with. "Hemophilic": Faulkner remained unprepared throughout his life—suffering rather than mastering what happened to him—because his resources for quarantining experience were inadequate. It was as though, figuratively, his inner "passages" were subject to leakages— leakages that would produce inner hemorrhaging. Is it any wonder that in his fiction the range of intricately channeled, bodily engagements with the world—drinking, eating, smelling, touching, fornicating, vomiting— emerges as though too hot, electrically charged, headed for trouble? It is in this sense—rather than through any retrospective grasp that might come later—that Faulkner is a diagnostic writer. Like the canary taken down deep into the mine, he possessed senses keen enough to scent the coming disaster just before it struck. To scent it, not to ward it off or escape.

Powerful as Mink's troubled relation with his wife is, the scenes sub-sequent to the murder of Houston are even stronger. Mink kills Houston because he feels insulted by Houston going to court to make him pay for damage done by his cow on Houston's land. The reasoning is dubious, and Faulkner spends no time bolstering or undermining it. He focuses on the murder's aftermath. During forty pages as stark as Macbeth's experience after murdering Duncan, Mink finds that—like his creator more gener-ally—he cannot get *done* with his deed. "I thought that when you killed a man, that finished it, he told himself. But it dont. It just starts then" (HAM 958). One remembers Macbeth staring at the ghost of Banquo and mutter-ing: "the time has been / That when the brains were out, the man would die."

Faulkner begins by juxtaposing Mink's ominous silence against an unwanted Snopes cousin's ceaseless chatter (he wants to exploit the murder by finding and rifling the dead man's wallet). Mink has no interest in profit; his concerns are more fundamental, beginning with disposing of the body. Then, thanks to the "pitch blackness" in which his attempt to do so occurs, as well as to Houston's wounded dog that—in inconsolable grief—stays near the body and attacks Mink whenever he approaches it, Mink begins to lose all forward motion. A number of daytime activities in *The Hamlet* reference the full moon of fertility—a folkloric belief buttressing communal continu-ity over time—but no moon shines during these death-haunted pages. No time seems to pass either. Here is Mink awaiting the dog's attack:

> Then the dog's voice stopped, again in mid-howl; again for an instant he saw the two yellow points of eyes before the gun-muzzle blotted them. In the glare of the explosion he saw the whole animal sharp in relief, leaping. He saw the charge strike and hurl it backward into the loud welter of following

darkness…with the gun still at his shoulder he crouched, holding his breath and glaring into the sightless dark while the tremendous silence which had been broken three nights ago when the first cry of the hound reached him and which had never once been restored, annealed, even while he slept, roared down about him and, still roaring, began to stiffen and set like cement, not only in his hearing but in his lungs, his breathing, inside and without him too, solidifying from tree-trunk to tree-trunk, among which the shattered echoes of the shot died away in strangling murmurs. (HAM 946)

Time and space have congealed, become arrested: he is over and over repeating the unfinished murder. Nightmarishly, he cannot relocate the dead body in the "pitch blackness." When he finds it, he cannot dislodge it from the hollow tree trunk into which he earlier hurled it. In trying to do so, he nearly falls in himself, too deep to climb out. Meanwhile—Poe-like—the dog, though wounded repeatedly, will not die. The stuck corpse Mink is struggling to retrieve suddenly comes free, and as he carries it (half again his size) into the coming dawn, he discovers that one of its limbs is missing. He rushes back in a panic to the tree stump to find the telltale limb, tries to ward off again the still ferocious dog, and is at last arrested. Mink's final attempt at freedom involves leaping from the surrey that is carting him off to jail, hoping to brake it somehow with his foot, but instead catching his neck in the surrey's stanchion. As the surrey continues to move, "something struck him a terrific blow at the base of his neck and…became…a pressure, rational furious with deadly intent" (HAM 972). He briefly passes out. Once in jail, surrounded by black prisoners and barely able to make his damaged throat utter words, he croaks: "'I was all right…until it [Houston's body] started coming to pieces. I could have handled that dog.'" "'Hush, white man,' the Negro said. 'Hush. Dont be telling us no truck like that.'" As the jail food gets passed around, Mink reflects (these are his last thoughts): "Are they going to feed them niggers before they do a white man?" (973–4).

The sequence captures hypnotically the experience of man alone and stumbling, caught beyond control in the mire of his own doings. Mink is perpetually unprepared, yet determined to persevere. Faulkner seems to have known since the early 1930s that Mink would make a final appearance. His obsessive journey—after thirty-seven years in Parchman prison—to find and kill his cousin Flem would provide *The Mansion*'s most compelling vignette. Unrepentant, incorrigible, going down, Mink—like Labove and Houston—gives us a measure of *The Hamlet*'s obsessive concerns. Ratliff's shrewd imperturbability makes him uniquely appealing among Faulkner's cast of characters. But if we want to take the temperature of Faulkner's imagination, we turn to the outraged, unvanquished Mink Snopes.

The Hamlet most echoes *If I Forget Thee, Jerusalem* by way of its invest- ment in the madness of human bondage. We might conclude by consider- ing the vignette in the novel that literalizes such madness: the idiot Ike Snopes's infatuation with a cow. Told in a pastoral and overheated Latinate vocabulary, this love affair reconnects with Faulkner's earlier, supremely moving Benjy Compson. But *The Hamlet*'s idiot hardly resembles the earlier novel's idiot. Benjy served largely as a lens on the stumblings of the Comp- son family (he had little "plot" himself). By contrast, Faulkner grants Ike his own project, allows him to celebrate an ecstatic union with his beloved: "So he leaves the crib…breathing in the reek, the odor of cows and mares as the successful lover does that of a room full of women, his the victor's drowsing rapport with all anonymous faceless female flesh capable of love walking the female earth" (HAM 898).

Sanctuary: a stay against confusion, a sheltered space permitting self-ful- fillment. Is idiocy the requisite mental stance for any male lover who might actually manage to enjoy his woman's "anonymous faceless" fertile body? Labove, Houston, and Mink—each afflicted with normal consciousness— come to grief on entering this identity-shattering arena of erotic encounter with the beloved. But idiot Ike is freed from normal thought and social custom, unaware of his beloved's difference, unashamed of his body's animal propensities: "They eat from the basket together. He has eaten feed before— hulls and meal, and oats and raw corn and silage and pig-swill…things which the weary long record of shibboleth and superstition had taught his upright kind to call filth" (HAM 899–900). Filth: the uncleanness connected with on-the-ground animal ingestion and love-making, as well as with menstrua- tion. "Periodic filth between two moons balanced," so the horrified Quentin Compson in *The Sound and the Fury* imagined female sexuality. "Woman- filth," so the enraged Doc Hines in *Light in August* screamed. The reality of sexual congress and the liquid-filled foulness of the female womb within which it must occur: apart from idiot Ike, Faulkner's dreamy males tend to encounter this bodily realm as dizzying, scandalous, ungraced by spirit.

One remembers a related passage from "Wild Palms": "how the four- legged animal gains all its information through smelling and seeing and hearing and distrusts all else while the two-legged one believes only what it reads" (HAM 566–7). The animal, lodged in its body and trusting its senses, is at ease—as the human never can be—with the orientation the senses provide. Aiming higher, "upright" humans repudiate sensory orientation, yet they lack instinctual resources that might guide a trajectory more worthy of the spirit. Thus humans depend—grievously—for orientation and procedure on the faulty reading matter (the defective maps) provided by culture. Is this one of the reasons Faulkner so immerses his reader in the sense-directed movement of his culturally deprived, spatially disoriented characters—Benjy, Joe Christmas, the overwhelmed convict, Mink in the dark, Ike on the move? Unconcerned with disembodied realms like truth or goodness, the body stays on the ground; it neither lies nor errs. For his part, Ike experiences his mental blankness as bacchanalian plenitude: nothing in the career of his body can make him vomit. Even being showered by his beloved cow's copious defecation fails to disturb his epithalamion. For him, the unbridgeable difference between human and animal does not exist.

Unbridgeable difference: only mindless Ike spans the unspannable. Normal humans in thrall to animal urgency are not so lucky. Faulkner and Estelle, Faulkner and Meta, Harry and Charlotte, Labove and Eula, Houston and Lucy, Mink and his sexually soiled wife: these couplings are impossible to resist or sustain. Mules appealed to Faulkner because—naturally unrelated to the rest of the animal kingdom—they steadily and (if need be) fiercely stayed what they were: separate, unreachable, beyond coupling. "We don't want him tame," Sam Fathers had said of the great dog Lion. At his core, the Faulkner male—animal or human—wants to be intact, individual, beyond merging. When he falls or is compelled into relationship, something primordial in him rebels. Insofar as sanctuary is a ruse for temporarily escaping one's embattled foreignness to one's world—for experiencing life as untroubled by the entry of others—sanctuary must fail. Because erotic love heedlessly seeks to bridge what cannot be bridged, it emerges—in Faulkner's life and in these two novels of his early forties—as a species of sublime madness. However his males crave it, they abhor it with equal intensity. They are never ready for it, and it will not submit to domestication. It is beyond owning.

Near the end of *The Hamlet*, Ratliff and Uncle Will are chatting together, standing near the wounded Henry Armstid. The latter had believed, despite all evidence, that he could actually own the wild pony he has bought. He has paid for his mistake after trying to take possession. Kicked unconscious, his leg broken, writhing "Ah. Ah. Ah," the groaning Armstid awakens in Uncle Will Varner a larger meditation on human unpreparedness for encounters. Reflecting on how we suffer when we seek to domesticate the world's shocking otherness, Varner murmurs, "There's a pill for every ill but the last one." Without missing a beat, Ratliff replies, "Even if there was always time to take it." Silent for an instant, Uncle Will rejoins, "Even if there was time to take it. Breathing is a sight-draft dated yesterday" (HAM 1019).

Breathing, as a sight-draft dated yesterday, is radically at risk. It may be cashed in at any time by "the Ones that set up the loom." Whatever the sinister gods had in mind, it was not our prospering. We do not nicely, cumulatively, "become" ourselves over time. We muddle along, often well enough protected by the tattered garments of habit and expectation. Sooner or later, habit will fail, expectation come a cropper, and the trap will spring. We will find ourselves reduced once again to the naked amazement in which it all began—as Yeats put it, "the foul rag-and-bone shop of the heart." Born to encounter a final death—that ending for which we are never prepared—we encounter on the way any number of smaller deaths, some of them potentially mortal themselves. When they hit, we suffer, but we are also, once again, alive. No one knew this better, in 1940, than William Faulkner.

"THE MAELSTROM OF UNBEARABLE REALITY"

The deepest logic in both Faulkner's life and his work is that disaster strikes—when it strikes—prior to any preparation for it. In the moment of crisis, one is never ready. For that reason I have opened this chapter, like the preceding ones, in the midst of trouble, without explanatory framing. I have sought to render something of the texture of Faulkner's stumbling in the present moment. It is time for further meditation on those would-be shelters Faulkner sought for protection and coherence. Each in its way— alcohol, love affairs—delivered its boon en route to failing him over time. The protection was temporary, the coherence illusory. There was no long-term escaping the troubles that beset his life.

The quest for refuge emerges as a groundswell in the work as well—a quest perhaps most memorably dramatized in *Absalom*. "*A might-have-been that is more true than truth*" (AA 115, emphasis in the original): so Rosa Coldfield thought of sanctuary. It was protection against the onslaught set loose by the "sinister gods." The quoted clause articulates Rosa's thinking at a moment of sudden unpreparedness. Having been ignored throughout her orphaned childhood, this needy child had invested her older niece Judith's coming marriage—to her peerless fiancé Charles Bon—with all the emotional fulfillment lacking in her own life. Suddenly their betrothal was shot out from under her, hurtling her into "*the maelstrom of unbearable reality*"

(120, emphasis in the original). Stunned by Wash Jones's brutal announcement that Henry had killed Bon, Rosa rushed to Sutpen's Hundred. There she encountered not Bon's corpse (she was never to lay eyes on him) but instead an apparently serene, unreachable Judith. She encountered as well—invisibly filling the space around her—the collapse of her long-sustained and sustaining dream. "*Why did I wake*," she wondered, "*since waking I shall never sleep again?*" (AA 118, emphasis in the original).

Waking into unbearable reality: Faulkner's work explored—from start to finish—the human need for fictions that would ward off disaster lurking somewhere at the "*prime foundation of this factual scheme*" (AA 118, emphasis in the original). His fiction represented the world as a space that could not be confronted on its own brutely inhuman terms. A "*miasmal mass*" Rosa called it in *Absalom:* the world as a swamp ultimately inhospitable to human designs invented to make it hospitable.

What sounds like metaphysical nihilism was rooted in specific cultural dilemmas. Writ large, Faulkner's novels powerfully illuminated an early twentieth-century South looking back, bewildered, on the collapse of antebellum dreams. *Absalom* lingered over the antebellum aspirations invested in Sutpen's construction of his mansion: naked men covered in mud to ward off mosquitoes, working from dawn to dusk as they dredged from the swamp a dwelling that would match Sutpen's dream of himself. The South had taught him to pursue precisely this figure in the world. Like all such sanctuaries—race- and class-shaped to the hilt—this one was primed to backfire over time. Finally secure inside his plantation, Sutpen denies entry to his part-black son Charles Bon—even as he himself had been denied entry, forty years before, into Pettibone's plantation. Class abuse (white trash may not enter) repercusses as race and gender abuse (a discarded part-black wife and her part-black son who cannot be acknowledged). The unanticipated consequences of disowning Charles Bon leads to Sutpen's being disowned himself—abandoned by his second son Henry—and eventually killed by his poor-white retainer Wash Jones. One's desires get entangled—all the puppet strings inextricably knotted—with the desires of others. Sutpen's precious mansion—at once shelter, antidote against earlier humiliation, and crowning glory—ends by burning in the night. Clytie—his slave, servant, daughter, victim, and avenging destroyer—sets it aflame. It reads as metaphysical rebuke. It reads more deeply as the murderous consequence of Southern class, race, and gender belief systems.

Faulkner's earlier masterpieces—*The Sound and the Fury, As I Lay Dying, Sanctuary,* and *Light in August*—grappled no less movingly with the same thematics of psychic exposure and protection: assaults beyond negotiation, futile attempts to secure safety. Macbeth's soliloquy on time gone wrong would haunt Faulkner for his entire life. Time had become treacherous: we dream outdated dreams, lie our ways into wars that end before we can enter them, love women we cannot possess when we seek them, and no longer desire when they become ours. Our attempts to extricate ourselves from untimeliness are themselves untimely, burying us more deeply. The dilemma was at first existential—outrage at untimeliness—but the longer he endured it, the more he glimpsed its cultural underpinnings.

Caddy's virginity, like Dewey Dell's and Temple's, harbored a cultural insistence—a mandated sanctuary—that Faulkner thought to be indefensible in theory and knew to be punitive in fact. Between life's unanticipated abrasiveness and youth's sexual urgency, female virginity had little chance of enduring. Virginity's meaning, like the larger one embodied in his region's defeat in 1865, centered on the inevitability of Southern loss, and the pathos of defending it nevertheless. In like manner, as Joe Christmas's story would testify, the violence engendered by crossing the color line rested on racial convictions—airy conceptual sanctuaries—unsupported by biological data, physical evidence, or repressed (but unrepressible) human desire. White male designs, insofar as they were built on the backs of others who could not be acknowledged, necessarily collapsed—and were followed by repercussive aftershocks affecting generations to come. The defeat of Quentin Compson, Joe Christmas, and Thomas Sutpen was not just existential bad news. It carried in its wake a larger diagnostic portent. Ultimately it revealed, in excruciating detail over time, that the gendered and racial maps these Southerners lived and died by—the priorities and distinctions that furnished Southern identity itself—were suicidal at their core.

In *As I Lay Dying*, Faulkner had one of his characters point out the difference between weightless words that rise into the air and unspeakable realities that take place on the ground. Faulkner had come to see that human values—"designs," as he would call them in *Absalom*—locate in the air. There they take the form of the socially inculcated fictions we live and die by. Because they have no natural rooting, because they privilege some by exploiting others, they eventually come crashing down. By his early thirties, Faulkner grasped not only that words can be mendacious. He saw that the systemic project of culturally driven narratives—however benign—was to produce (retrospective) order by way of mendacity. Narrative lived in the air, even as it sought to make credible a verbal world of thought and feeling and belief at odds with the real in its on-the-ground, strife-ridden complexity.

In this way, Faulkner took on—doubtless without identifying it thus—his novelistic project. He would reconfigure inherited verbal structures (narrative forms) so strenuously that against their own will, they would intimate the unmanageable realities their purpose was to massage into order. *Absalom, Absalom!*—with its array of cultural dreams along with their inevitable collapse, with its proliferation of narrative shapings along with their confessed inadequacy—embodies this project at its highest point.

Finally, and this is inseparable from Faulkner's grandeur, no individual blame attaches to the array of collapses his great work records. Not that he narrated his stories of destruction and damage amorally, with Nabokovian detachment. Rather, sharing imaginatively the insistences of his protagonists—even as he saw that these were grounded in illusion or privilege—Faulkner did not pass judgment. He managed to place himself in his characters and outside them at the same time. To judge, one has to see past the dilemmas that bedevil one's characters, to know not only that they are wrong, but how they might have been right. Faulkner neither knew nor pretended to know this. Thus the remarkable honesty of his best work, the reason for its heartbreaking power. No alternative exists—while reading it—to the agony his people are suffering or inflicting or both. His later work—I shall address this point more fully soon—tended to possess answers, to turn stumbling into error. It tended to do what fiction usually does: identify solutions that retroactively transform abiding dilemmas into manageable problems.

"The maelstrom of unbearable reality": Faulkner not only wrote that condition, he lived it. More—and this was perhaps his rarest resource as a writer—he respected it. He grasped that stumbling is how humans negotiate present moments that are too much for them. Because we live inescapably in the present moment, we cannot be prepared for the ramifications of our experience. We enter a scene that began long before our moment of arrival. The scene harbors, as well, concealed consequences that long outlast our moment of departure. A childhood sweetheart he couldn't bring himself to elope with; a war he sought unsuccessfully to enter; a plane he bought to make up for lies he had earlier told, and that he bequeathed to his brother Dean; a first child whom he lost, followed by another too precious to relinquish (as divorce would have required); a white Southerner who viewed blacks as other and inferior yet sometimes saw in them—within the mirror they put before him—his undeniable dark twins: none of these life experiences is spectacular as such. Any Southerner might have had them. But if you add them together, they can be haunting, as any life is open to being haunted. Being haunted depends not on the unusualness of the stimulus but on the imaginative depth of the response. Faulkner's imagination was hemophilic.

These were the interrelated liabilities and resources he carried with him throughout his life. Hemophilic: channels that remained open, outside the aegis of will. His lifelong stance of impenetrability—his recourse to silence and impassivity—implies, as its counterpart, an immensely threatening inner responsiveness. Silent did not mean phlegmatic. From childhood forward, he took in everything that was happening around him and forgot little of it—its look, feel, smell, sound, and unacted possibilities. He maintained greater control by absorbing silently rather than performing out loud. Eventually, his indirect mode of performance would involve the creative probing and reshaping of what he had already absorbed—his labor as an artist. Inside his head a teeming, many-peopled world was already under way. Excessive drinking was at first a normal part of his childhood and youth. Later, it became a summoned—eventually fatal—dimension of his maturity and older years. He was a man who solved little, and who rarely fooled himself about what he had failed to solve. By his early thirties he had become badly married, given to bouts of uncontrollable drinking, determined to put onto paper the cluster of novels already roiling around inside his head. He was also in need of more money (as a Southern paterfamilias) than he could hope to earn by his fiction.

The many trips to Hollywood follow in almost predictable fashion— how else pay the bills that his inherited model of identity tells him he must incur and pay if he is to be both successful and honorable? Once in Hollywood, the gathering emotional trap is set and ready to spring. Hollywood solicits everything awry in his married life: his loneliness away from home, his alienation from the medium of film and from those who produce it, his incapacity to adapt to a world of rented dwellings and apparently interchangeable faces, each lacking its specific history. He meets at work a charming and gentle Southern woman—a decade younger, recently divorced, in awe of his reputation. They begin an affair—this will be the sanctuary that frees him from matrimonial misery—and they fall in love (this seems to be the correct sequence). He cannot divorce, begins to drink more heavily, plunges more deeply into his affair. He learns that erotic love is ecstasy and torture, incompatible with everything else he has come to know and endorse about himself. He is caught in the quagmire of his own contradictions. All along, the big book—the one that will once and for all establish him as America's greatest—keeps eluding him, telling him that he is not yet the writer he must be.

Such is the becoming of William Faulkner—a movement through space and time that calls into question the usual meanings of "becoming." It is nearer to a sustaining than a becoming—a sustaining of burdens whose weight increases over time. Like Mink Snopes desperately using his own neck to spring himself free from an otherwise straight path heading to jail, like the convict bleeding anew at every encounter but grimly determined to get the job done though he had nothing to do with its assignment, like the mule persevering in its speechless direction, regardless of others' commands or beatings: so Faulkner endured the contradictions that made him up. By the early 1940s the picture is tolerably clear, the portrait more or less complete. What remains is what he called in *Absalom* the "rubbishy aftermath," the later years of hospitalization, frustration, and international fame.

CHAPTER 5

TOMORROW AND TOMORROW
AND TOMORROW

Late in the second act of *Requiem for a Nun* (1951), Gowan Stevens and his wife Temple (miserably married for eight years now) ponder the painful sequence of events that has brought them to their current dilemma. Gowan's uncle Gavin has gathered them together to figure out how they might have avoided the disaster at Frenchman's Bend—the drunken car accident and subsequent rape that launched the vicious mayhem of *Sanctuary*. Looking back, they cannot imagine anything other than what occurred: "Tomorrow and tomorrow and tomorrow," Temple murmurs, and Gavin ("speaking her thought, finishing the sentences" [RN 611]) says without missing a beat, "—he [Gowan] will wreck the car again against the wrong tree, in the wrong place, and you will have to forgive him again, for the next eight years until he can wreck the car again in the wrong place, against the wrong tree—" (611).

Faulkner was fifty-three years old when he wrote this hybrid text—half epic prose history of Yoknapatawpha County, half stage play in which Temple Drake Stevens seeks to reclaim her soul. Despite strenuous attempts—by Gavin, the Governor, and (behind them both) Faulkner—to "confess" Temple, the project of self-recovery does not succeed. Looking back over the unenlightened years that had passed, Temple is unable to come upon a retrospective insight that might allow her, cathartically, to liberate her future. Rather than analyze *Requiem for a Nun* further, I stress the failed project of recognition. Temple cannot resee her past so as to begin anew. Nor could her author, with respect to his own life. Faulkner's last two decades reenacted conflicts that had arisen earlier and remained irresoluble. What had gone wrong earlier would inevitably go wrong again.

Faulkner passed half of the 1940s in Hollywood, trying to write *A Fable* while drafting screenplays. Probably blacklisted as an unwise alcoholic risk, he now obtained film work only at a risible salary—less than half the weekly rate he had received in the 1930s. It was rumored that Jack Warner liked to brag about paying America's greatest novelist only (what in Hollywood was considered) a pittance. Almost none of Faulkner's scripts made it to the screen. Throughout this decade he remained immersed in the on-again, off-again relationship with Meta Carpenter. In addition, Estelle's alcoholism flared during the 1940s as uncontrollably as his did; these were arguably the worst years of their marriage. Going off to Pine Manor Junior College in 1951, Jill was happy to escape the family nest. She would later remember "the meals eaten mainly in silence at the polished dining-room table where she would be the only channel of communication between her parents, and the periodic crises" (F 546).

The 1950s might have been a happier decade for him, if he had been the kind of man who enjoyed public recognition. Such recognition had begun massively to arrive: the Nobel Prize (1950), the National Book Award (1951, for *Collected Stories*), the French Legion d'Honneur award (also 1951), another National Book Award and the Pulitzer Prize (both in 1954, for *A Fable*). He had become financially at ease as well. An iconic figure honored the world over, he now took on (with what interior grimace who can know?) the role of a "sixty-year-old smiling public man" (as Yeats wryly put it in "Among School Children"). Managing to act in accord with the Nobel image others assumed to be his genuine identity, Faulkner served often during this decade as a traveling spokesman for the State Department. To be sure, government officials micromanaged his tours, anxious to head off trouble before it worsened. But trouble rarely arrived. Faulkner had learned how to negotiate such occasions; he was at ease delivering prepared remarks and answering unscripted questions. It is hard to imagine him in the 1940s either being invited to such assignments or assenting and carrying them off so well. This was also the decade in which he was repeatedly onstage politically, publicly pursuing a civil rights solution whose terms few others (black or white) deemed viable.

Beneath these 1950s public performances, the deeper profile of the man changed little. His broken marriage did not heal, nor did he find a satisfactory way of escaping it. The self-destructive drinking, like the spine-damaging horseback riding, continued unabated. In the late 1950s—after noting his near-falls and unskilled moves—a fellow rider once asked him if he *liked* horses. Faulkner responded, "I'm scared to death of horses, that's why I can't leave them alone" (F 658). The unvanquished: however rocky the road he had chosen, retreat was not an option, and he carried on. No more than Temple was he able to look back and discover in hindsight what in himself he might change, so as to arrive at peace. Peace would remain beyond his reach. To his agent Harold Ober he had written in 1945, "For some time I have expected, at a certain age, to reach that period (in the early fifties) which most artists seem to reach where they admit at last that there is no solution to life and that it is not now, and perhaps never was, worth the living" (SL 199). There is little reason to believe that these nihilistic sentiments lifted much during the 1950s.

Rather than find his way into new insights and the breakthroughs they might permit, Faulkner persevered in his long-established rituals. We need not rehearse further the alcohol-caused hospitalizations—including probably electroshock therapy and certainly psychoanalytic sessions—that befell him throughout the 1950s. "Befell him" is the accurate phrasing. He never sought these therapies—he sought no therapy at all—but his friends and family could not simply look on as he descended deeper into self-destruction. "Befell him" is another reason why the psychoanalytic cure never worked for Faulkner. As Freud had known from the beginning of psycho-analysis, the patient must want to be cured if he was ever to overcome the resistances that the treatment deliberately provoked and engaged, in order to do battle with them.

Tomorrow and tomorrow and tomorrow. In 1946—home again, his relationship with Meta on the skids, for how long he did not know—Faulkner decided it was time for fresh blood. He would seek it in the same form that he had attempted to find it a decade earlier. To Malcolm Cowley he wrote, "It's a dull life here [in Oxford]. I need some new people, above all probably a new woman" (SL 245). Meta Carpenter—probably the unique love of his life—diminishes in this later phrasing to just a "woman": a generic category permitting subsequent replacements. Three years after this letter, he would have his chance at a new one. A sensitive, twenty-year-old Memphian, Joan Williams, adored his work from afar. She yearned to become a writer, and she needed to get her life back on track. She had recently gone through an elopement and its annulling. Her parents, she was sure, understood neither her feelings nor her ambition. Perhaps this godlike fellow Southern artist would share some of his insight.

Thus charged, she gathered her courage and—determined to seek him out at home—headed to Rowan Oak. To her embarrassment, Faulkner responded to the uninvited knock at his door coldly, with unconcealed annoyance. Mortified, Joan beat a hasty retreat, then wrote a profuse apology from her parents' home. Identifying some of her reasons for wanting to see him, Joan's letter piqued him, brought her before his mind's eye as the surprise visit had not. Thus it began. Interested, he wrote back, and she warmly continued the correspondence from Bard College, where she was a student. Her letters teemed with questions about how she might become a novelist, but he was soon responding in a quite different register. "These are the wrong questions," he wrote back. "A woman must ask these of a man while they are lying in bed together" (F 507). Shocked by this sexual advance, yet encouraged by his sympathy, she sought to redirect the relationship onto an artistic plane.

There ensued, at a pace lurching between frustrating stasis and agonizing slow motion, a three-year relationship marred by awkwardness and incompatible longings. Twenty-year old Joan Williams, on the voyage out, did not want an affair with fifty-three-old William Faulkner—much as she admired him. But she could not see her way to relinquishing his attentions either. It was a comedy waiting for someone other than Faulkner to write it. Bernard Shaw had already captured in *Pygmalion* something of the wry pathos wrought into their different positions. A restless Henry Higgins, Faulkner sought strenuously to straddle the roles of lover and teacher. The project was false from day one, and it could not be made true. His bad-faith letters to her read as recurrently double-edged—an erotic tug skewing and sugaring his artistic advice. Her letters must have been troublingly mixed in their motives as well, for Estelle became enraged once she intercepted some of them. She had put up with Meta Carpenter, but this twenty-year-old Memphis girl was too much. Estelle challenged Joan face-to-face, telephoned her parents and complained, then took more heavily to the booze. Intent on keeping her letters coming, Faulkner directed Joan to send them to "Quentin Compson," care of General Delivery, at the Oxford post office. Some disguise!

His amorous moves resisted but not quite rebuffed, Faulkner assiduously pursued the courtship. Finally, by the summer of 1953 they became— briefly, unsatisfyingly—lovers. (She would later fictionalize this relationship in her novel *The Wintering*.) Faulkner's letters of artistic advice to her were generous, if useless; he knew them to be useless. No one could help anyone else become a writer; no one could have helped him. Rather than give advice as such—a stance he had avoided his entire life and would have avoided here if the letters had really been about advice—he urged her to trust her own thoughts and feelings, to ignore others' rules and models. He invited her to help him write *Requiem for a Nun*, a collaboration she wisely refused. Throughout it all he was seeking the bodily and psychic reassurance of a consummated sexual relationship. Whatever else Joan meant for him, he envisaged her as a sanctuary in which he could keep at bay his advancing years and—visible in the distance—the specter of sexual waning. For her part, she must early on have sensed an erotic denouement approaching. Somewhere inside her psyche—where the deeper quid pro quos take place—she must have decided to accept him as a lover. If that was the price for keeping his precious attention, she would pay it. This cannot have been easy. In her imaginary, Faulkner would have combined, incoherently, aspects of her parents and her ideals, her prison and her escape. It was perhaps sympathy rather than strategy that led her to consummation. She could not have failed to realize how badly he needed her. Years later, at a Faulkner conference in the early 1990s, I sat opposite Joan Williams at dinner. As she spoke off and on with Faulknerians whom she had met before, I watched the tears repeatedly gather in her eyes. Forty years after their affair, thirty after his death, she seemed freshly wounded. I wondered: did he ruin this woman's life, too?

As for Faulkner's role in this misguided affair, surely Labove—depicted so authoritatively a decade earlier—should have taught him (if these things can be taught) that pedagogy and eros make strange bedfellows. Rising from different intentions and pursuing different ends, they are all too likely to encounter each other comically, pathetically. By the fall of 1953, Joan would end the affair and become engaged to a man her own age. Within the next year, she and Faulkner would begin to go their separate ways. What perhaps redeemed this relationship—transcending the banality of his sexual insistence and her reluctant submission—was the care he gave her during their time together and by way of letters. For her part, she responded with kindred generosity, doing what she could to address his alcoholism—finding New York doctors, helping him recover from binges. Between them, they may have managed to bestow on their foredoomed relationship something of grace after all.

Later, in the mid-1950s, Faulkner would meet in Rome the bohemian Jean Stein (only nineteen years old—younger even than Jill—but sophisticated and already well traveled in several senses). They would soon engage in a more carefree physical relationship. Jean Stein was no tortured Southern girl in need of advice and acknowledgment. Descended from a wealthy family, intellectually adventurous, she was already perhaps more worldly than he would ever be. More, she admired his work—producing, with his help, the best interview of him that would ever be written, published in the *Paris Review* in 1956. Jean served as well as an epistolary lifeline of understanding during Faulkner's embattled civil rights encounters. She may finally have meant as much, to him, for her generous free spirit as for her sexual acceptance of this self-enclosed, sixty-year-old Southern writer—possessed of genius, but afflicted by it, too.

THE LATER FICTION 1: FAULKNERESE

It is one thing to attempt to persuade my reader how and why Faulkner's great work is great. It is another to try to persuade my reader why the lesser work is lesser. It is distasteful—and serves little purpose—to linger on what is lacking in a supreme writer's lesser work. I do not recant my conviction that Faulkner's contribution to the world of letters began in 1929 (*The Sound and the Fury*) and concluded in 1942 (*Go Down, Moses*). Apart from a small number of scholars who argue otherwise, this has long been the consensus about Faulkner's work. In terms of my argument, those were the years in which Faulkner's unpredictable becoming found its way into his experimental masterpieces. These works narrate poignant dramas of time—unpreparedness before the onslaught of experience, incapacity to map it in the present moment—such as no other Western novelist has matched.

The years between *Go Down, Moses* and *Intruder in the Dust*—from 1942 to 1948—stand out as uniquely barren in Faulkner's career. Six years would be a notable gap for any prolific writer; for one with Faulkner's habits of composition, it is astonishing. In the later 1920s, he published at a clip of a novel a year. Seven novels appeared during the 1930s, and four in the 1950s. Apart from the dry spell of 1942–48, the largest temporal gap between novels is three years: this 1940s drought begs to be explained. Rather than speculate on its causes, I want to identify its fallout. The writer who emerged in 1948 has changed: less a different man than a different writer. For the next six years, his novels would provide the quarry for what later came to be called (by all who dislike his work) "Faulknerese."

What rhetorical traits combine as "Faulknerese"? I begin with a rough definition, to be followed by a couple of examples. "Faulknerese" is a verbal practice given to proliferating syntax and Latinate/polysyllabic vocabulary. Its insistence manifests in seemingly numberless clauses that thunder onward. "Faulknerese" does not pare down; it has no interest in the Flaubertian mot juste. It refuses to pause, to let readers catch their breath, by supplying that (increasingly longed for) period that would announce: this sentence has now *ended*. Such "Faulknerese"—either previously encountered or dreaded in advance—is a major reason many readers are skittish toward Faulkner's work. It appears full-blown in *Intruder in the Dust* (1948), *Requiem for a Nun* (1951), and *A Fable* (1954). To see what is at stake, we might examine part of the first sentence of *Requiem's* opening section, "The Courthouse":

> The settlement had the records; even the simple dispossession of Indians begot in time a minuscule of archive, let alone the normal litter of man's ramshackle confederation against environment—that time and that wilderness;—in this case, a meager, fading, dogeared, uncorrelated, at times illiterate sheaf of land grants and patents and transfers and deeds, and tax- and militia-rolls, and bills of sale for slaves, and counting-house lists of spurious currency and exchange rates, and liens and mortgages, and listed rewards for escaped or stolen Negroes and other livestock, and diary-like annotations of births and marriages and deaths and public hangings and land-auctions, accumulating slowly for those three decades in a sort of iron pirate's chest in the back room of the postoffice-tradingpost-store, until that day thirty years later when, because of a jailbreak compounded by an ancient monster iron padlock transported a thousand miles by horseback from Carolina, the box was removed to a small new leanto room like a wood- or tool-shed built two days ago against one outside wall of the morticed-log mud-chinked shake-down jail; and thus was born the Yoknapatawpha County courthouse. (RN 475)

Each detail is saliently put before us, but they relentlessly accumulate into a sort of overwhelming. One adjective ("meager") gives birth to four more ("fading, dogeared, uncorrelated…illiterate"), in turn followed by—it seems—every possible item that might have been preserved as "records." When Faulkner thinks "settlement records," he thinks exhaustively. The collection is overfull; one has little sense that the twelve different categories of archival material will later take on selective significance. (They don't.) Rather, the Faulkner imaginary has become plenary. This is how he *sees* that historical "archive." He seems compelled to note not only every item or object there but its metamorphosis in time or extensiveness in space ("postoffice-tradingpost-store").

We go for a second example to Faulkner's "biggest" novel, *A Fable*. There the reader learns immediately that the crucial plot-event has already taken place. The Great War has unexpectedly, without orders from above, ground to a halt, in a small village in France. The rest of the novel will invest this mutual cessation of fighting with extraordinary significance—moving toward the Christian passion on which the text is openly modeled. I cite the swift arrival (a few pages into the book) of a military car carrying the three top generals. They have come to crush the incipient rebellion:

> It [the car] came fast, so fast that the shouts of the section leaders and the clash of rifles as each section presented arms and then clashed back to "at ease," were not only continuous but overlapping, so that the car seemed to progress on one prolonged crash of iron as on invisible wings with steel feathers,—a long, dusty open car painted like a destroyer and flying the pennon of the supreme commander of all the allied armies, the three generals sitting side by side in the tonneau amid a rigid glitter of aides,—the three old men who held individual command over each of the three individual armies, and the one of that three who, by mutual consent and accord, held supreme command over all (and, by that token and right, over everything beneath and on and above the distracted half-continent)—the Briton, the American, and between them the Generalissimo: the slight gray man with a face wise, intelligent, and unbelieving, who no longer believed in anything but his disillusion and his intelligence and his limitless power—flashing across that terrified and aghast amazement and then gone, as the section leaders shouted again and the boots and the rifles crashed back to simple alert. (FAB 678)

This is a carefully meditated piece of writing. If I claim that its cumulative insistence makes it hard on the reader, one might remember my earlier claim that Faulkner's difficulty was inseparable from his importance. Indeed, the opening page of *Absalom* is more daunting than this passage. But there is difficulty, and there is difficulty. Like the other earlier masterpieces, *Absalom* proceeds in such a way as to test a reader's willingness to sustain confusion: not to know, not yet. Its first page moves from Rosa and Quentin talking intensively together, one afternoon in September 1909, to the two-generational family history of the room they are talking in (the closed shutters, the tomblike atmosphere). From there it moves to the absent nineteenth-century company haunting that room: the ghost of Thomas Sutpen, musing on them. Then it turns to something earlier yet, and apparently inaugural: Quentin's imagining (thanks to Rosa's words) the spectacular imposing (in 1833) of Sutpen's Hundred—"Be Sutpen's Hundred!"—on the land. A slew of characters and events and settings are hurled at an unprepared reader: yet each of these elements becomes (eventually) crucial to *Absalom*'s still-to-unfold range of meanings.

The difficulty of the passage from *A Fable* has nothing to do with not knowing enough in present time, unpreparedness for all that is at stake in a moment of experience. By contrast to the opening of *Absalom*, the later passage is oddly static—a sort of monumental tableau—as it presses us to attend to the stature of its cast of officers. The prose is at pains to insist that the Generalissimo's "supreme command" goes beyond present company, extending to everything "beneath and on and above the distracted half-continent." That quoted phrase is slack, as are "by mutual consent and accord," "by that token and right," and "terrified and aghast amazement." We are in the presence of a "big" scene full of grandiloquent phrases—a scene whose author pulls out the stops to make sure we see how big it is. We are to be impressed by military pomp and circumstance, the arrival of men of unparalleled power. Faulkner's prose draws attention to specific commands and positions, described to impress: presenting arms, returning to at ease, rifles moving to alert. *A Fable* rarely ceases underlining the gravity and importance of its major players. (In some ways, its rhetoric oddly reminds the contemporary reader of the 2003 phrase, "Operation Shock and Awe," during the Iraq War.) Thematically, the book's plot is unambiguously antimilitary. But its relentless declaiming—its verbal onslaught as a series of massive set pieces, a parading of the author's biggest verbal guns—seems suggestively to echo the same military grandeur that the plot works to undermine.

THE LATER FICTION 2: "WE DON'T WANT HIM TAME"

I have cited before these words of Sam Fathers (in *Go Down, Moses*), after he has captured the wild dog Lion and has begun to train him to take down Old Ben. Faulkner's fiction aspired more broadly to the condition of untamedness. "When something is new and hard and bright," Cash had said in *As I Lay Dying*, "there ought to be something a little better for it than just being safe, since the safe things are just the things that folks have been doing so long they have worn the edges off and there's nothing to the doing of them that leaves a man to say, That was not done before and it cannot be done again" (AILD 85–6). Cannot be done again: the 1929 breakthrough that took Faulkner from *Flags* to *The Sound and the Fury* required a refusal of novelistic safety. Faulkner had good reason for believing that no publisher would take on the risk embodied in his latest novel. Yes, *Ulysses* had appeared in 1922—and without Joyce's Stephen Dedalus (presented to the reader through interior monologue) there might well have been no Quentin Compson—but Benjy's narrative is pure Faulkner. More, Faulkner choosing to open *The Sound and the Fury* in that untamed idiotic mind involved a greater risk than Joyce opening *Ulysses* in the comparatively accessible first chapter, "Telemachus." (*Ulysses* becomes increasingly bewildering once it moves past its initial investment in characters, but it begins familiarly enough.)

Each of Faulkner's novels that followed *The Sound and the Fury*—from 1929 through 1936—pursued its version of untamedness. Retaining an interior monologue format, *As I Lay Dying* departed dramatically from Compson dysfunction. Its world was rural, vernacular, and comic rather than once-aristocratic and tragic. Its cast of characters—each granted an interior lens—expanded from the earlier book's three to a dizzying fifteen. *Sanctuary*, for its part, ran a different kind of risk: embarking on a sequence of the most sordid sexual misdeeds and their unmoralized consequences. ("Good God, I can't publish this," Hal Smith had remonstrated after reading the manuscript; "we'd both be in jail" [F 239].) *Light in August* opened up a new territory of unsafe materials: the murderous territory of Southern race relations that Faulkner would continue to probe in *Absalom* and *Go Down, Moses*. Each of these novels was never far from offending its reader in its own way. Next came the rhetorically overwrought *Pylon*, soon followed by *Absalom*. In the magisterial *Absalom*—difficult to write not least because it was so freighted with historical, racial, and personal troubles—Faulkner's thematic range and technical inventiveness surpassed the capacity of all of his American contemporaries. He had become a writer of stunning risks taken and made good on.

Of the next four books—*The Unvanquished* (1938), *If I Forget Thee, Jerusalem* (1939), *The Hamlet* (1940), and *Go Down, Moses* (1942)—only the first could be called tame. Each of the others reached into high-risk zones of analysis and implication—his own sexual experience, the broadest repercussions of racial injustice in America—that put the writer at risk. The form of each was new; Faulkner was continually reinventing himself. Then, following the six-year hiatus, came the three novels of "Faulknerese." Shrill to the point of seeking to outshout God himself, these ambitious novels failed less because they were "tamed" than because they escaped rhetorical control. Faulkner had long admired Thomas Wolfe's project of "trying to put the whole history of the human heart" into a single sentence (FIU 144). Thus formulated, this would be a disastrous program for fiction, and Faulkner's great work happily eluded it (whatever lip-service he paid). In that unbridled trio of "Faulknerese" novels, however, he seems in some ways to have attempted to out-Wolfe Wolfe.

It is possible to glimpse—in Faulkner's own early fifties, the years in which he wrote these rhetorical monsters—a cumulative despair rising and overflowing its earlier unstable boundaries. It was probably the period of his greatest personal misery and self-doubt as a writer, joined by his most damaging attempts to elude these by way of sanctuary. By the later 1950s, however, it is as though Faulkner had emerged onto the other side of a climacteric (both imaginative and experiential). The "sinister gods" remained in charge, to be sure. Life remained something that was "not now, and perhaps never was, worth the living." But his intensity had diminished, his sense of outrage seemed to have lessened, and his last novels began to escape a "Faulknerese" compulsion to insist. He became tame(r). The doting grandfather (Jill's first child was born in 1956), the amiable (though still impenetrable) Charlottesville gentleman and sartorial fox hunter, the serviceable teacher at the University of Virginia and global spokesperson for American culture: this more presentable persona began to emerge. Not that Faulkner's underlying anxieties and misgivings got resolved, but they seemed—for periods of time during his last five years—to weigh less heavily. "Pappy really changed," Jill said, reflecting on his silent delight in her two young sons: "He became so much easier for everyone to live with....He was enjoying life" (F 671). This older, tamer Faulkner wrote *The Town* (1957), *The Mansion* (1959), and *The Reivers* (1962).

The Town—the second volume in the Snopes trilogy—suffers when compared to the earlier *Hamlet*. Many of the same characters reappear, but it is as though they, too, have passed through a sort of climacteric. The book is domestic, more polite, at moments almost genteel. The Ratliff who shares the narrative focus with Chick Mallison (the child protagonist of *Intruder*) and with Gavin Stevens has lost much of his earlier force. His task here—as narrator—is shrewdly to counterpoint the ever-verbose Gavin Stevens. Other than narrating about Flem, Eula, her lover De Spain, her daughter Linda, and a few other odd Snopeses, the narrators have little to do. (The voyeuristic dimension of *The Town* is extensive and a touch unpleasant.)

The Mansion (two years later) is stronger. Eula's illegitimate daughter Linda Snopes, as uncompromising as her mother, has grown up, traveled abroad, and returned home, endowed with radical convictions. A left-wing politics begin to manifest itself. It is as though the reactionary racism that Faulkner tried to confront throughout the 1950s produced finally its fictional antagonist: a fearless girl who pursues the projects her benighted fellow white Southerners abhor. But this last Snopes volume comes most alive when it dilates on Mink Snopes's fanatic pursuit of his treacherous brother Flem. In this pursuit Mink is abetted by Linda—who has long detested Flem for ruining her mother's life. Finally, Mink emerges (exiting from Parchman prison thirty-seven years behind the time) as a sort of walking anachronism. Through him, Faulkner intimates his own nostalgia for the early twentieth-century South of his childhood—the world as it used to be.

"I listen to the voices, and when I put down what they say, it's right" (FCF 159): so Faulkner had long ago described to Malcolm Cowley his creative procedure. Most readers caught up in the vortex of his greatest characters' dilemmas would grant the claim. Unlike Henry James or James Joyce, Faulkner rarely proceeds by way of a modulated authorial stance— intricately nuanced and carrying latent judgments—enacted upon his fictional universe. When Faulkner is great, he is inseparable from his characters—immersed utterly in their voices, gestures, and actions. Perhaps it is that dream-like projection into his materials—neither subtly judgmental nor sentimentally endorsing—that is most missing from these two tamer Snopes novels.

Such intensity is missing from *The Reivers* as well. Filled with light-hearted adventures whose pathos rarely turns toward tragedy or obsession, this last novel was written for—and dedicated to—his grandsons. (Its opening words are "Grandfather said.") Mink's long backward glance has now stretched into reminiscence of events that took place a lifetime ago. These involve derring-do vignettes—a stolen car, betting on and fixing horse races, several sorts of Memphis mayhem. Miss Reba's whorehouse features as prominently here as it did in *Sanctuary*, but this time shorn of menace. It has become an all right place for boys to read about. Often compared to Twain's boy books on the one hand and to Shakespeare's valedictory *Tempest* on the other, *The Reivers* possesses little of *The Tempest*'s inexhaustible resonance. Insofar as it is Twain-like, it is closer to the shenanigans of Tom Sawyer than the more brooding inwardness of *Huckleberry Finn*. "The human heart in conflict with itself": so Faulkner had identified, in his Nobel Prize speech, his signature concern. The raging, conflicted heart is what (apart from Mink in *The Mansion*) these last novels lack—a lack one can only hope softened their author's final years as well. Less driven once he had passed the age of sixty, perhaps more accepting of his inescapable conditions, Faulkner seems to have stumbled less, even if peace remained beyond his grasp. His valedictory novel, at any rate, hardly stumbles at all: a testimony to its lightness and charm.

"MUST MATTER"

You get born and you try this and you dont know why only you keep
on trying it and you are born at the same time with a lot of other
people, all mixed up with them, like trying to, having to, move your
arms and legs with strings only the same strings are hitched to all the
other arms and legs...like five or six people all trying to make a rug
on the same loom...and it cant matter, you know that, or the Ones
that set up the loom would have arranged things a little better, and yet
it must matter because you keep on trying...and then all of a sudden
it's all over and all you have left is a block of stone with scratches on
it...and after a while they don't even remember...what the scratches
were trying to tell, and it doesn't matter.

—*Absalom, Absalom!*

"Cant matter" is primordial in Faulkner's understanding of life and is never
gainsaid. In the passage from *Absalom* that I opened this book with and
quote again here, the pathos of "must matter" is sandwiched between a
"cant matter" and a "doesn't matter" that remain inalterable. All the "Kil-
roy was here" scrawls on all the walls in the world do not change the fact
that the human being is a puny creature up against the "sinister gods," "the
Ones who set up the loom." Life is not a winning situation, and Faulkner
never forgot that it wasn't. Yet he tenaciously insisted on writing his books
as though they "must matter." No less, this stumbling man persevered
throughout his life as though (against all better judgment) somehow it, too,
must matter.

His abiding tenderness toward children shines through the biographical data. One notes it first in his volunteering to be local scoutmaster (a
post he held in the early 1920s, until church dignitaries found him morally
unworthy of this trust and forced his resignation). Toward his daughter
Jill—"Missy"—he remained deeply attached from her birth until his death,
perhaps most so during the "salt mine" years (much of the 1940s) that he

spent in exile in Hollywood. Learning from Estelle that his nine-year-old daughter had had her hair cut, he responded:

> Pappy misses that yellow hair that had never had an inch cut off of it since you were born, but Pappy knows and can remember and can see in his mind whenever he wants to every single day you ever lived, whether he was there to look at you or not....So any time he wants to think so, that hair is still long, never touched with scissors. So, that being the case, your hair can be cut like you want it, and it can still be like Pappy wants to think of it, at the same time. So I am glad you had it fixed the way you like it, and I want you to enjoy it and write me about it. (SL 173)

Like a Keatsean "still unravished bride," Jill lived both in and out of time for her father: a growing woman disappearing Eurydice-like from him, an immortal child housed securely in his mind. Two years later, he was brooding over her parting words to him about "Lady Go-lightly" (the horse he had bought for her in Hollywood): "Pappy, I've got to have that horse. It hurts my heart," she had said (F 468). For $125 he bought a two-wheeled horse trailer and paid $350 more to have others help him haul Lady to Mississippi behind his car. ("I've got a mare that's going to foal," he told a Hollywood colleague, "and I want it to foal in Mississippi" [467–8].) Driving at top speed for three days across country (with brief motel stops), they arrived at Rowan Oak after midnight. Jill was awakened. Sleepily, she made her way down the stairs, then saw him standing there next to the horse trailer, and started running: "It's my horse," she said, incredulous, as she embraced Lady, "it's my horse."

Toward his stepchildren Malcolm and Victoria his relations were complex, sometimes involving disciplinary gestures they would remember. But he was there for Victoria during her own crisis in early 1938. A young mother with a baby only a few months old, and suddenly abandoned by her husband, she had sought refuge at Rowan Oak. Faulkner kept her occupied, gave her typing to do, worked crossword puzzles with her, and read Keats and Housman to her during the terrible evenings. "He kept me alive," she later said of his care. But it was his niece Dean to whom—apart from Jill—he must have felt the greatest emotional and financial responsibility. His role in her father's crash in 1935 had never ceased to torment him, and he steadfastly supported her during her years of growing up, college education, and subsequent travel, as her father would have done. When, in the fall of 1958, she married John Mallard in Oxford, he and Estelle hosted the wedding events. He gave her away at the altar. After the newlyweds had left for their honeymoon, he and Estelle took the altar flowers to the St. Peter's cemetery late that night, and he laid them on the grave where Dean was buried. As Blotner interpreted this gesture, "the flowers told his brother that he had seen his daughter through childhood and adolescence, from maidenhood to marriage. He had fulfilled the vow made twenty-three years before by the wreckage of the Waco" (F 655). If I forget thee, Jerusalem: Faulkner honored at least this vow, among the vows he made.

His generosity toward his extended family was unfailing but far from sentimental. In June 1942, he wrote his agent Harold Ober (who, ever reserved, must have been shocked by reading it) the following complaint: "I have been trying for about ten years to carry a load that no artist has any business attempting: oldest son to widowed mothers and inept brothers and nephews and wives and other female connections and their children, most of whom I don't like and with none of whom I have anything in common, even to make conversation about" (SL 153). Though doubtless penned in a moment of irritation, the letter remains telling. Its terms presage his larger lover's quarrel with his state itself. "Loving all of it even while he had to hate some of it," he would write in 1954 about Mississippi, "because he knows now that you don't love because: you love despite; not for the virtues, but despite the faults" (ESPL 42–3). These blood-kin and family-kin were his world—partly shaped by him, more deeply simultaneous with him and inherited. His honor was at stake in the quality of his treatment of them. Although the puppet-strings of their desires may have interfered with his own, he was not free to abandon them. The difficult, silent loner and the embroiled, responsible family man came together—in irresoluble tension— as one William Faulkner.

His stance toward Phil Stone reveals the same underlying loyalty. More than anyone else, Stone helped to launch the young Faulkner's career. But his mentoring became at times insufferable. Promoting (and paying pro- duction costs for) *The Marble Faun* (1924), Stone had informed the Yale *Alumni Weekly:* "This poet is my personal property and I urge all my friends and class-mates to buy his book" (F 123). As Faulkner's fame increased, the darker side of Stone's attachment to him emerged more often. In the *Oxford Magazine* in 1934, Stone launched what he proposed as a six-installment narrative of Faulkner and his family. Granting that Faulkner was one of the "most noted exponents…of modern technique," Stone denied his pro- tégé any "trace of genius" and opined that "he has gone as far as he will ever go" (331). Happily, the magazine fizzled out after three issues. Against this emotionally intricate backdrop, we can measure Faulkner's generosity when Stone himself fell into overwhelming money troubles. When his father's bank collapsed in 1930, Stone assumed his considerable debts. Ten years later, the same debts were crushing Stone, and foreclosure on one of the notes was fast approaching. Desperate, Stone turned to Faulkner, who immediately wrote Bob Haas at Random House: "I have a friend here, I have known him all my life, never any question of mine and thine between us when either had it....Of course I will sign any thing, contracts, etc....I will sell or mortgage....$6000 is what we have to raise" (SL 111)—in three weeks. Borrowing $1,200 against future royalties on *The Hamlet*, and collecting $4,800 as the cash value of his own life insurance policy, Faulkner got the $6,000 to Stone just in time. Over a decade later, in an *Oxford Eagle* tribute to Faulkner for having won the Nobel Prize, Stone remembered his friend's generosity: "A lot of us talk about decency, about honor, about loyalty, about gratitude," Stone wrote. "Bill doesn't talk about these things; he lives them" (F 526).

A demonstration of virtue without the verbal claims that so often go with it (and at times substitute for it): Faulkner's French translator, Maurice Coindreau, noted the same rare trait a few months after Faulkner's death: "If he wanted to speak well of you," Coindreau wrote, "he preferred to do it when your back was turned" (F 98). Recognition and gratitude were exactly what he did not seek in return. Faulkner's acknowledgment had nothing to do with appearances or applause, and everything to do with a silent ethical gauge he carried within. Following his returning to Oxford in December 1950, flush for perhaps the first time in his life—thanks to Nobel largesse—Faulkner headed to his Uncle John's office: "I want you to do something with that damned money," he told his uncle the judge. "I haven't earned it and I don't feel like it's mine. I want to give some money to the poor folks of Lafayette County" (535). This meant poor blacks as well as whites.

Even a cursory reading of Faulkner's letters reveals another virtue sometimes missed by readers of his work: humor. In the spring of 1958, addressing a class of English majors at Princeton, he received one especially sententious question: "I have read all your books and short stories," the young man said, "and I want to know, is there one character that is saved by grace?" Pausing for a moment to take this in, Faulkner responded, "Well, I have always thought of God as being in the wholesale rather than the retail business" (F 650–1). Earlier, in 1948, he had written to Cowley of a handsome invitation to address Yale's English Department and receive $200: "I don't think I know anything worth 200 dollars worth talking about…so I would probably settle for a bottle of good whiskey" (SL 271). Turning down recognition from Yale—like his later refusal to accept President Kennedy's invitation to join other Nobel laureates for a dinner at the White House—were moves determined and sanctioned by that inner ethical gauge. (When Blotner asked Faulkner what to say to reporters amazed by his decision, he replied: "Tell them I'm too old at my age to travel that far to eat with strangers" [F 703].) Often the humor would be wrapped around a financial offer that he wryly conceded could still tempt him. To Ober he wrote in 1959:

> Having, with THE MANSION, finished the last of my planned labors; and, at 62, having to anticipate that moment when I shall have scraped the last minuscule from the bottom of the F. barrel; and having undertaken a home in Virginia where I can break my neck least expensively fox hunting, I am now interested in $2500.00 or for that matter $25.00. (SL 433)

Putting in the oo cents: this is the sign of humor by a man who for much of his life had been beaten up by money negotiations he never respected and rarely got the better of. Faulkner's humor emerged not at the expense of anyone, unless of himself. Because he knew he was a fool in the hands of the gods, he could laugh at—and sometimes share with others—the predicaments he found himself in. Beaten up by money arrangements, but not corrupted.

Faulkner distinguished acutely between financial complications and financial dishonor. For a period of over four years (in the 1940s), he was hounded by a literary agent named Herndon, who had offered to sell some of his stories in Hollywood as materials for film. These transactions soon became sticky, as East Coast and West Coast agents jockeyed to get into the act. When Faulkner wrote Herndon that he was going with a West Coast agent and that their arrangement was off, Herndon turned aggressive. He concocted an elaborate argument about having suffered damages, and he threatened to sue if Faulkner did not comply. Faulkner was both openly defiant and inwardly aggrieved. He wrote Herndon, "You accused me of deliberate underhand dealing, which is not true, and inferred that I could be forced by threats into doing what is right, which I will take from no man." After a genuine attempt to negotiate Herndon's claims, Faulkner closed his letter as follows: "If this is not satisfactory to you, then make good your threat and cause whatever trouble you wish" (F 158). The tone is sublime: one would associate it more with dueling gentlemen like Hamilton and Burr than with a 1940s quarrel between writer and agent. Certainly no lawyer working for Faulkner would have encouraged him to respond thus! The aftermath is likewise revealing. Faulkner wrote Ober, "I have failed in integrity toward him [Herndon]. I was not aware of this at the time, yet and strangely enough perhaps even if it is not true, I do not like to be accused of it" (SL 160). Faulkner's sense of honor is a critical dimension of his identity. He does not compromise with it nor suffer others to cast aspersions on it. Learning of Hemingway's death (a year before his own), Faulkner immediately sensed it was a suicide. This form of exit obscurely ruffled Faulkner's unspoken code of integrity: "I don't like a man that takes the short way home," he told a friend (F 690). Living just is the courage to stay with a bad hand until the game is over (and most hands are bad hands: the sinister gods hold the trumps).

Against these odds, Faulkner made good on the single successful bid for sanctuary that gave his life its form: his undeviating determination to write novels. That activity was deforming as well. Deforming because writing served—as intoxication and affairs could not—as socially sanctioned escape, abiding alibi for nonaffiliation. Writing legitimized his disappearance from the socially commanded performances that dot most people's lives from maturation onward. It gave Faulkner extended absence not only without leave but without requiring leave. Musing on the role of the map of his fictional kingdom that Faulkner drew for *The Portable Faulkner*, Cowley recognized that "intellectual solitude" was the "precondition of his writing. Only in solitude could he enter the inner kingdom—'William Faulkner, sole owner and proprietor'—that his genius was able to people and cultivate" (FCF 166). Only inside the space silently generated by his words was Faulkner able to hear the voices soliciting him.

Much as he required this sanctuary provided by words, he recognized its noninnocence from the beginning. Writing stands in for doing. In the South, serious men did not write. As Addie Bundren savagely put it in *As I Lay Dying*, "words are…just a shape to fill a lack." Faulkner had learned throughout his twenties to craft a range of fictions that more insidiously took the place of the real. The Canadian RAF uniform simulated a war experience he never had. He used lies—a plate in the head, another in the knee—to persuade others of wounds never incurred. Faulkner grasped, early on, that the very idea of fiction is steeped in falsehood. His great work never succumbs to sentimental confusions between the invented and the real that lies behind all convention. What is the tireless drive for the truth of things—a drive that marks his masterpieces—if not a core conviction that the truth differs from simulations of it? This even if one can never summon forth more than speculative simulations.

If writing was for these reasons deforming, it was also the most heroic and form-providing mode of sanctuary Faulkner was to know. Intoxication was the hopeless strategy of a man seeking to outrun his demons by dulling their inner distinctness. But writing was the successful strategy of a man seeking to escape life's outer clamor so that he might negotiate the maelstrom of conflicting voices inside his own head. So that he could grasp the fact that they all inhabited *him*. Inhabiting him, the voices surged as possibilities within, and they were set in motion—by his raging "hemophilic" imagination—not as mistaken stances to be corrected but as irrepressible dimensions of identity. Intoxication—by expelling others from consciousness—served as mental meltdown (mimicking infancy's blankness, precursor of the final sanctuary that is death). Writing, by contrast, was how he creatively "dried out" and took the fullest measure of his private and social being. It provided the priceless medium within which he was able to access the broadest implications of his own experience. There, as he encountered others again within the precincts of his imagination, he envisaged who would meet up with whom, what would precede their encounter, where it would take them, what its consequences would be. Such arranging gave the inner voices all their spoken and unspoken resonance, inserted them into their most troubling, repercussive interrelationships. The imaginative restaging did so not so much bypass judgment as arrive at a grasp of the human drama that moved beyond judgment altogether.

Writing—the arduous, agonizing, and enlivening time of conceiving, composing, and revising—was how Faulkner reckoned with what had happened to him in life. It was how he experienced as drama both his multiple identities and his disastrous mistakes—how, by doing it, he learned who he was. His writing, whenever it is great, refuses didacticism; he has no interest in pointing a moral. Instead, it was through writing that he imagined his way into how "five or six people all trying to make a rug on the same loom" would impinge on each other, and what this would look like as it unfolded in time. Faulkner was so alert to the value of this generative activity that he never ceased to protect it. When he made it clear that he did not like to talk about either himself or his work, he was not concealing information others had a right to know. Rather, everything that mattered about him mattered because he wrote. "He made the books and died"—so Faulkner fantasized his brief epitaph. Those shapely urns of words would constitute at once his private self-making and his lifelong letter to the world. If you wanted to get the good he had to give, you had to go to the labor of engaging him where he most vividly lived—in his books. No biography, including this one, could substitute for that encounter.

Most who knew Faulkner for any length of time noted both his courtliness and a self-containment bordering on silence. To these traits we should add his scrupulous self-respect (Faulkner never groveled) and his respect for others, coupled with his vigilant demand that others respect him. He never ceased to be astonished at how this demand was regularly overrun by those who sought to exploit him. There was finally a lifelong stubbornness in Faulkner—extending to ruthlessness: it is not for nothing that his favorite animal is the mule. Perhaps from his mother he learned not to back down if he thought he was in the right. Another term for such stubbornness bordering on ruthlessness is endurance: Faulkner endured his life. As Edouard Glissant glossed that verb in its French provenance, he was equal to the abiding hardness of his life.

Endurance joins together "must matter" and "cant matter," taking us far into his emotional and conceptual economy. He respected blacks most, it seems, for their unillusioned capacity to endure—to accept the worst that whites had inflicted on them without losing their grace and humanity. Relatedly, but in a different key, he lived out his life unbendingly himself, even self-damagingly himself. Not that he sentimentalized this hardheaded insistence on who he was. It was as well the source of an abiding inner critique. But he was who he was—not tall, not especially handsome, not smart about his life. He rarely failed to hear the silently sounded inner chorus of his own mistakes. Why else would he have so sought out sanctuaries of escape? He was stumbling man, off-balance man, man in the present moment and under duress—man who endured but (despite occasional rhetoric) rarely prevailed.

Unless one were to say that in one arena only he prevailed: as an artist. For the first twenty years of his nearly forty-year career, he tirelessly persisted in producing and marketing his work. This meant facing down hundreds of rejection slips (as he told a budding writer once, you needed a hundred rejections before you made it to zero). So it is finally as avatars of his own incorrigibility, perhaps, that we recognize the company he keeps. Bayard Sartoris, Quentin and Benjy and Caddy and Jason Compson (yes, Jason too), all the Bundrens male and female, Joe Christmas, Sutpen, Lucas Beauchamp, Labove and Houston and Mink, Charlotte Rittenmeyer, even the tall convict: these are the unteachable ones, heading into disaster as he would himself head into another painful rehearsal of who he was. "I don't understand it," the suffering but undefeated Houston would say to himself as he lay down rigid in his bed: "I dont know why. I wont ever know why. But You cant beat me. I am strong as You are. You cant beat me" (HAM 220). Such grim fortitude suffuses the figure Jay Parini describes when he ends his biography on the note of Faulkner's grit:

> Faulkner pushed ahead like an ox through mud, dragging a whole world behind him....There is something primordial about the unfolding of Faulkner's work, which often came rushing to the fore, as if unpremeditated, although stories and characters would lie at the back of his mind for years. When they emerged, they did so with terrifying force. Faulkner rode them like wild horses, tamed them, brought them to book. (OMT 429)

Over and against these "primordial" figures there is *The Hamlet*'s Ratliff—the virgin messenger, the voice who makes possible the community. Nourished by vernacular wisdom, Ratliff is Faulkner's greatest figure of balance. He releases much of the humor in Faulkner—the humor of endurance—a humor that hardly pretends to change things but wryly recognizes their makeup. Ratliff is who Faulkner might have been if he had enjoyed living in the company of others. Ratliff is the gift Faulkner makes to the community, in place of himself. All but unflappable, serenely inscrutable, Ratliff is his creator's moral compass and would perhaps be his major figure if Faulkner's fictional world centered on ethical judgment. But it doesn't. At its best, it is not about making the right decisions, not about children outwitting parents and repressive elders or even a mob who would lynch Lucas Beauchamp. At its best, the work is not crazily—à la Thomas Wolfe—seeking to put the whole impossible history of the human heart into one sentence, as Faulkner attempted in the swollen portions of *Intruder in the Dust, Requiem for a Nun,* and *A Fable.* At its best, the fiction hardly brings to mind the avuncular figure who worked in behalf of the State Department, who lectured at the University of Virginia (politely taking questions from the students)—the man who donned his elegant fox-hunting uniform, rode with the Charlottesville aristocrats, and let himself be photographed in his displayed finery.

Rather, the Faulkner whose work—and life—inspired this book is the writer Evelyn Scott recognized when, astonished, she first read *The Sound and the Fury*. "Here is beauty sprung from the perfect *realization* of what a more limiting morality would describe as ugliness," she wrote. "Here is a humanity stripped of most of what was claimed for it by the Victorians, and the spectacle is moving as no sugar-coated drama ever could be" (CH 78). It is the spectacle of being off-balance and lurching—being seen and respected and pitied as we move through the stages of our fall, heading toward the earth. Cant matter and must matter: Faulkner takes the drama of the human heart in conflict with itself too seriously to either console or pretend to resolve. The self in free fall—not knowing why, but not trying to escape either. Later it might all make sense, later, when the storm yielded to calm, as confusion gave way to recognition. That story of retrospective recognition is perhaps the greatest we have—the story that narrative was invented to tell—and some of Faulkner's later work participates in it. But at his most moving, he shows how life in ongoing time necessarily involves stumbling. To be buffeted by storm is to know the reality of "cant matter." To endure it—and to continue seeking, impossibly, to put the storm into words—is to insist on "must matter."

NOTES

PROLOGUE

1. As "larger cultural loom" implies, the collapse of one's dreams is caused by something more than metaphysical malice. Judith Sutpen inhabits an antebellum Southern world of sanctioned aspirations and agreed-on taboos. Her defeat in *Absalom, Absalom!* has everything to do with racial and economic protocols shaping her hopes and shattering them too. But—caught up as an individual merely endowed (like all individuals) with partial perspective—Judith *registers* this confounding as incomprehensible disaster. Faulkner's great novels home in on the emotional tenor of such collapse. He centered his work on the subjective vertigo of coming undone, even as that work suggests, all along its periphery, the larger, interwoven, cultural dimensions of collapse. I argue throughout this book that his novelistic signature consists in *respecting*—and inventing ways both to represent and pass on to his reader—the experience of unpreparedness, of shock. Shock goes deeper—is more telling—than retrospective explanations for it. Faulkner's great work was invested in writing how it felt to stumble, and in suggesting (but only later) what contributed to the stumbling. It had less interest in proposing cultural analyses that might make future stumbling obsolescent.
2. André Bleikasten's *Faulkner: Une Vie en Romans* (2007) provides an extraordinary account of the novels, along with a scrupulous account of the life. But, as he would have been the first to admit, Bleikasten saw no way meaningfully to interconnect his parallel accounts. This important work has not yet been translated into English.
3. No one has better expressed this point than Madeline Chapsal, a French journalist who observed Faulkner's cornered moves at a party given for him in Paris, in 1955, by his grateful publishers, Gallimard. Faulkner's recalcitrance, she noted, "is built of the most exquisite but the most obdurate politeness" (LG 229). She concluded: "There is no use looking at Faulkner. You must read him. To someone who has read him, Faulkner has given all that he has, and he knows it" (230).

CHAPTER 1

1. My account of the divorce proceedings is indebted to Judith Sensibar's *Faulkner and Love: The Women Who Shaped His Life* (New Haven: Yale University Press, 2009), 470. Sensibar revises not only Blotner's account but more broadly—as I shall address in subsequent notes—his understanding of the relationship between Faulkner and Estelle. Sensibar's study appeared in print only as I was copy-editing my own manuscript. In the form of footnotes I seek recurrently to engage its argument: that Faulkner's work owes more than has been acknowledged to the formative influence of three women—Mammy Callie, Maud Falkner, and Estelle Faulkner.

2. Drawing on interviews with the Faulkners' daughter Jill, Sensibar argues in *Faulkner and Love* that Estelle's part in the larger drama of her marriage to Franklin and her divorce from him (ten years later) has little to do with flirtatious behavior and its troubling consequences. Sensibar believes that the "southern belle" role Estelle performed, during her late adolescence and the early years of her marriage, was merely "a part she [Estelle] played to the hilt when necessary. 'Mama played up the "clinging vine" "Southern Belle" business when required, but she was really the least clinging person I've almost every known,' observes the Faulkners' daughter" (5). Relying heavily on the unpublished manuscript stories Estelle wrote during the years of her marriage to Franklin, Sensibar proposes an Estelle at once savvy, self-aware, and victimized. Since none of Estelle's letters has been preserved, Sensibar's revisionary portrait depends on circumstantial and indirect evidence (the unpublished manuscripts) freely and speculatively interpreted. Essentially, she argues that not only did Estelle's unconventional writing fertilize Faulkner's own and make possible *The Sound and the Fury*, but that their marriage has been broadly—and misogynistically—misconstrued as a failed union. "To suggest that Faulkner spent his life with a woman with whom he had no real relationship debases both partners" (10), Sensibar claims, although the number of troubled marriages that fit that description is unfortunately legion. Sensibar's painstaking research enriches Faulkner studies by deepening and widening our portrait of Estelle. Yet the darker dimensions of their marriage—on which I focus in my own narrative—remain stubbornly intact. Faulkner's desperate letter (June 1929) to Ben Wasson, the eery echo of June 20 as Temple's perjury date and his marriage date, the references to "scratching" in *Sanctuary* and "mire" in *As I Lay Dying*, Estelle's suicide attempt during their honeymoon at Pascagoula, so many of Jill's (and others') comments about her parents' dysfunctional union: these persuade me that, however loving their marriage might have been at times, it was also—and extensively, for years on end—a deeply troubled bond that both spouses saw all too often as bondage. None of this is to imply that Estelle, rather than Faulkner, is to blame. I believe they both—because of who they were, in all their intricacy—contributed to the marital suffering that they both assuredly experienced.

3. "There was not even an employment contract for Murry under the terms of the sale. Not only had his father arbitrarily stripped Murry of his profession, but he also substituted in its stead the operation of a much less prestigious means of

transportation, a livery stable. Overnight he demoted his son from the twentieth century to the nineteenth" (*Faulkner and Love,* 172).

4. Much of this paragraph's argument—as well as my orientation in the two pre-
    vious paragraphs—is indebted to Sensibar's earlier, provocative reading of the
    Falkner family history as a narrative of paternal wounds inflicted on, and then
    recycled by, the sons, once they become fathers in their own right (OFA). Sen-
    sibar is equally sensitive to forms of racial and gender abuse wrought into this
    family history. John Irwin's *Doubling and Incest, Repetition and Revenge* posits
    both *The Sound and the Fury* and *Absalom, Absalom!* as obsessively returning
    to and reconfiguring a Freudian drama of abusive fathers and injured sons, of
    inflicted wounds that repeat and replay rather than heal. Though Irwin has little
    interest in Faulkner's life, his reading of the work uncannily echoes patterns
    found in the family's troubled history.

5. There is both internal and external evidence suggesting that Faulkner knew
    Joyce's book well. His library contains a 1924 copy of *Ulysses,* with his name on
    it; Stone claimed to have given it to him as "something new…something you
    should know about" (F2 1:352).

CHAPTER 2

1. Sensibar's revisionist account of the Faulkner-Estelle relationship considers this
    elopement crisis to be no crisis at all. Speaking of them both as "adolescents"
    trying to figure themselves out—though each was already twenty years old in
    1918—Sensibar claims that, for his part, Faulkner "did not need or want a wife"
    (*Faulkner and Love,* 320). She provides no evidence for this claim other than the
    insouciance that appears in Faulkner's letters to his parents written later that year
    from New Haven and Toronto. Faulkner's published letters, however—as is widely
    known—virtually never reveal his more troubling thoughts or feelings. As for
    Estelle, Sensibar understands her agreeing to marry Franklin in 1918 as something
    sinister imposed on her. Lem Oldham and Cornell Franklin—Estelle's father and
    fiancé—pressured her to consent to this union, Sensibar argues, because they both
    saw it in their interest for her to do so. On this reading Estelle is a pawn caught
    up in a marriage "market" (Sensibar's emphatic and repeated term) controlled by
    males. Estelle accordingly succumbs because of a complex mix of daughterly obe-
    dience, guilt over the loss of her own younger brother (whom she would "replace"
    with the child she hoped soon to conceive), and anger that Faulkner had already
    deserted her, years ago, for the attentions of Phil Stone. None of this is implau-
    sible, but no less, none of it is supported by more than speculation and indirect
    circumstantial evidence. In my reading—which of course I cannot prove either,
    but for which I offer the evidence available (Blotner, after all, did a good deal of
    homework)—their failed elopement was indeed a crisis, with reverberations for
    Faulkner's life and art that would endure indefinitely.

2. Susan Snell, *Phil Stone of Oxford: A Vicarious Life* (Athens: University of Geor-
    gia Press, 1991), 77. My interpretation of Stone's likely social resonance for
    Faulkner is indebted to the opening chapters of this study.

3. Snell, 140.

4. As the references embedded in this and the next two paragraphs suggest, my argument is here indebted to James G. Watson's astute reading of the strategic dimension lodged in Faulkner's intricate negotiation of photos of himself. See his *William Faulkner: Self-presentation and Performance* (Austin: University of Texas Press, 2000), 35, for the passage cited.

5. André Bleikasten reads Faulkner's sustained fictionalizing of his own life as follows: "c'était bien un simulateur, il aimait tricher. Mais tricher, ce n'est pas seulement tromper, c'est aussi corriger le hazard....Tout au long de sa vie, Faulkner s'employa à corriger le hazard, à dissimuler les défauts. Il rusait avec la vérité, la contournait, la détournait, en inventait d'autres. Il mentait pour mieux respirer" (*William Faulkner: Une vie en romans* [Paris: Editions Aden, 2007], 103).

6. Faulkner used this phrase in one of the interviews he gave in Japan in 1956. Speaking of his phenomenal creativity between 1929 and 1936, he said: "there's a time in his life, one matchless time, when...[the speed and the talent are] matched completely" (LG 149). Jay Parini took the phrase as the title of his 2004 biography of Faulkner.

7. Blotner puts it thus: "Meanwhile, almost unbidden, the staff [Uncle Ned and Mammy Callie] was beginning to gather....There was no money for salaries...but he was responsible for their food, shelter, clothing, health care, and pay when he could afford it. That he should do this was exactly what Mammy Callie and Uncle Ned expected" (F261–2).

8. *Soren Kierkegaard's Journals and Papers*, tr. Howard V. Hong and Edna K. Hong (Bloomington: Indiana University Press, 1967–1978), 7 vols, 1:450.

9. See Bleikasten: "L'une des très rares photos à nous faire voir un Faulkner heureux est celle qui le montre, en chemise et pantalon de lin blanc, la cravate négligemmant glissée entre deux boutons de sa chemise, souriant, radieux, devant son Waco" (364).

CHAPTER 3

1. C. Vann Woodward, *The Burden of Southern History* (Baton Rouge: Louisiana State University Press, 1960), 8.

2. Judith Sensibar explores at length the premise that, thanks to Faulkner's extensive childhood exposure to Mammy Callie and her world, he would have registered— deeply and disturbingly—both the emotional realities of Callie's world and the white-mandated ordering system that feared, mangled, and repressed those realities. "Callie Barr taught him uncolored love," Sensibar claims; "from her he learned the courage to plumb the terrible psychic and cultural consequences of denying and being ashamed of that love" (*Faulkner and Love*, 20).

3. However attentive to data that previous historians and biographers overlooked, Williamson's narrative reconstruction remains speculative. With respect to one claim—the age of Emeline Falkner, the mulatto woman who entered the Colonel's household in 1858—it may even be self-contradictory. The 1860 census

gives this mulatto woman's age as twenty-seven, which would make 1833 her birth year. But the birth year engraved on her tombstone in the Ripley Cemetery, as Williamson himself labored to identify (by rubbing hard at the at-first-indecipherable stone) is 1837. Are two different women involved, or is there an error in the data? In support of the latter idea, the census information may have been mistaken, or it may have been mistakenly reported. Alternatively, the tombstone date might be erroneous. Finally, as Williamson makes clear, the writing on Emeline's tombstone was at first illegible and (as is corroborated by others who have seen Williamson's evidence) its carved dates are still—despite his rubbing—difficult to decipher with certainty. The larger argument loses nothing of its resonance, but some of its factual underpinnings seem insusceptible (at this point in history) to definitive proof or disproof.

4. "Letter from Birmingham City Jail," cited in Grace Elizabeth Hale and Robert Jackson, "We're Trying Hard as Hell to Free Ourselves," in *A Companion to William Faulkner*, ed. Richard C. Moreland (Malden, Mass.: Blackwell, 2007), 43.

5. *What Else but Love? The Ordeal of Race in Faulkner and Morrison* (New York: Columbia University Press, 1996), 12.

6. See the entire essay, Hale and Jackson, "We're Trying Hard as Hell to Free Ourselves," 28–45.

7. Cited in Arthur Kinney, *Go Down, Moses: The Miscegenation of Time* (New York: Twayne, 1996), xix.

8. James Baldwin, "Stranger in the Village," in *The Price of the Ticket: Collected Nonfiction, 1948–1985* (New York: St. Martin's Press, 1985), 88.

9. I explore the South's interracial "love story" only insofar as Faulkner's greatest novels reveal the suppressed white longing for passage across the race-barrier, even as they continue to register such crossing as a taboo to be maintained at all costs, including murder. Such experience is more broadly fraught, however. The impress of black mammies on the countless white children they suckled and nourished—an unavoidably shaping force regardless of the forms of denial mandated by racist ideology—lies at the heart of a larger psychic disfigurement from which the South has still to recover. Lillian Smith's *Killers of the Dream* focuses powerfully on the causes and fallout of this disfigurement. Among Faulkner's critics, Eric Sundquist, Richard Godden, and Judith Sensibar have dealt extensively, though in quite different ways, with the psychic scars imposed by Southern racist arrangements. See Sundquist's *Faulkner: The House Divided* (Baltimore: The Johns Hopkins University Press, 1983), Godden's *Fictions of Labor: William Faulkner and the South's Revolution* (New York: Cambridge University Press, 1997), and Sensibar's *Faulkner and Love*.

CHAPTER 4

1. Tom Dardis, in *The Thirsty Muse: Alcohol and the American Writer* (New York: Ticknor and Fields, 1989), devotes some seventy pages to arguing otherwise. Focusing on the alcoholism of Faulkner, Fitzgerald, Hemingway, and O'Neill, Dardis maintains that neither moralizing nor psychologizing is pertinent:

"Most alcoholics do not drink because they're emotionally ill to begin with. They drink because they're alcoholics" (13). Dardis provides information about Faulkner's history of drinking but offers no explanatory frame for making sense of it other than chemically.

2. See Dardis's account (citing Herbert Asbury, *The Great Illusion: An Informal Account of Prohibition*): "Probably the worst drink that appeared during Prohibition was fluid extract of Jamaica ginger, popularly known as Jake, which was about 90 percent alcohol....As far as is known, nobody died from drinking it, but even small quantities nearly always caused a terrible form of paralysis" (41).

3. Dardis, *Thirsty Muse*, 93.

4. Sensibar reads the cause of Faulkner's drinking more narrowly as the narcotic he drew on his entire adolescent and adult life, in order to manage the deliberate— and indirectly suicidal—rejection of the black maternal (Mammy Callie) that Southern culture demanded of its white males. Drink, she claims, served for Faulkner "as an anodyne for unbearable loss that cannot be mourned" (*Faulkner and Love*, 3).

5. Faulkner to Bob Haas (June 1946): "I believe I see a rosy future for this book, I mean it may sell, it will be a War and Peace close enough to home, our times, language, for Americans to really buy it" (SL 238).

6. This is not the more famous film entitled *Battle Cry* (starring Aldo Ray) that appeared several years later.

7. Hugh Kenner makes this claim in *A Homemade World* (New York: Knopf, 1976), 205–6.

INDEX

Note: page numbers in italics indicate sustained discussion of novels